THE JAINA PHILOSOPHY OF NON-ABSOLUTISM

THE JAINA PHILOSOPHY OF NON-ABSOLUTISM

A Critical Study of Anekāntavāda

Dr. SATKARI MOOKERJEE
Author of the *Buddhist Philosophy of Universal Flux*

With a Foreword by

Prof. S. N. DASGUPTA

MOTILAL BANARSIDASS
Delhi :: Varanasi :: Patna

Indological Publishers & Booksellers
Head Office : BUNGALOW ROAD, JAWAHAR NAGAR, DELHI-7
Branches : 1. CHOWK, VARANASI-1 (U.P.)
2. ASHOK RAJPATH, PATNA-4 (BIHAR)

ISBN 0 89684 021 2

First Edition : *Calcutta*, 1944
Second Edition : *Delhi*, 1978

Printed in India
BY SHANTILAL JAIN AT SHRI JAINENDRA PRESS, A-45, PHASE-1, INDUSTRIAL AREA, NARAINA, NEW DELHI-28 AND PUBLISHED BY NARENDRA PRAKASH JAIN, FOR MOTILAL BANARSIDASS, BUNGALOW ROAD, JAWAHAR NAGAR, DELHI-7

TO

Dr. SYAMAPRASAD MOOKERJEE,

M.A., B.L., D.Litt., LL.D., M.L.A., Barrister-at-Law,

Ex-Vice-Chancellor of Calcutta University,

President of the Royal Asiatic Society of Bengal,

Working President of

The All India Hindu Mahāsabhā

This book is respectfully dedicated as a token of gratitude and admiration for his untiring services to the cause of the regeneration of India's Culture and for the unfailing inspiration and encouragement received from him

by

the Author

FOREWORD

The earliest parts of Jaina literature are earlier than the Buddha. We find the latter referring to Mahāvīra who was his contemporary, but in all probability the earliest Jaina literature, though not extant, is much earlier than Mahāvīra. The Buddhists and the Jainas have been opponents from the beginning and the idea of the lay and uninformed public that they are advocates more or less of the same type of thought because they both praise non-injury or Ahiṁsā as supreme moral conduct is absolutely false. Though Buddhism has always contested with the systems of Indian thought that are avowedly loyal to the Upaniṣads, yet a careful analysis will show that much of the ideas of Buddhism have sprung from a hostile response to the Upaniṣadic ideas as interpreted in Buddha's time and that much of it can be regarded as being reconstructions on the Upaniṣadic ideas, but we cannot say the same of Jainism. It reveals an ideology entirely different from the Vedic. It cannot however be gainsaid that in the later days the Jainas contested the Buddhists, the Vedāntists and the Naiyāyikas and they participated in some of their ideas and have adopted some of their stock arguments. The study of Jainism in its earlier aspects suggests a view that there must have been some kind of animistic philosophy among the inhabitants of the country though we are unable to say who they were. The Jaina literature was written in Prakrit and from its general trend one would regard it as a sort of folk-philosophy interested in overstraining the moral aspects without any theistic bias. This folk-philosophy had however elements in it which in the hands of later writers were connected into logical doctrines remarkable for their originality, acuteness and subtlety. This took place by way of writing commentaries on the old Āgamas and also by way of independent treatises, written in abstruse Sanskrit of the commentary literature that prevailed between the 8th and the 12th centuries.

Dr. Mookerjee has undertaken to give us in this treatise a thorough shaking of a logical tree that was planted in the Āgamas. The fruits were inaccessible in the high branches in the concealment of the foliage but now after thorough shaking Dr. Mookerjee has given, they are lying at the foot of the tree and one who passes may well pick them up. The difficulty of such a task will be apparent only to those that are acquainted with the difficulty of the texts which form the basis of Dr. Mookerjee's work. The interminable shades of controversy hinted at often in cryptic language make it impossible to glean the ultimate result for any one who has not within his grip the logical and dialectical literature of the different schools of Indian philosophy — a qualification not easily acquired.

It is curious that Jainism should have the misfortune of not being able to attract scholars to rediscover it for our new age unlike Buddhism and other systems of Indian philosophy. When I was toiling on the subject in the early days of the first quarter of the century there were but two scholars who had turned their attention to this subject. It is a curious fact that no professor of philosophy in Europe is conversant with Sanskrit and practically no Sanskritist in Europe is conversant with European philosophy. To rediscover an ancient system of Indian thought in a modern language one should have not only a professed mastery over Sanskrit but also a technique of philosophic expressions which necessarily depends on a good knowledge of European philosophy. My pupil and friend Dr. Satkari Mookerjee possesses, I feel pride in saying, a mastery of Sanskrit that is required in handling difficult Sanskrit texts and he has also the knowledge of European philosophy which has given him the facility of transvaluing old Indian thoughts in modern ways in a correct manner — a power that a few that I know possess. I must congratulate both Dr. Mookerjee and Jainism that Dr. Mookerjee undertook to explain a most difficult problem of Jainalogy in such a lucid and clear manner. I have glanced over the pages and I am delighted to discover how clearly and with what precision he has been able to present the Jaina logical thoughts before his readers. Dr. Mookerjee's earlier work on the Buddhist doctrine of flux has been well appreciated by those who have read it and I feel sure this book will add to his reputation not only as a scholar of eminence but as the Head of the Department of Sanskrit in the Calcutta University.

S. N. Dasgupta

PREFACE

The present work is not an exhaustive account of Jaina thought, but an analytical study of its foundation. In it the doctrine known as *syādvāda* or *anekāntavāda*, which is so basal to the structure of Jaina metaphysics and constitutes its most original contribution to philosophical speculation, has been thoroughly dealt with all the relevant problems. A critical student of Philosophy, Indian and European alike, will find in it a fresh and vigorous approach to problems which have engaged the thought of all philosophers of the world. Jaina philosophy is frankly realistic and so stands in a close relation of kinship to the other realistic schools of thought, particularly Nyāya, Mīmāṁsā and Sāṅkhya. I have drawn out the relationship that exists among these systems and discussed their points of contact and their points of departure with equal emphasis. The systematization of Jaina philosophical speculation is chronologically a later phenomenon. The Jaina Masters entered the arena of philosophical polemics after Dignāga and Dharmakīrti and their redoubtable successors had shaken the philosophical conscience of the time. This belated arrival of Jaina philosophy, though it had its moorings in the *āgamas* which were licked into shape in the early centuries of Pre-Christian era, was responsible for its added vitality and enhanced strength. Jaina philosophy was saved from dogmatism, which was smashed to pieces by the vigorous polemics of the Buddhist philosophers. Uncritical avowal of faith was taboo in those days and this called for philosophical justification of one's articles of faith. The Jaina had to accept the rule of the game and the result is a full-fledged philosophy, that has come down to us as an invaluable heirloom.

The philosophy of *syādvāda* has been more maligned than understood. I have spared no pains to give a loyal representation of it and have shown that it is not a philosophical monstrosity that rival philosophers in their unphilosophical impatience have tried to make it out. Though born in an orthodox Brahmin family and though my personal philosophical convictions are rather enlisted on the side of Śaṅkara's Vedānta, I felt a close affinity of Jaina thought to Vedānta, which however a superficial observer may find to be diametrically opposed in their attitude and findings. It must not be forgotten that Vedānta is frankly realistic in its logic and epistemology. And the logical evaluation of phenomenal reality as a mass of irrational surds and contradictions by Vedānta is almost endorsed *in toto* by Jaina thought subject to a fundamental reservation, *viz.*, its peculiar attitude of logical thought. The Jaina accepts the findings of Vedānta, but refuses to draw the same conclusion. Herein lies the originality of Jaina thought in that it seeks to reorientate our logical attitude and asks us to accept the exposure of contradictions as the true measure of reality. The academic world and the average man of culture have heard much of Vedānta, though its vigorous polemical apparatus still lies hidden in inaccessible Sanskrit works; and the impression of the generality of mankind is that India has produced only idealistic systems of thought. It is hoped that a critical student of Indian thought will feel the necessity of revising his opinion in this regard. Suffice it to say that Vedāntic idealism was not a facile overgrowth and it is necessary to understand realistic philosophy with all its strength in order to be able to appreciate idealism. Indian philosophy does not stand by mysticism, though it culminates in it. But the mysticism is not the result of dogmatic faith. It is reasoned out of logical thought and is rather an overflow. The inadequacy of logic was realized at the end of the journey and the necessity of cultivating a superior power of vision, which is not satisfied with the negative findings of reason, was realized as the key to unlock the mystery of ultimate reality.

All schools of philosophy in India, except the Cārvāka School of Materialism which seems to be the direct antithesis of philosophy, are agreed that philosophical speculation is a necessary discipline of the mind which steels convictions and attenuates doubts. But the ultimate truth cannot be realized by philosophical discipline alone, which is only a means to that end. Indian philosophers are agreed that the plenum of knowledge can be attained by the development of a super-vision which is a potentiality in all of us. The progressive development of knowledge and the instinctive discontent with partial conquests of science and philosophy in the domain of knowledge are the augury and the assurance of infinite perfection which is the logical consummation of our destiny. The Jaina is emphatic that omniscience is the condition as well as the result of perfection, and however much we may advance in our philosophical enquiry and scientific pursuit, which are not antagonistic in their aim in spite of their difference in method and lines of approach, it cannot by itself bring about the final consummation. But there is no alternative short cut to this. One must proceed on the road of philosophical speculation and elect to pass through the grind of the intellectual drill that philosophy prescribes until the terminus is reached. The terminus of philosophy is the beginning of spiritual career. The necessity of the pursuit of philosophy is vindicated by the fact that no thoughtful man can get rid of it. Even the man, who decries philosophy and condemns its culture, can hope to make out his case by only having recourse to philosophy. The denunciation of philosophy itself results in the setting up of a rival philosophy.

India's philosophical culture is characterized by a sincerity of purpose and seriousness of outlook which cannot fail to extort the unstinted admiration of all but the cynic. Another characteristic of Indian speculation is the unfettered freedom of thought which was unknown in other climes. There was no state persecution for philosophical opinions, and censorship of thought was unknown, provided it did not instigate the subversion of the moral order. The same was true of religion. India has been the land of freedom of religion, which is however a recent growth in the West. This was made possible in India for the reason that Indians did not seek to make political and economical capital out of their religious persuasion. They never confounded things of Caesar with things of God. Another reason seems to be the perfect agreement and unanimity on the necessity of moral discipline. Indian thought was agreed on the moral condition that the animal in man was to be supplanted by the divine. There may be some truth in the contention that India's tolerance of other faiths has resulted in the weakening of her political power. Indians are not even today intolerant of other creeds; but the political consequences are to be set down to the account of the proselytizing zeal of alien faiths which seek to strengthen their political interests by multiplication of converts. India in the past has effected the solution of religious differences by pinning them down in their respective spheres of influence as spiritual forces; and I am convinced that the solution of her present-day problems can be achieved if political labels cease to be put on the difference of faith — religious, philosophical and intellectual.

It may not be out of place to speak a word on the genesis of the present work. I was invited by Mr. S. C. Seal, the Secretary of the Bhāratī Mahāvidyālaya, to deliver a course of twelve lectures on Jaina Philosophy under the auspices of the Bhāratī Jaina Pariṣad. I accepted the offer and have subsequently retouched my lectures and added to them on the request of friends who are interested in my academic pursuits and in the propagation of Indian thought. One thing I may be permitted to claim as the special feature of the present work, *viz.*, that I have kept my philosophical convictions completely in the background and have endeavoured to give as thorough and powerful an exposition of Jaina thought as could be done by an adherent of the Jaina faith. And this has been possible because my philosophy is broad enough to embrace all differences of approach and conclusions. Though an idealist by temperament and conviction I do not believe that the cause of idealism and of truth will thrive only on the degradation of realism. On the contrary I am convinced of the fact, paradoxical though it may sound, that a powerful realistic philosophy is the foundation on which a powerful idealism is to be erected. Up till now I have written little on Vedānta barring a few papers and I consider that my treatment of Buddhistic and Jaina Philosophy will prepare the ground for the reception of my contemplated work on Vedānta, which will take considerable time and labour.

I must thank my pupil Mr. Nathmal Tatiya, M.A., Puranchand Nahar Research Fellow, for preparing the contents. The index and abbreviations have been done by Mr. Anantalal Thakur and my best thanks are due to him. I cannot express my gratitude to Prof. S. N. Dasgupta in adequate terms for having furnished a Foreword in spite of his indifferent health and multifarious preoccupations. My debt of gratitude has become heavier to Dr. Syamaprasad Mookerjee by his approval of my dedication of the book to him. Lastly I must thank Mr. Shantiprasad Jain, Mr. Satischandra Seal, and Mr. Chhotelal Jain for their interest in the propagation of Jaina thought. It will be a sacred investment of their money if the multi-millionaires of the Jaina community shed their indifferentism to Jaina culture and make it worthwhile for scholars to devote their labour to Jaina thought by presentation of books and other forms of aid, the lack of which was seriously felt as a handicap by the present author. One word and I finish. Mr. Nathmal Tatiya, M.A., and Mr. Sitamsusekhar Bagchi M.A., B.L., have been my critics and they helped me with their words of appreciation. These two scholars are carrying on researches on Jaina Philosophy under my guidance and I wish that they should be liberally patronized by lovers of Jaina culture. Dr. Satindra Kumar Mookerjee, M.A., Ph.D. read the book in typescript up to Chapter VI and I owe a good deal to his criticism and suggestions. I wish it were possible for him to go through the whole book and I had the benefit of his criticism of the remaining chapters — a fastidious scholar, that he is, who lets nothing pass unchallenged either in the way of linguistic form or of matter of argument. The present writer wished to incorporate a chapter on *Naya,* but the press could not wait and so this has to be postponed for a second edition, if one is called for. A word of explanation seems necessary for my elaborate treatment of the Nyāya Conception of Universals in a book on Jaina Philosophy. My apology is that in this I have only followed in the footsteps of Yaśovijaya, who in his *Nyāyakhaṇḍakhādya*, a remarkable exposition of Jaina Philosophy in the manner and terminology of the Neo-logicians of Bengal and Mithilā, has incorporated in his work all the arguments of the *Ātmatattvaviveka* with the exposition of its commentators, Raghunātha Śiromaṇi, Guṇānanda and Nārāyaṇa. Yaśovijaya has unbounded admiration for Raghunātha and has paid him handsome compliments for his originality of thought even while he differs from him. I have given the references to the *Ātmatattvaviveka*, but could have made the same to Yaśovijaya's work, which quoted from the former book *verbatim* and *literatim.* In this I have followed the plan and procedure of Yaśovijaya and I felt that a departure would make the treatment of this fundamental problem of philosophy inadequate and imperfect. I have however criticized the later exponents of Jaina thought and in this I trust I have only exercised the prerogative of an exponent, who need not be a yes-man. I have offered my criticism in honest faith and I have referred to Vimaladāsa in support of my position. I believe that the problem of the relation of universals to particulars is purely logical and not spatio-temporal. The universal is logically related to the particular and this relation is not capable of being understood in terms of space-time determination.

The universal is a fact which can be understood by logical thought alone and space-time does not constitute either a determination of or a barrier to its ontological status. It is everywhere and everywhen in the sense that it cannot be conceived to ontologically non-existent, though for self-manifestation it requires a spatio-temporal event as its medium, in between its media. It "is neither given nor presented but is taken" in the language of Bradley.

I shall consider my labour to be amply justified if it succeeds in stimulating the interest of a student of philosophy in Indian thought in general and in Jaina thought in particular.

Asutosh Building,
9th March 1944. SATKARI MOOKERJEE

CONTENTS

FOREWORD Prof. S. N. Dasgupta vii

PREFACE ix

CHAPTER

I THE LOGICAL BACKGROUND OF JAINA PHILOSOPHY 1-22

Sources of knowledge (1—2); Functions of experience and reflection (3); Origin and status of the Laws of Thought and their reorientation from the Jaina standpoint (4—19); Difference of philosophers and their progress towards consummation of absolute unanimity stressed (20—21); Original contributions of Jaina Philosophy (21—22).

II NON-ABSOLUTISM 23-48

An absolute real can neither be a cause nor an effect (23—27); The Jaina solves the difficulty by means of anekānta (27—29); Things cannot be held to be existent in an absolute sense; four kinds of non-existence; position of the Vedāntist elucidated (29—35); The Jaina position of non-absolutism (35—37); Sāṅkhya theory of causation and its criticism by the Jaina (37); The problem of the eternal existence of word of the Mīmāṁsist and its solution from the Jaina standpoint (38); The formidable array of arguments of the Cārvāka materialist who denies the reality of non-existence on entirely different grounds (38—43); The Jaina reply (43—46); The problem of post-non-existence (46—48).

III NUMERICAL DIFFERENCE AND ABSOLUTE NON-EXISTENCE 49-72

Meaning of numerical difference and absolute non-existence; The results of their denial; The Vedāntist and the Buddhist positions (49—51);

The Vedāntist's and the Śūnyavādin's denial of relation (52—55); Jaina reply (54—60); Sceptic's rejoinder and the Jaina reply; The problem of causation; Nāgārjuna on Sāṅkhya and Nyāya theories and the Jaina solution (60—61); The discovery of anekāntavāda as a solution of the problem of causation (62); The central thesis of the Jaina and the nature of reality; Jaina position compared and contrasted with other systems (64—72).

IV Absolute Negativism and Absolute Particularism 73-96

Fluxist on the objectivity of non-existence and the Jaina position (73—74); Voidist's position and the Jaina reply (75—80): Jaina conception of the nature of reality; The Sāṅkyha-Yoga position (80—82); Prefixing of *syāt* to propositions, a warning against reading absolutist sense; The meaning of 'inexpressible' (83); Fluxist's interpretation of 'inexpressible' and the Jaina reply (83—86); Buddhist epistemology of perceptual knowledge and the Jaina position reviewed (86—96).

V The Inexpressible or the Indefinite 97-116

Buddhist position and the Jaina solution recalled (97); The Mīmāṁsist view of reality and its defect and the Jaina position (98—100); Significance of *syāt* (100—101); Bhartṛhari's plea that the whole order of reality is but the manifestation of word and the sceptic's position which makes thought free from verbal association and the Jaina's reconciliation which is effected rather by going deeper into the nature of reality than in a syncretic spirit (101—114): Sceptic's condemnation of all knowledge as false; falsity — a relative concept — position of Saṅkara (114—115).

VI The Dialectic of Sevenfold Predication 117-176

Sec. I. The question why should the number of

assertions be seven, neither more nor less and its answer; genesis of sevenfold assertions (117—120); Vedântis 's denial of the second proposition; first two propositions logically valid and psychologically necessary (120); Logical and ontological considerations; propositions can be viewed both as analytical and synthetical according to our intellectual equipment and psychological interest (121—122): Unguarded predication — a source of confusion and misconception; *Syāt* a corrective proviso (122); Why further combinations not possible (123—125); The import of the seven propositions (126—133).

Sec. II. Import of each term of the propositions (133—136); The negative proposition is as much true as the affirmative one; non existence belongs to jar and not to what is not jar as the Naiyâyika would have us believe; The Vedântist complaint of contradiction and the Jaina answer; The Naiyâyika's belief that certain facts are always existent and their opposites are inconceivable and the vindication of the Jaina position (137—142); the determinate nature of existence and non-existence — conception of svarūpa and pararūpa — other determinants *viz.*, substance, time and location— external and internal determinations (142—148); The problem of the relation of subject and predicate in the proposition "the self exists" (148—150).

Sec. III. Survey of the remaining five propositions (150—151); each proposition constitutes an estimation of reality, which has been either advocated by a school of philosophers as a matter of historical fact or is capable of being entertained as possible evaluation (151—153); The theory of sevenfold predication regarded as a logical elaboration of the position of the Jaina; its universal application illustrated (153—159); Consideration of the objection advanced against the theory as a whole (159—165); The question which of the two; realism and idealism, possesses the final truth and its answer (165); The Jaina position in logic and the realistic philosophers (165—166); The contention of the Naiyāyika who believes in the opposition of being and non-being like the idealist and the Jaina reply (166—170); The position of Prabhākara and the Jaina solution (170—172); Jaina's dismissal of the fundamental accusation of contradiction entails the collapse of all other charges (173); The Jaina non-absolutism and its critics (174); The Sāṅkhya doctrine of identity of substance in the midst of its changing modes, the universal-cum-particulars of the Naiyāyikas, the perceptual cognition of variegated colour in a carpet of the Buddhist — are confessions of unity of the plurality; The Cārvāka and the Mīmāṁsist also endorse the Jaina logical standpoint (174—176).

VII RELATIONS 177-211

(I) Identity and difference — the presupposition of relation (177—178); Denial of relation — the Fluxist, the Vedāntist and Bradley; the charge that unreality of relation would make causal relation unreal does not affect the Buddhist; relation of terms only a subjective construction according to Dharmakīrti and Kant alike (178—181); Reciprocity of services the *conditio sine qua non* of objective relation — (181—191); Jaina conception of relation (191—195); The difficulty about the cognition of relation and the Jaina reply — perception of concomitance in agreement and difference the organ of the knowledge of causality (194—198). (II) The problem of inherence; the nature of inherence — proof of inherence and the source of its knowledge — difficulties regarding inherence and the Vaiśeṣika answer (198—206); The Jaina position (206—211).

VIII The Nyāya Conception of Universals 212-265

Meaning of relatedness — meaning of identity (212—213); Buddhist contention that the meaning of terms is negation of the opposite and that negation is a fiction is psychologically false and logically unjustifiable; source of knowledge of the universal according to the Naiyāyika: elaborate exposition of the Buddhist and the Naiyāyika position (213—241); A retrospective survery of the Buddhist arguments put forward to negative the objective reality of the universal and Udayana's criticism of the Buddhist position (241—253); The Buddhist theory which makes the particular responsible for the thought of the universal and its criticism (253—256); Examination of the objections advanced by the Buddhist against the possibility of an object universal (257—260); A difficulty raised by the non-absolutist and the Naiyāyika reply (261—262); The objection of Dharmakīrti and the Naiyāyika's answer (262—264); The problems whether our sense organs are competent to envisage universals and whether language is directly cognisant of reality as it is (264—265).

IX The Jaina Conception of Universals 266-286

Sec. I. Jaina conception of universals as represented by Jinabhadra, Akalaṅka and Vidyānandi down to Yaśovijaya (266); The position adopted by Samantabhadra (266—272).

Sec. II. Buddhist influence and the reinterpretation of universal by Jinabhadra, Akalaṅka. Vidyānandi and Prabhācandra down to Yaśovijaya (272—274) Criticism of the same (275—289).

INDEX 287-289

ABBREVIATIONS

AM—Āptamīmāṃsā
AMI—Āptamīmāṃsā
AS—Aṣṭasāhasrī
ATV—Ātmatattvaviveka (Bibl. Indica)
ATVB—Ātmatattvav veka Com. by Bhagīratha Thakkura (Bibl. Indica)
ATVD—Ātmatattvaviveka-Dīdhiti (Bibl. Indica)
ATVS—Ātmatattvaviveka Com. by Śaṅkara Miśra (Bibl. Indica)
BSŪ—Brahmasūtra
KP—Kāvyaprakāśa
Nar. Com.—Com. on ATV. by Nārāyaṇa (Benares)
NKC—Nyāyakumudacandra
NKU—Nyāyakusumāñjali
NS—Nyāyasūtra
NVi—Nyāyaviniścaya of Akalaṅka
PDS—Padārthadharmasaṃgraha
PKM—Prameyakamalamārtaṇḍa
PV—Pramāṇavārttika
SBHT—Saptabhaṅgītaraṅgiṇī
SBT—Saptabhaṅgītaraṅgiṇī
TSB—Tattvārthasūtrabhāṣya
TSV—Tattvārthaślokavārttika

CHAPTER I

THE LOGICAL BACKGROUND OF JAINA PHILOSOPHY

The Jaina Philosopher maintains that existents are possessed of an infinite number of attributes and characteristics which can be discovered by experience alone. Even the primal attribute of existence, which is the foundational element of the nature of an entity, is not capable of being ascertained by *a priori* logical considerations. Our knowledge of things and of their relations starts from experience, and reason can at best serve to organise the experienced data and build a system of thought, the elements of which together with their relations, must be ultimately derived from this fundamental source of knowledge, in other words, from direct acquaintance furnished by observation. The Jaina does not draw a line of distinction between internal and external sources of knowledge so far as their logical value is concerned. He refuses to put a premium on internal intuition. The mind, even with its active contributions, which the Jaina does not seek to deny, is believed by him to be an instrument of discovery and not a creator of facts. If we undertake to institute a comparison between the Jaina and Kant, a risky venture in all conscience, we may observe that the Jaina would have no difficulty in accepting the latter's finding that mind and matter both co-operate in producing knowledge. But the Jaina would not agree with Kant and for that matter with the Buddhist logicians, Dignāga and Dharmakīrti, who anticipated many of the conclusions of the German Philosopher, that the categories, or forms of understanding, as he calls them, are but mental phenomena. Such concepts as causality, substance, attribute and the like, are no doubt the ways in which the mind works up the data of experience, but this does not mean with the Jaina that they are true of the mind only and not of the extra-mental reality which they purport to understand. The Jaina would take them to be the instruments of discovery of the nature of reality, internal and external, which render the same kind of service as the sense-organs do.

If our experience is not to be denounced as a false traitor, there is no reason why external reality should be condemned to the status of a mystery. If it is to be condemned, there are again no *a priori* grounds for believing inner experience and thought to be valid, since they are as much concerned with reality as external experience is. The denial of validity of all thought and experience involves self-contradiction, inasmuch as the denial would at any rate claim validity for itself. If the experience of outer reality cannot carry a guarantee of its truth, there is no reason for preference of internal experience also. The truth of the doubt as a fact, albeit mental, is also to be equally called in question. But this means the impossibility of all predication — be it affirmation or negation as the case may be.

There is another point on which the Jaina again would emphatically differ from the rationalists. Both Kant and the Buddhist philosophers hold that sense-experience can give insight into particulars and the universal forms are contributed by thought or the mind. The Jaina does not see any reason why things should be particulars alone. Things are, according to the Jaina, both universals and particulars together — rather they are concrete universals, if we may be permitted to use this respectable term with due apology to Hegelians. Reflective thought certainly enables us to analyse the two aspects in a concrete real, but that does not argue the inability of experience to take stock of reality in its universal character. A real is a particular which possesses a generic attribute. There is no reason why experience should fail to take cognisance of the generic aspect, though it is present in it. This is also the position of the Naiyāyikas and the Mīmāṁsists who agree with the Jaina in their conception of the nature of reality. The Jaina does not find any difficulty in accounting for the emergence of concepts. It is reflection, no doubt, which is necessary for the evolution of conceptual thought, but reflection is grounded in experience, which, in its turn, directly derives from reality. Experience furnishes unanalysed data with the universal and the particular rolled into one. Reflection only distinguishes the two elements and this has been misconstrued to be the original contribution of thought. But thought does not impose the universal. It only discovers its existence in the real. If the universals were subjective creations, our experience would have to be denounced as valueless, as particulars, even if perceived, would yield no knowledge, as Kant has proved and the Buddhist has admitted. If experience be not unnecessarily condemned to take stock of particulars only, for which there is no logical necessity, and if again universals be not denied an objective status and basis, for which again there is neither warrant nor justification, and if, in conformity with the plain verdict of experience, the nature of reals is admitted to be made up of both the elements — universal and particular and to be cognised as such by perceptual knowledge, the difficulties of philosophers would be reduced to an appreciable extent. We shall presently show how the Jaina solves the problem of the origin and status of the Laws of Thought in the light of his reflections recorded here.

It will be seen in the course of our speculations that the number of qualities and characteristics of a particular existent is infinite, if original qualities and derivative characteristics induced by relations are taken into consideration. Everything is related with every other thing, and this relation involves the emergence of a relational quality. The qualities cannot be known *a priori*, though a good number of them can be deduced from certain fundamental characteristics. For instance, we can deduce, from the fact that things are existent and diverse, the fact of the existence of characteristics that impart individuality to each thing. It can be further deduced that things being numerically different are bound by relations of similarity and dissimilarity — by similarity, so far as they are things of the same kind, substance, quality and so on, and by dissimilarity, so far as they are of different kinds. But this *a priori* deduction of qualities does not argue that the qualities are subjective. The Jaina would rather interpret this deduction as an analysis of the nature of reals quite as objective and realistic as the chemical and physical analysis of physical substances. The human faculties are not in antagonism to the objective reality, but are rather the organs of discovery of its nature and behaviour. There have been aberrations and errors in the interpretation of the functions and services of these organs, and the resulting incongruities have been a source of confusion. The subject has to use his faculties to find out the behaviour of objects and the laws of such behaviour without any preconceived bias. And the results achieved by science by the pursuit of this procedure prove the soundness of the Jaina attitude and standpoint. The expression 'Laws of Thought' is not free from ambiguity and has been a source of confusion of thought and issues. That these are self-evident principles is a proposition which can be accepted subject to a reservation. We shall endeavour to elucidate the Jaina position by examination of the Laws of Thought one by one. The Jaina thinks that the Laws can be true and valid only if they are laws of reality. It cannot be supposed that they are the laws of our thinking and not of the objects of thought, because the supposition involves preposterous issues. It makes not only agnosticism inevitable, but perforce deprives human thought of the faintest claim to validity. The Jaina does not agree to draw a line of cleavage between existent and existent. The subjective thought is as much existent as the objective datum and both have to be determined by experience to be what they are. That our consciousness and the modes of consciousness are known by themselves does not confer any privilege on them in so far as the question of their validity and truth is considered. The problem of truth is a logical problem and must be determined with logical means. The criterion of falsity is contradiction. If a judgment is found to be contradicted by another judgment of unquestionable truth, the former is to be rejected as untrue. Subjective experience, as illustrated by dream, is rejected as false because it is contradicted by our waking experience. There is no intrinsic characteristic of falsity. The problem of falsity is thus ultimately a question of experience. The problem of truth is no less a matter of experience and *a priori* logic is absolutely incompetent to deal with it. What are usually called self-evident principles do not derive their self-evidence so much from logic as from psychology. Of course our thought movement has a logic of it, but, the logic is not in antagonism with experience. Logic has to work upon the data of experience and is as much an instrument as experience is. Indian realists do not set an arbitrary limit to the denotation of the term 'experience.' They would include within its scope much that passes for pure thought. The Naiyāyika understands by 'experience' (*anubhava*) not only perceptual cognition, but inferential and verbal judgments as well. The Jaina is more liberal in this. He would include even memory within the fold of experience. It is absolutely necessary to bear in mind the comprehensive denotation of the term 'experience' which includes both internal and external cognitions. The Jaina's advocacy of the validity of *Ūha* (reasoning) as the organ of intuition of universal propositions shows that his empiricism is not of the narrow type. In fact the Jaina does not read a contradiction between reasoning and experience, which seems to be customary. He is impatient with the rationalists when they undertake to build their systems of thought in defiance of experience. Reasoning is a valued organ possessed by mankind, but it must be used with caution and circumspection. The meaning of the Jaina contention will be apparent from our speculations recorded in the course of our enquiry.

It is thought that sense-experience is incompetent to yield knowledge of universals. The proposition seems to be a corollary of a wider proposition that all existents are particulars, absolutely discrete and separate from one another. The Buddhist fluxist holds this view and accordingly regards universals as figments of thought having no objective status. There are again thinkers, who, though they believe in the objective existence of universals, assert that sense-experience is incompetent to take stock of them. The Jaina differs from both these classes of thinkers. Although the Jaina does not seem to believe in the existence of unitive universals,[1] he maintains the immanence of universals in particulars by virtue of which the individuals are placed under a class. As has been observed the Jaina is a believer in concrete universals. Things are neither exclusively particulars, nor are they exclusively universals, but they are a concrete realization of both. The two elements can be distinguished by reflective thought, but cannot be rent asunder. So our experience of one particular individual is not confined to that individual alone, but extends to unperceived individuals also in so far as the latter typify the universal as a part of their constitution. Individuals, even when they belong to a class, will vary from one another and no inference of their variations is possible from the observed instances. But it is certain that the unobserved

1. We propose to discuss the Jaina conception of universals in the last chapter.

individuals will exhibit the same fundamental characteristics which are involved in their possessing, each and all, the universal, characterizing the observed individual. Repetition of experience only helps us to take stock of the universal in its true character, but once the latter is known, it does not stand in need of verification or confirmation by further observation. Thus, when a man perceives a cow, he perceives the individual cow together with the cow-universal (*gotva*) and he is certain that any other cow would also possess the same fundamental characteristics that are implied by the presence of the cow-universal in it. Further experience may confirm his conviction, but the added strength of conviction is due to the added strength of the cognition of the universal, which was derived even in the first case. The Naiyāyika and the Jaina and other realists of India are agreed on this question of the complex nature of existents as well as the competency of direct experience with regard to this complex character. Although the complex nature of reals is emphasised by the Naiyāyikas and the Mīmāṁsists also, the logical implications of this ontological doctrine were worked out by the Jaina alone; and the result has been a momentous revolution in the evaluation of the Laws of Thought. It is maintained that as the nature of existents can be determined by experience alone, no *a priori* cosiderations should be allowed to give a twist to the unmistakable deliverance of the former. Logic is to be checked by reference to this primary source of knowledge. The failure to compare the consequences entailed by unfettered logical thought with the plain verdict of experience and to check the results has been responsible for such widely divergent views of the nature of reality as to make philosophy appear to the neophyte as a veritable Tower of Babel.

It is necessary that we should first examine the Laws of Thought as propounded in the traditional schools and understand their ontological implications. Secondly, we should test these Laws in their application to the workings of Nature and mind as to how far the laws function as a measure of reality. Thirdly, we should give rigorous consideration to the consequences and conclusions, that have been deduced by the Jaina philosophers. I must confess here that the present dissertation is not found ready-made in any Jaina work and, as presented here, it is but a construction and development of the Jaina logical standpoint. But the deduction is so obvious that there would be little room for doubting its fidelity to the Jaina point of view. It may be looked upon as a development necessitated by the demands of modern thought, and it is hoped that it will help the understanding of the Jaina metaphysical position, as interpreted in the following chapters.

Now, the Laws of Thought are formulated as follows: (1) *The Law of Identity* — "Whatever is, is" (2) *The Law of Contradiction* — "Nothing can both be and not be" and (3) *The Law of Excluded Middle* — "Everything must either be or not be." These principles are undoubtedly true and are intuitively perceived. But the abstract formulation proves inadequate to deal with actual data with their infinite complexity, unless the laws are qualified by necessary reservations. The Jaina does not believe in the *a priori* validity of these laws and he thinks that these laws of thought are derived from the fund of experience, which is the ultimate source of knowledge and the final court of appeal in a dispute about the nature of things. Now the nature of things is believed to be dynamic in character from the observation of the data of experience, and these laws, the Jaina would insist, should be in consonance with the concept of change and all that it implies. The abstract formula of identity "A is A" is bound to suffer from the defects of symbolism, which seems to lay stress on the static character of things. But nothing is static according to the Jaina and so the symbolic representation does not give any insight into the nature of reality as it is. The point will be made clear if we substitute a concrete substance for the symbol A, say, a pen. The proposition will then be "A pen is a pen." But a pen, being a real, is constantly undergoing change, and change means that the changing substance is becoming different at every stage of change. So a pen at a particular moment is not absolutely the same pen at the next moment. It was fresh and new when it was turned out of the factory and with the efflux of time and the wear and tear of constant use it will lose its freshness as it continues in its career. The same pen was new at one time and becomes old at another time. The new and the old pen are not absolutely the same entity. But they are not, on the other hand, absolutely different also. The identity of the pen persists in spite of the change of characteristics and this demands an explanation. The Vedāntist idealist has declared change to be illusory on the basis of this Law of Identity. The pen 'black' and the pen 'white' are not absolutely the same identity, and the difference in qualities undoubtedly implies a difference in identity. The matter will be fully discussed in a subsequent chapter when we shall discuss the problem of change. It will be proved that change connotes difference and identity, and both should be accepted as true. What the Jain maintains is that the nature of reals can be understood from experience, and reflective thought only helps to clarify our conception. It cannot and should not ascribe to the real any attribute or element that does not belong to it in its own right. This is the fundamental position of all realistic philosophy. But realists, as a matter of historical fact, have not been able to maintain their loyalty to this fundamental position without compromise.

A slight consideration will show the inadequacy of pure logic to give us the full knowledge of a real unless it is supplemented and reinforced by experience. Thus, the pen in question is a pen, no doubt, but that is not the whole of it. A pen is a substance, good or bad, soft or hard, black or blue, or white and infinite other things, which are to be gathered from the progressive expansion of knowledge of its nature. If anybody were to argue on the basis of the Law of Identity that a pen should not be anything else than the pen as it was at the first moment of its existence, certainly his argument would be false. The logician may contend that the identity of the pen includes all these possibilities within its own ambit and so the law does not suffer. Yes, it is exactly the case, but the law does not help us in the least so far as our knowledge of the identity is concerned. The identity is accepted to be true in the midst of all these varying attributes, because experience certifies the continuity of the pen all the while. This should be a pointer in the case of change of attributes. The pen does not forfeit its identity with the change of characteristics, that is entailed by the efflux of time, as it is recognized to be the same pen. There is no reason to call in question the reality of change or of the identity, as both are perceived facts. Every entity is subject to change and maintains its identity throughout its career until it is supplanted by something different. To be explicit, the position, we maintain, may be stated as follows. The pen is a pen so long as it exists as a pen; it was not a pen when it was a piece of raw material; it will not be a pen when it will cease to exist as a pen and become something else. Again, a pen is existent in its own place and time, in its own nature as a pen, and not in another place and time and in a different nature. The Vedāntist draws a distinction between essential and non-essential characteristics of reality. The characteristic, which continues unmodified, is believed to constitute the essential nature of the real, and the changing attributes, which occur and disappear in time, represent the contingent and unessential appendage, which according to the Vedāntist, obscures its true nature from our view. The Jaina does not subscribe to this position, as it amounts to denial of the reality of change. When as a matter of fact we are to depend upon experience to make us aware of the very existence of a real and *a priori* reasoning is absolutely of no avail in this respect, why should we distrust its testimony with regard to other attributes, which are equally intuited along with the attribute of existence? As to the problem of *a priori* knowledge of the behaviour of things unobserved on the basis of the observation of a particular instance, the Jaina does not see any difficulty in it, which makes appeal to an *a priori* source of knowledge inevitable or imperative. Observation of one instance, say a pen, is not confined to that individual alone, but extends to other individuals in virtue of the possession of the universal, which makes a pen what it is. So it does not require any transcendental source of knowledge to meet the situation. The Jaina thus concludes that the formula of identity has to be hedged round by so many qualifications that in its abstract, symbolic form it turns out to be absolutely vague, useless and misleading.

What is true of the Law of Identity will be found to be true with equal force of the Law of Contradiction also. A cannot both be and not be — is the formula of the Law of Contradiction The proposition seems to be self-evident in its abstract form. But as soon as it is converted into a concrete fact, it is found to require so many provisos and restrictive qualifications to be true to reality that in its abstract form it seems to have little or no logical value. 'A pen cannot both be and not be' seems to be a self-evident proposition. But a little reflection will show that its self-evidence is only apparent. 'A pen cannot both be and not be' — is a proposition which is understood to illustrate the Law of Contradiction. Let us try to understand the relation of being and non-being. Being and non-being, that are thought to be incompatible, may be understood in an absolute or relative sense. Absolute being is never other than being irrespective of difference of time, place and circumstances in which it may manifest itself. But such absolute being is only an idea and an abstraction, and in so far as experience is regarded as a proof, it must be asserted to remain unproved. So also with regard to absolute non-being. If the incompatibility of such absolute being and absolute non-being is denied, that does not give us any aid in the determination of the status and relation of facts experienced by us. If, by the terms 'being' and 'non-being,' however, we are to understand concrete being and concrete non-being as exemplified by the objects of experience, the law as formulated is misleading and untrue. Is it a fact that the pen cannot both be and not be? The pen is a pen in so far as it is a pen, that is to say, in so far as it retains the character of pen. It is again a pen so long as it exists as a pen, that is to say, in its own time. It is again a pen only in the area of space where it is and in so far again as it possesses the qualities and functions that belong to it. The being of the pen is thus to be understood in reference to a definite individuality that it possesses in virtue of its intrinsic determinations. It is not a fact in respect of a different setting and of a different individuality. It is thus a fact and not a fact even at the same time. It is a fact *quâ* pen, but is not a fact *quâ* other than a pen. Again, as a determinate existent it occupies a particular span of time and area of space, outside which it is not a fact. Again, as possessing a magnitude it is a plurality of parts. The parts do not, taken by themselves, possess the pen-character, but the pen is not absolutely different from the parts, as it has no being outside them. As viewed in other relations the pen is not a pen. The pen is a substance, but substance is not the pen. The terms 'being' and 'not-being' as elements in the formula have thus to be understood in a very restricted sense, *i.e.*, only in relation to a definite context, which can be known from experience alone. The validity of the Law of Contradiction should thus be held to be determined by the testimony of experience and not *a priori.* Experience certifies the dual nature of entities, *viz.*, existence in respect of its own individuality and non-existence apart from and outside this nature; and there is no reason why we should reject either of the two. Not only this, but whatever can be predicated of anything as its characteristic can have a meaning and purpose only if it implies its negation. Existence can be the characteristic of a real, if it implies non-existence also of that of which it is predicated. Existence is a determinate characteristic and when affirmed of A implies its non-existence as B. Similarly with regard to non-existence and all other affirmative and negative characteristics. A thing is determined to be what it is only when it is differentiated from what it is not. If A is asserted to be existent, the assertion is significant only if it negates its non-existence in its own context and implies its non-existence in a different context. It cannot be legitimately contended that the implication of the opposite by the affirmation of a positive characteristic is only a necessity of conceptual thought and so does not argue its objective status in a real. Conceptual thought is not unfounded in reality. If things were absolute particulars having no character apart from its own self-identity and if the predication of characteristics were only a figment of the intellect, it would not be possible to explain the emergence of different concepts and their affiliation to different entities. A 'blue' is determined to be characterized by blueness and a 'red' by redness. If the characteristic 'blue' were as destitute of objective status as 'red' in blue is, it passes our understanding why red should not be conceived as blue and blue as red. It must then be admitted that conceptual thought is as much controlled by the objective real as perceptual intuition is. Moreover, intuition uninterpreted by conceptual thought is an unrelieved blank and hence as good as non-existent. Abstract speculation moving *in vacuo* is a reckless venture and a blind enterprise. If philosophy is not to stultify itself in its mission to organise our thought and experience into an ordered whole, it must directly approach reality and study its character and behaviour free from preconceived bias. Dispassionate study reveals reality to be a synthesis of opposites — existence and non-existence, and we have no warrant to override the plain delivery of experience in deference to abstract considerations. The Vedāntist starts with the premise that reality is one universal existence; the Buddhist fluxist believes in atomic particulars, each absolutely different from the rest and having nothing underlying them to bind them together. The Naiyāyika believes both to be combined in an individual, though he maintains that the two characters are different and distinct. A real according to him is rather an aggregate of the universal and the particular, and not a real synthesis. The Jaina differs from them all and maintains that the universal and the particular are only distinguishable traits in a real, which is at once identical with and different from both. A real is neither a particular nor a universal in an exclusive manner, but a synthesis which is different from both severally and jointly though embracing them in its fold. A real is *sui generis*.[1] Such a real answers to all the demands of experience and meets all the requirements of thought.

Such being the case, the Law of Contradiction as propounded by formal logic cannot be accepted as the measure of reality as it is. There is no absolute contradiction between being and non-being, when understood in relation to definite contexts and settings, abstracted from which they would have no reality of their own. The differences of views about the nature of reality are due to the unwholesome influence of the cultivation of pure formal logic, and to the propensity of philosophers to build systems of thought *in abstracto*. If experience is found to come in conflict with the Laws of Thought and the system built by philosophers does not resemble in the least the real world of our experience, these philosophers do not feel the slightest scruple to condemn experience. There might be some plausibility of abstract reason being the determinant of reality, if there were agreement among philosophers regarding the function and results of reason. But the fact is entirely the reverse of unanimity. The fluxist and the nihilist both put their absolute reliance upon the self-evident validity of the Laws of Thought,

1. As., pp. 147-48.

but the results achieved by them are entirely incompatible with one another. So also with regard to the Vedāntist and the Buddhist idealist. The Jaina also believes in the truth of the law of contradiction, but he insists that the source of the law should be sought not in *a priori* thought, but in concrete experience of the behaviour of things.

What should then be the criterion of contradiction and incompatibility? The Jaina affirms, "We consider a position to be incompatible, which has not the sanction of valid experience. But no amount of *a priori* cognition can dismiss a situation as incompatible, if it is found to be cognized by an accredited instrument of cognition. As regards contradiction between two facts, it is ascertained to hold between them when they are never found to co-exist in one substratum. There can be no co-existence between two facts which are contradictorily opposed to each other and in such a situation one is invariably superseded by the other. Light and darkness, heat and cold, are believed to be mutually contradictory, because they are never found to co-exist. But if the co-existence of any two things is attested by uncontradicted experience, there is absolutely no earthly reason why they should be regarded as mutually contradictory." The Buddhist does not believe in the unity of a whole, since he scents contradiction between the existence and non-existence of a selfsame quality in it even in respect of different parts. A piece of linen may be red in one half and black in the other half. The Naiyāyika and the Jaina do not find any contradiction in the situation, — the linen is both red and black, but not in the same part. The Jaina is an empiricist so far as the knowledge of reality is concerned. But the Buddhist logician thinks that the linen in question is not one, but a conglomeration of atoms arranged in a certain juxtaposition, The 'red' is numerically different from the 'black', because the two are incompatible — thus would the Buddhist argue. The Jaina would assert that it is experience that makes us aware of the existence of 'black' and 'red' and also that they are not found in the selfsame part. Black and red are thus opposed only in reference to the selfsame specific part. But so far as the whole is concerned it is not subject to such a limitation. It actually embraces the two qualities in its own self, as it is found to do so by experience.

Why should the Buddhist or any other adherent of abstract logic take exception to it ? To be consistent the Buddhist should assert that the whole *quâ* a unity is not perceived. But if the cognition of the whole be a fact and the co-existence of black and red in it be equally a matter of unmistakable experience, we should accept it to be so. But the Buddhist denounces the cognition of a unitive whole as unfounded thought on the ground of the incompatibility of the two qualities. Thus he reverses the whole position. The Jaina realist goes to experience when in doubt about the possibility of the occurrence of a fact, and if experience confirms it, he accepts it to be true. But the Buddhist believes a concurrence to be contradictory *a priori*, and if experience is found to record such a situation, the Buddhist idealist does not hesitate to declare it to be false. The difference between the realist and the idealist hinges upon this fundamental difference of view of the validity of the Laws of Thought — whether they are known empirically or *a priori*. It seems that the difference between them is irreconcilable, being more or less bound up with the innate difference of our predispositions and tendencies from self to self. The result is an uncompromising antagonism between our respective outlook and attitude.

The Law of Excluded Middle is not a necessary deduction from the Law of Contradiction, but a new finding. If A cannot both be X and not-X, it must either be X or not-X. The implication of the Law of Contradiction is negative, whereas the Law of Excluded Middle enables us to determine what the nature of a thing should be. It is either X or not-X. The Law of Contradiction affirms that it cannot be both. In other words, it enables us to assert what it is not. The Law of Excluded Middle enables us to assert what it is, or to be precise, what it should be. We know for certain that it cannot be neither. Not only this, we know that it must be something. The Jaina accepts the validity of the law, but does not believe in its aprioristic character. He believes in the truth of these Laws of Thought only because they are laws of reality. And as laws of reality they can be discovered by experience alone. The idealist also has to appeal to experience in the case of the Law of Excluded Middle at any rate to determine what a thing is in actual fact. Supposing that a man asserts that a horse is either red or not-red, we may take the assertion to be true so far as it goes. But as a source of knowledge of the horse and its colour, it is not very helpful, though it narrows down the scope of possibilities. Its verdict is non-commital. It may help us to avoid a mistake, but as an instrument of positive knowledge it is absolutely valueless. We shall have to observe the horse, and then and then alone can we say that it is red or not-red as it is in actual fact. Moreover, the alternative 'not-red' is indeterminate and it can have a determinate value only when experience supplies the knowledge we require. What is true of the Law of Excluded Middle is also true of the other two laws. It is experience alone that can give meaning and validity to them, without which they are useless formulas and unreal symbols. The nature of things, including the foundational element of their 'being', can be known from experience and experience alone. *A priori* thought is incompetent even to assure its own existence.

Even if we believe that 'thoughts' as modes of consciousness are self-intuited, bare existence and intuition should be distinguished. They are not the same thing, though inseparable. Thought is self-intuitive because it derives this capacity from consciousness of which it is an example, but its 'existence' is a fact by itself owing to the possession of a nature which it shares with all existents. It is a coincidence that consciousness has being and self-intuitive capacity. The belief in the *a priori* validity of consciousness and its activities is perhaps due to this coincidence.

The Law of Contradiction and the Law of Excluded Middle are rather the Laws of Opposition. That one thing is opposed to another thing can be determined by experience alone and not by pure thought. This is the contention of the Jaina realist and in this he is fully endorsed by the Naiyāyika and the Mīmāṁsist. But the idealist does not subscribe to the realist's contention *in toto*. The idealist maintains four types of opposition, *viz.*, (1) The opposition of being and non-being, existence and non-existence, is and is-not, which is called *absolute opposition*; (2) *Destructive opposition* found to hold between hostile facts (*vadhyaghātaka-bhāva*); (3) The *opposition of non-congruence*, subsisting between facts which cannot exist together in one substratum (*sahānavasthānalakṣaṇa*); and (4) the opposition of obstruction (*pratibadhyapratibandhakabhāva*), found to obtain between two facts, when the presence of one prevents the occurrence or activity of the other. Now of these four, the last three types of opposition are known from experience and not *a priori.* The idealist agrees with the realist in his contention that the relation of opposition should be ascertained from experience alone so far as these three types are concerned. But the first type of opposition is, according to the idealist, known *a priori* and without appeal to experience. It is known by intuition, pure and transcendental. It can be verified by experience, but experience is not the determinant of its validity. It is valid universally and necessarily. It is argued that the apodeictic certainty and the universal necessity of this law of opposition cannot be derived from empirical knowledge, which is by its very nature vitiated by contingency and particularity. Experience cannot furnish any corrective to its verdict. The Law of Contradiction is based upon this type of opposition and so also is the Law of Excluded Middle. The opposition between being and non-being is known *a priori* and does not stand in need of verification to validate it. Its validity is self-certified, and though experience may illustrate its truth, it does not confer validity upon it. Its validity is intrinsic, being derived from the aprioristic constitution of our thought-principle. If experience is found to be in consonance with this law, as known *a priori*, it is true and valid, and if it is found to be at variance with it, it must be rejected as false. What is said to be true of the Law of Contradiction is true of the other laws in the same way and in the same degree. The idealist, in arguing the consequences of the *a priori* validity of these laws, observes that these Laws of Thought are also the laws of being. It cannot be supposed that being and thought are opposed to each other. On the contrary they are the same stuff, though 'thought' is rather prior to being so far at any rate as the nature of reality is revealed to us. Thought seems to have chronological precedence, if not logical or ontological priority. To take a concrete instance, let us consider the opposition between square and circle. We cannot conceive that a square can be a circle, as the very idea is repugnant. The opposition of the two is known *a priori*. If experience were the source of the knowledge of this opposition, our knowledge at best could be contingent in character and not universal in reference. We can actually experience only a limited number of squares and circles and our knowledge of opposition would necessarily be confined to the actual data, if experience were the only determinant of it. The opposition of blue and red is equally a necessary opposition. The necessity and universality of the opposition between these empirical facts are derived from the basic opposition of being and non-being. To be a square implies that it is not not-square and it is thought to be not-circle, because the concept of square implies the concept of not-circle. So the opposition of square and circle is one of being and non-being, square and not-square at bottom. We depend upon experience only to acquaint us with a square and a circle, and with what is red and what is blue. But once this is known, the opposition between them is certified *a priori* without appeal to experience. If I know a pen I can assert with apodeictic certainty that it is not not-pen. Of course experience alone can supply me with the knowledge of the infinite plurality of things that are not-pen. But the relation of opposition is known *a priori* and the experience of opposition does not add an iota to the strength of my conviction. That the knowledge in question is *a priori* is proved further by the fact that the multiplication of instances does not improve the conviction and the diminution of the number does not detract from its strength. The conviction is at its maximum and this should demonstrate its aprioristic character.

The Jaina admits the truth of all the premises, but does not admit that the conclusion that the knowledge in question is trans-empirical follows from them. The main grounds for inferring the metempirical character of the knowledge are two *viz.*, universality and necessity. Kant also thought these two characters to be incompatible with empirical knowledge. The Jaina would assert that the proposition "All empirical knowledge is contingent and particular" is only an assumption, based upon the wider assumption that all reals are particulars, and that universals are only hypostatized concepts. It has been shown in the very beginning of this chapter that the Jaina does not believe that reals are particulars or that empirical knowledge is contingent, being confined to these data. He concludes that reals are concrete facts embodying the universals in themselves. In fact, the Jaina would go further and maintain that particulars have being, because universals form an essential ingredient of them. As has been observed by an ancient thinker the universal is the very life of particulars. A cow is not recognised as a cow unless it is known to be informed with the universal, cow-hood. When it is seen at a distance too great to allow a distinct perception of all its features, it is perceived to be an individual, which cannot be classed under the head of cow or not-cow.[1] This shows that particulars cannot be bereft of universals, which alone give them the status of reality. The knowledge of the universal again in the particular gives in one glimpse the knowledge of all the individuals as possessed of the universal. Each individual may exhibit variations, but in spite and in the midst of these variations the universal is cognized as the essential factor. There is no ground for denying its objectivity. The Buddhist contention that the universal is only a subjective idea fails to explain why the different individuals belonging to a class should generate one self-identical idea of a universal. If the cow-universal be as unreal as the horse-universal, why should not the horse-universal be felt as affiliated to cows and the cow-universal to horses. The Buddhist has no convincing answer. But the situation admits of an easy explanation if the universal is regarded as an essential part of a real and the assumption of the idealist that reals are particulars and universals are contributions of pure thought is rejected.

We have endeavoured to explain that the knowledge of universality can be accounted for by experience. Now the knowledge of the element of necessity remains to be examined. We have shown how the Laws of Thought are to be qualified by so many provisos in order to make them applicable to reality. But it must be admitted that in spite of the provisos or rather within the framework of the provisos the laws hold as a matter of necessity. A pen, subject to the limitations of time, place, intrinsic nature and determinations, which may be termed as its

1. na hi gauḥ svarūpeṇa gauḥ, nāpy agauḥ, gotvābhisambandhāt tu gauḥ Bhartṛhari. Comp. the elucidation by Jagannātha in his *Rasagaṅgādhara* p. 144 (Nirṇayasāgara Press, 1916).

context, certainly has being as a pen, and not as a not-pen and thus has an exclusive character. It thus satisfies the requirements of the Laws of Thought. A pen is a pen and thus satisfies the Law of Identity. A pen is not not-pen and thus satisfies the Law of Contradiction. A pen again is a determinate existent as a pen and not an indeterminate nothing-being both pen and not-pen. It thus satisfies the Law of Excluded Middle. It is a truism that what holds good of the pen, holds with equal certitude of all existents. We are intuitively certain that the nature of things cannot be otherwise. What is then the source of the certitude of necessity ? The idealist or the pseudo-idealist is of the opinion that the certitude is due to the fact that the laws are *a priori* known. But the Jaina does not believe in the *a priori* validity of these laws or in the existence of pure intuition absolutely unmixed with empirical elements. But can empirical knowledge satisfy the claim of necessity that is undoubtedly felt to attend these Laws of Thought ?

'Whatever is, is', 'A is A', are the formulas of the Law of Identity. The Jaina thinks that the element of necessity follows from an analysis of the nature of A. The being of A is a part of it and so long as there will be A, A will have being. So the universality and necessity of A being A follows from the very nature of A. The being of A and its specific determination are known when A is known. It is also known that bereft of this nature, A will cease to be A. So the predicate being an amplification of the nature of A, or, in other words, the proposition being analytical, the necessity of the predicate is only a matter of deduction. As regards the Law of Contradiction, it is also not synthetic. A has a being that is determinate and definite. Determinate being implies being in a particular context and non-being outside this context. If A were not a being even in its own context, it would not be A. So the Law of Contradiction follows from the determinate character of its being as known from experience. The Law of Excluded Middle likewise follows as a deduction from its very nature. Even if the laws be regarded as synthetic propositions, there is no difficulty in accounting for the element of necessity. One need not necessarily adopt Kant's solution that the necessity is due to the *a priori* necessity of our ways of thought. One can easily explain the situation on objective lines. The nature of things may be supposed to involve that they should behave in a specifically characteristic way. Instead of regarding the Laws of Thought as the Laws of our way of thinking, one can take them to be expressions of the way of behaviour of things. If the ways of thought can be necessary, there is nothing repugnant in the supposition that the ways of reality may illustrate a necessary law. It is not merely a question of possibility or probability. If experience be incompetent to discover the element of necessity in outer reality, we do not see how it happens to transcend this limitation in the case of internal reality. The matter has been discussed in the very beginning and we need not reiterate the arguments produced before.

The difference of philosophers is, however, a matter of conviction deeper than reason can probe, though ratiocination is their common instrument. Although absolute unanimity has not yet been achieved among different schools of thought, it may be claimed that differences have been narrowed down and obscurities and confusion of thought have been clarified to an appreciable extent. If we look deeper and do not unnecessarily magnify the differences, the amount of agreement will be seen to be not inconsiderable. It is again by discussion and exchange of thought and comparing our notes that we can hope to progress towards the consummation of absolute unanimity, though it is neither desirable nor possible in the present state of our knowledge that we should not stand by our convictions. But what is required is purity of motive and honest, unwavering pursuit of enquiry into truth. It is again imperative that the mediaeval spirit of jealousy and the quest of personal or communal triumph instead of the triumph of truth should be shed unconditionally. It cannot be too much stressed that philosophers should not forget that it is as important to try to understand the opponent's point of view as to understand the nature of ultimate reality. And where we cannot agree, we should at least have the charity to agree to differ. It has been made a matter of complaint that philosophy has not made as systematic progress as science has done. But there must be a difference between science and philosophy even in respect of advantages. Philosophy being more or less a matter of abstract speculation and its problems more intangible and elusive than those of science, its progress must be less spectacular. But the path of progress seems to me to lie in understanding to evaluate the different lines of approach that have been made by our predecessors. Inspired by this faith and personal conviction that the Jaina's contribution in this regard should be studied afresh and made known to the modern world, I propose to give a survey of the fundamental ground of Jaina philosophy. I do not attempt anything like a complete study of Jaina metaphysics in this volume. The present venture will serve to prepare the ground for detailed study of Jaina thought with all its problems and doctrines. That must be postponed for the present. Meanwhile I wish that the evaluation of the foundational problems of Jaina philosophy, that is attempted in this work, should reach the thinkers of the present day. The discussion of categories, however, in Jaina philosophy has not so much originality or freshness of approach, as the enunciation of the Law of Sevenfold Predication called the *saptabhaṅgīnaya* possesses. The Jaina's stand against scepticism and abstract speculation and his demand for incorporating all the possible angles of vision into a synthetic approach to reality have not outlived the necessity that called Jaina philosophy into existence. The problems of thought are evergreen, though fashionable terminology that crops up from time to time may serve to camouflage the old problems and give them the appearance of novelty. The Jaina is a realist out and out. The world has got much to think that Indians produced idealistic systems, which for their majesty and perfect technique and bold conclusions cannot but attract attention and admiration. Vedānta seems to be the perfect philosophy from the idealistic standpoint, and Jaina philosophy, being the complete antithesis of Vedānta, should be entitled to equally extensive study. What is presented here is only a fragment. In it we may succeed to lay the foundation, but the superstructure with all its glories and drawbacks is to be raised upon it in future. This much may be claimed for Jaina speculations that however much there may be room for difference of opinion in regard to the evaluation of particular problems, the value of the sevenfold dialectic as an instrument cannot be overestimated. The idealist undoubtedly will refuse to accept its validity. But realism will find in the Jaina philosopher a powerful champion. It cannot be expected that all the findings of the Jaina will meet with approval. Much of it may be antiquated and may appear to be quaint so far as its doctrinal side is concerned. But the new orientation imparted to logical thought and epistemological speculation by the sevenfold dialectic will not be antiquated, however much philosophical speculations may advance and whatever results the progression of science may achieve.

CHAPTER II

NON-ABSOLUTISM (*Anekāntavāda*)

We have elucidated the logical background of Jaina philosophy and we have shown that the Jaina evaluation of the Laws of Thought differs *toto caelo* from that of the idealists, which gave an ultra-intellectual orientation to philosophical speculation. The Jaina pleads for soberness and insists that the nature of reality is to be determined in conformity with the evidence of experience undeterred by the considerations of abstract logic. Loyalty to experience and to fundamental concepts of philosophy alike makes the conclusion inevitable that absolutism is to be surrendered. A thing is neither real nor unreal, neither eternal nor non-eternal, in absolute sense, but partakes of both the characteristics; and this does not mean any offence to the canons of logic. The dual nature of things is proved by a *reductio ad absurdum* of the opposite views. Thus the law of causation, whether in the moral or in the physical plane, is divested of its *raison d'etre* if absolutism is adhered to. An absolute real can neither be a cause nor an effect. An effect already in existence has no necessity for a cause, and an eternal cause unamenable to change is self-contradictory, inasmuch as an eternal cause would produce an eternal effect. But both the terms 'eternal cause' and 'eternal effect' have no meaning. It may be contended that the issue does not affect the position of the Vedāntist or the Absolute Negativist (*Śūnyavādin*) since they do not believe in the reality of causation. But the contention is not sincere as they believe in it on this side of transcendental realisation. And their plea, that truth is of one sort in the plane of theoretical and practical activity, and of another kind in the transcendental plane, seems to be a make-believe. We postpone the consideration of the metaphysical issue to a subsequent chapter, and it should suffice for the present to observe that these two metaphysical systems have gained a haven only by making a holocaust of all our cherished beliefs and ingrained convictions. Whatever may be their logical merits they have failed to carry conviction to an enormous number of men and women who respectfully decline to be satisfied with their negative findings, whether qualified or unqualified. As regards the position of the advocate of flux (*Sautrāntika*) the difficulty alleged does not find a satisfactory solution from him as well. In this system all existents are believed to be momentary in duration. A moment is the indivisible atom of time which stands absolutely detached and discrete from its antecedent and consequent units. If an existent can occupy only such a moment, it cannot function as a cause. Exercise of causality is possible either in succession or non-succession, but both are incapable of being predicated of a momentary real A 'momentary' has no duration and consequently no succession. Simultaneous production of effects is also not admitted by the Buddhist fluxist. Moreover, absolute affirmation of a characteristic, reality or unreality, eternity or non-eternity, implies by the very force of its inherent opposition the negation of the opposite characteristic. So if a thing is affirmed to be real or momentary the predication is not of a simple characteristic, but of a complex one. The thing is not only real but not not-real, not only momentary but also not not-momentary. This militates against the absolutist standpoint of predication of simple characteristics.

If things were real in an absolute sense there would be no causation, as it is possible if only an event which was non-existent is brought into existence. But an existent by its very nature, that is to say, irrespective of such external conditions as time, space and the like, is not in need of the services of a cause. If, on the contrary, the effect were unreal in an absolute sense it could not any more be called into existence, since an unreal fiction such as a barren woman's son or a square circle is never found to leap into existence. The *Śūnyavādin* may contend that the whole show of causal order is only an appearance and the effects that are seen to be produced are as unreal as the so-called fictions. No reliance, again, can be placed upon experience, they would plead, as experience in dream also exhibits the same characteristics as so-called normal experience; and the objects perceived or inferred are nothing but chimeras. So the objection on the ground of the failure of causation is futile so far as the sceptics are concerned. But this denial of causation again involves a difficulty. If the perceived objects in dreams were unreal and so uncaused events, why should they cease to exist, or, to put it the other way about, why should they appear at all ? So experience, normal or abnormal, would have no *raison d'etre* in the *Śūnyavādin's* scheme of metaphysics. If nescience is held out to be the cause of such appearance, the question would naturally arise whether nescience *per se* is real or unreal. If it were unreal, there would be no causal activity and consequently no appearance. Even if the order of experienced objects be declared unreal, there must be a cause of this order of appearance. A real cause is necessary even for the production of unreal experience. The optic illusion of the double moon has its cause in the positive disorder of the eye, which is real as any thing. So the dilemma is inescapable, whether the order of causality is held to be real or unreal in an absolute manner. If the effect were real irrespective of time and place and conditions of causality, there would be no necessity for positing a cause. If it were unreal, no amount of causal activity could bring it into existence. If, again, it were uncaused, there would be no time in which the effect would be existent or non-existent.

The same deadlock emerges even in the philosophy of flux. The Yogācāra, who denies extra-mental reality, seeks to explain our experience of the phenomenal world on the analogy of dream experience. But he believes that consciousness, which is the only reality according to him, is in a state of perpetual flux. It is momentary and so ceases to exist at the next moment, when it is replaced by another consciousness-unit. The previous unit produces the subsequent unit and the chain of consciousness-units goes on for eternity, being governed by the law of causation. So the law of causation is the very corner-stone of Yogācāra metaphysics, as it is of the *Sautrāntika*,[1] both being agreed upon the fluxional nature of reality and the law of causation as the supreme ruling principle of the order of reality. The difference between the two lies only in the denial or affirmation of extramental reality. But the law of causation cannot be supposed to

1. For a thorough-going exposition of the *Sautrāntika* philosophy the reader is referred to my work *The Buddhist Philosophy of Universal Flux*, published by the University of Calcutta.

operate in the case of momentary entities. Of course the Buddhist would maintain that the previous moment is the cause of the subsequent moment and causation presupposes only this sequence and nothing more. The absence of the cause at the moment of the emergence of the effect is no bar to the operation of causality, as synchronism of the cause and effect is not relevant. If synchronism were determinant of causality one would not search for the cause in the previous event. And between two synchronous events nobody commits the fallacy of regarding one as the cause of the other, as between the two horns on a cow's head. But the Jaina philosopher maintains that neither sequence nor synchronism alone can account for the law of causation, but that both combined give us the correct estimate of the operation of causality. That the relation of cause and effect does not hold good between two co-existent facts, such as the two horns on a cow's head, is admitted by the Jaina also. But the absence of synchronism between the cause and the effect at the moment of the latter's emergence would make the effect independent of the cause. The effect was not in existence when the cause was in existence and it comes into existence when the cause has ceased to exist. So if the effect is independent of the cause when it comes into existence and is not found to be dependent upon the cause either before or after, the bearing of the cause upon the effect becomes a fiction. The previous existence of the cause is absolutely irrelevant. If an effect could come into existence even in the absence of the cause at the moment of its origin, there is no logic why it should not come into being at other moments when the cause is absent likewise. It has been contended by the Buddhist fluxist that if a permanent cause enduring for more than a moment could produce an effect, why should it not go on producing like effects for all the time of its existence ? If the 'permanent' comes to lose the causal power at a subsequent moment, the possession of power at one moment and the loss of power at another moment would entail the co-existence of two contradictory attributes in the former, and this is incompatible with its integrity. The supposed permanent would be split up into two — in other words, there would be no one entity but as many as the varying attributes and causal operations. The Jaina philosopher, however, refuses to be convinced by such tactics of abstract logic. The identity or otherwise of a real is to be accepted on the verdict of uncontradicted experience and the possession of varying attributes or powers is not incompatible with the identity of a thing. Even the Buddhist cannot deny that the selfsame real, *e.g.*, light, produces diverse effects, *viz.*, the expulsion of darkness, the illumination of the field of perception, radiation of heat and so on. Certainly the diverse effects cannot be produced by the selfsame causal energy. If a plurality of energies can be possessed by a self-identical entity without offence to logic, why should the spectre of logical incompatibility be raised in the case of a permanent cause possessing diverse powers ? The Jaina solves the difficulty by means of the law of *anekānta,* which affirms the possibility of diverse attributes in a unitary entity. Strictly speaking, a thing is neither an absolute unity nor split up into an irreconcilable plurality. It is both unity and plurality all the time. There is no opposition between unity of being and plurality of aspects. The opposition would have been inevitable if the unity of a real had varied with each aspect. But the varying aspects are affirmed of the self-identical subject and this proves that the unity is not affected by such predication. A thing is one and many at the same time — a unity and a plurality rolled into one. This view of the nature of reality avoids the fallacy of uncaused production, which is insurmountable in the other philosophies. The cause is both non-synchronous and synchronous with the effect — the former before the origin of the effect and the latter at the time of its origin. Nor does the non-emergence of any further effect in the presence of the cause after the production of the first effect occasion a difficulty. The nature of things is to be determined in consonance with their behaviour as observed with normal human faculties. When the cause is not seen to produce an effect more than once at a time, it must be postulated that the cause undergoes change of power, and the change of power is not incompatible with the identity of the causal entity as it is certified by the unchallengeable verdict of experience. That experience is the ultimate determinant of contradiction or non-contradiction and not *a priori* logical considerations is to be admitted even by the Buddhist, who swears by logic in season and out of season whenever it suits his convenience. The Buddhist idealist holds that cognition assumes the form of cogniser and cognised in one. The same cognition is transformed into the likeness of an object, which becomes the content, and in its rôle as pure cognition it functions as the cogniser. This is the epistemology of perception of the Sautrāntika realist, according to whom the direct object of cognition is never the external object, but the content as part and parcel of the cognition. The external object is a matter of inference according to the Sautrāntika. Barring this difference of metaphysical position, both the Sautrāntika and the Yogācāra are agreed on the dual character and the dual rôle of cognition. In the case of non-perceptual cognition also the same dual rôle is asserted with equal emphasis. The content, which is identical in being with the cognition, is believed to stand for the unperceived object, *e.g.*, the fire as inferred from smoke, and the cognition in its cognitive capacity is assumed to be the cogniser. The opposition of the cogniser and the cognised is evident, but still their coalescence in the selfsame cognition is believed to be a fact and that without spelling a contradiction. If the contradiction is denied on the strength of the undisputed testimony of experience, the same solution cannot be discarded in the case of cause and effect, as experience is unmistakable in its verdict in this case also. This is not the only advantage in the Jaina position. It gives us a satisfying explanation of the law of causation, the belief in which is irresistible for all human beings and is the *conditio sine quâ non* of all scientific and practical activity. The absolutistic standpoint of the other schools of thought fails to offer any explanation. The heroic course adopted by the Vedântist and the Śūnyavādin does not again commend itself as the only alternative metaphysical explanation. The result is identical. Both the fluxist and the Vedântic idealist fail to render a realistic explanation of the law of causation, as the condition of causal operation, succession or non-succession,[1] which are the necessary concomitants of time-continuum, are denied, and the chain of cause and effect is reduced to the position of an intellectual construction. The Jaina theory avoids the fallacies incident to

1. For the elaborate exposition of succession and non-succession as the condition of causal operation I refer the reader to my book *The Buddhist Philosophy of Universal Flux*, Chapters I and IV.

extremism as the cause is both permanent and fluxional and the effect is both existent and non-existent. The point will be elaborated later on.

Again, if things were held to be existent in an absolute sense, that is to say, if existence were their only characteristic and non-existence were denied as ideal fiction, the result would be equally disastrous. There would be no distinction of one thing from another. Everything would be everything else having nothing to distinguish them. Secondly, there would be neither beginning nor end for anything. Thirdly, nothing would be possessed of an individuality. In other words, things would be nothing—entity would be reduced to non-entity. We propose to demonstrate how the absurd issues alleged above follow inevitably on the denial of non-existence as a characteristic feature of things. Now, non-existence is recognised to be of four types, *viz.*, (*i*) absolute non-existence, *e.g.*, the non-existence of colour in air (*atyantābhāva*); (*ii*) pre-non-existence, *e.g.*, the non-existence of the effect in the cause (*prāgabhāva*); (*iii*) post-non-existence, *e.g.*, the non-existence of an effect after destruction (*pradhvaṃsābhāva*); and (*iv*) mutual non-existence or numerical difference or non-existence of identity of things (*itaretarābhāva*). If existence were the whole nature of things, there would be no non-existence anywhere; and in the absence of the fourth type of non-existence, all entities would be lumped together into one thing. *viz.*, Existence. The Sāṅkhya does not believe in the reality of non-existence. But in that case the enumeration of the different categories and the evolution of the categories from primordial *Prakṛti* in a descending scale and the dissolution of each succeeding category into its immediate predecessor would have no meaning. The existence of a second entity implies that the first is distinct and different from the second and this presupposes the reality of mutual non-existence. The emergence of lower and later categories from the preceding ones presupposes that they were not existent before at least in their developed form. The presupposition of such unprecedented emergence is the second type, *viz.*, pre-non-existence. And the retrograde course of evolution, in which the lower categories are said to be re-absorbed into the higher one, presupposes that they cease to exist at any rate in their finished form. This presupposes the third type of non-existence. And the non-existence of Primordial Matter (*Parkṛti*) in the Spirit (*Puruṣa*) and of the latter in the former is evidently an admitted fact, and this necessitates the postulation of the first type of non-existence. Thus, non-existence cannot be denied by the Sāṅkhya without stultifying the whole scheme of ontology propounded by him. But the Sāṅkhya might maintain that the denial of non-existence on his part does not entail these consequences. He does not believe in the reality of non-existence apart from and independent of the reals as the *Vaiśeṣika* does. The denial of non-existence thus amounts to the negation of independent non-existence. But if non-existence be regarded as a formative element in the nature of reals he would have no objection to its reality with all its four varieties. But this is also the position of the Jaina and of the Mīmāṁsists. If, however, such be the position of the Sāṅkhya and the Mīmāṁsist, they should no longer characterize reals as existent only. Things, on the contrary, should be characterized as existent-and-non-existent. What the Jaina objects to is the uncritical, simple characterization of reals in terms of existence as opposed to non-existence. The nature of reals is always a complex of existence-cum-non-existence. As regards the affirmation of non-existence as a separate and independent category by the later exponents of Vaiśeṣika philosophy, the Jaina, too, does not subscribe to it. According to the Jain non-existence is as much an element in the constitution of a real as existence is. Accordingly a real can be said to exist or not to exist. The predication of existence and non-existence in respect of the same subject, though under different circumstances, is proof of the dual nature of reals.

But the aforementioned consequences of the denial of non-existence would not affect the validity of the position of the Vedāntist. The Vedāntist denies all differences and distinctions. The plurality is only an illusory appearance called into existence by the inherent nescience of individual selves. There is no plurality of selves either. The difference between self and non-self is also a fiction. But the question may be legitimately posed to the Vedāntist: 'How would you establish your position? You deny all differences, but by what instrument of knowledge would you substantiate your denial ? Certainly not by perception, nor by inference, nor by scripture, as all these instruments of knowledge record only positive findings. The Vedāntist, however, does not bank upon any one of these accepted instruments of knowledge. He maintains that the non-existence of differences is only a necessary deduction from the failure of the opponent to establish the existence of differences. All the arguments that can be advanced by the opponents would be shown to be inconclusive. After all, the experience of plurality is the sheet-anchor of the opponent. But this experience of plurality is not incompatible with the unity of the Absolute Brahman, which is divested of all differences, intrinsic and extrinsic. Consciousness, undifferentiated into modes and attributes, is the only reality, and experience of plurality is only an illusion. It is common knowledge that space is one and devoid of all differences and distinctions taken by itself. But the person suffering from a defect of sight would see it divided into lines. It is a truism that this experience of linear divisions in space is only an illusion. So there is no inherent impossibility in the association of plurality with the Absolute Brahman on the part of a person whose power of vision is infected with the defects induced by nescience.[1] The contention of the Buddhist idealist who believes in the multiplicity of consciousness-units has no substance. He believes in the unity of each consciousness-unit, but denies the subject-object polarization as due to the association of contents. The contents of consciousness are held to have no reality apart from consciousness. Thus when one becomes aware of blue, the awareness of blue does not establish the independent existence of blue. The 'blue' is only a content of consciousness and is non-different from it. It is due to the inherent proclivity of our thought movement for the belief in the separate existence of the content that the latter is not felt as identical with consciousness. To be more precise, the manifestation of consciousness informed with an apparent content has no *raison d'etre* outside the separatist tendency of our thought-activity, which is the legacy of false knowledge or ignorance from which we all suffer.

1. yathā viśuddham ākāśam timiropapluto naraḥ. saṅkīrṇam iva mātrābhir bhinnābhir abhimanyate. tathe 'dam amalaṃ Brahma nirvikalpam avidyayā. kaluṣatvam ivā "pannaṃ bhedarūpaṃ prapaśyati. Attributed to Bhartṛhari.

But the Vedāntist would urge that if the appearance of a content as an *other* to consciousness be only an illusion as admitted by the Buddhist idealist, then why should one consciousness be held to be different from another consciousness? The difference is felt owing to the difference of contents associated. But when contents are illusory and their association is only a false appearance, why should the difference of contents be made the ground of assertion of difference in consciousness ? The difference of subject and object, the cognizer and cognized, in the same consciousness-unit is a felt fact. But still the experience of the two poles is not believed to argue a real difference in the consciousness-unit on the ground that the difference is only illusory. Parity of logic and consistency of argument demand that the difference of contents, illusory as they are, should not affect the unity of consciousness as such. Not only this. The affirmation of absolute identity between consciousness and content on the part of the Buddhist idealist would, on the contrary, make it impossible for him to meet the criticism of the Buddhist Śūnyavādin who would deny the reality of consciousness and its content alike. If consciousness is identical with its content, which is admitted to be a false appearance, why should not consciousness also be regarded as a false appearance ? Certainly between two things held to be identical, one cannot be regarded as real and the other as unreal. If a content is denied independent reality on the ground that it is never cognised outside and apart from consciousness, such also should be the case with consciousness, which is never felt apart from a content. If the variation of contents and the unvariant continuity of consciousness be the proof of the superior status of consciousness, why should the Buddhist believe in the multiplicity of consciousness-units ? Moreover, the relation of content and consciousness cannot be regarded as one of real identity, as the difference of content from consciousness is felt in experience. So not only identity but also difference are equally felt facts and as this is not compatible with real identity, the relation is held to be one of illusory identity by the Vedāntist, since identity-cum-difference is according to him a contradiction in terms. And illusory identity of different contents thus cannot split up the identity of consciousness.

The Vedāntist would thus successfully deny the reality of non-existence, as the absurdities alleged are not regarded as absurdities, but as a true estimate of things. The Vedāntist also banks upon the failure of the opponent to prove the reality of difference and other types of non-existence which are the presupposition of plurality. But this is not his only resource. He maintains that there is no proof in support of the reality of non-existence. If perception were competent to envisage non-existence, there would be no occasion for taking note of existence. For one existent there is an infinite number of non-existents pitted against it. For instance a pen is one entity, but the number of not-pens is practically infinite. If one were to perceive the non-existence of not-pens in order to perceive a pen, there would be no occasion for the realization of the latter perception, as the percipient would be occupied for all his life with the perception of the non-existence of not-pens, whose number is admittedly unlimited. It might be contended against this argument that the mode of perception as observed does not lead to any such consequence. The non-existence of a thing is perceived only when the negatum in question is recalled. So only those things are cognized to be non-existent, which are recalled by the percipient on the occasion. As he does not recall all the possible things that are non-existent on the occasion of perceiving the non-existence of a particular fact, but only the negatum whose non-existence is the object of perception, the charge of infinite number of perceptions of non-existence falls to the ground. But the Vedāntist would not accept the explanation, which makes perception dependent upon memory. Moreover, perception, dependent upon memory, would not give a novel experience.

The Vaiśeṣika, who believes in the perception of non-existence, would assert that this amounts to a refusal to face the evidence of the psychology of perception as a whole. There are cases of perception which are independent of the services of memory, no doubt. But the perception of a thing as conducive to the attainment of a desired end is certainly dependent upon, and preceded by, memory. One perceives a mango in the dish and at once proceeds to eat it. This is made possible only by the memory of the sweet taste of mangoes experienced in the past. The perception of non-existence, as it occurs to a man of extraordinary powers acquired by the practice of *yoga*, is certainly independent of the aid of memory. The mystic would see everything, existence and non-existence both, in one act of intuition. But by a person of limited powers like us non-existence can be perceived only with the aid of memory. So there is no difficulty. But this defence has not satisfied the Vedāntist. In the first place, he maintains together with the Buddhist that perception is never a judgment. Perception gives us the knowledge of a thing as it is, uninterpreted by concepts. But the perception of non-existence would be a judgment as it is always cognized as non-existence of this or that. In the second place, the memory in question may be either of the negatum or of the non-existence. On the latter alternative, there would arise a vicious infinite regress. If the knowledge of non-existence be a case of memory, it would necessitate the postulation of a previous knowledge of non-existence. But as the latter would also be equally an act of memory, there would be no end of recollections. If, on the contrary, the cognition of non-existence at any stage is accepted to be independent of memory, why should the cognition under consideration be made dependent upon the same ? If, however, the recollection of the negatum is made the condition of the perception of negation, that also would give rise to a difficulty in another direction. Recollection, implicit or explicit, is certainly found to be an aid in the case of recognition. Here the object of perception is remembered to have been seen in the past and is then cognized to be identical with the perceived object. In recognition the two objects are same or similar and so memory is of help. But in the case of perception of non-existence one thing, *viz.*, the negatum, is recalled and another thing, *viz.*, its non-existence, is perceived. So the two situations are not similar. It should be recognised that perception is concerned with existent things and so cannot have jurisdiction over non-existence. The perception of non-existence is thus a false belief. Not only is non-existence incompetent to be perceived, it cannot be known by inference also. Non-existence is a non-entity and as such has neither an effect nor a characteristic, on the evidence of which it could be inferred. The absence of perception of a perceptible is held to be the source of such knowledge. But this is also a pretence. What is seen is the empty locus and this is believed to be the knowledge of non-existence. The knowledge of non-existence in all cases is found on analysis to be an intellectual construction arising on the perception of something else; and as the independent existence of non-existence is only a contradiction in terms such intellectual constructions are to be definitely recognized as unfounded illusions.

The Jaina philosopher would submit that the elaborate arguments of the Vedāntist may have succeeded in refuting the reality of non-existence as an independent category. But however successful may be his argument, he must believe in the difference of things. If he is to engage in a debate with an opponent and has to convince him by argument he must employ the logical syllogism, which consists of three terms. The difference of terms and of their logical value has also to be recognized by him. This implies that the denial of non-existence even as part and parcel of a real is only an academic pastime with him and not a sincere conviction.

The denial of pre-non-existence again would entail the existence of effect from the beginningless time and that of post-non-existence would make the effect continue unbroken without end. But origination and destruction of effects are experienced facts. Origination means the coming into existence of an event which was not in existence before and destruction means that an effect ceases to exist after having come into existence. If neither origination nor destruction can be repudiated without doing violence to experience, the reality of the two types of non-existence must be accepted, as without them the two phenomena referred to cannot be understood. The Sāṅkhya philosopher maintains that things are neither produced nor destroyed. A non-existent cannot be made existent and an existent cannot be made to cease to exist, because a thing cannot surrender its nature and yet continue to be the same thing as before. So he interprets origination as manifestation of a pre-existent effect and destruction as relapse of the manifest into the unmanifest state, which was its characteristic before origination. So nothing is produced or destroyed. The logical consequence of such a theory is the doctrine of absolute existence of things. But, as has been pointed out above, the absolutist position cannot be maintained by the Sāṅkhya without falsification of his whole scheme of metaphysics. Of course the denial of non-existence as an extrinsic principle does not involve any untoward consequence, but its denial as a formative element in a real has been shown to lead to absurdities. Consistency demands that the Sāṅkhya too should admit that there is a difference and intrinsic difference at that between a manifested and an unmanifested real. The 'unmanifested' and the 'manifested' should be recognized as possessed of different characteristics and so strictly speaking as not entirely identical. They are identical and different both — identical in so far as it is the same substance and different in so far as it undergoes a change of characteristic. This is the Jaina position of non-absolutism; and if it is accepted by the Sāṅkhya and the Mīmāṁsist, as they seem to show their leanings in its favour, in the entire extent of reality, there would be no difference between them and the Jaina. But on occasions both the Sāṅkhya and the Mīmāṁsist lapse into the absolutist attitude and the Jaina thinks this to be an error on their part.

The unqualified affirmation by the Sāṅkhya of the identity of the cause and the effect is due to defective use of language or misconception or both. Whatever be the meaning of such assertions, the issue is clear, *viz.*, that the cause and the effect are not entirely identical, but different also. If the effect were entirely identical with the material cause, there would be no occasion for the exercise of activity to bring it into existence. The Sāṅkhya may contend that the activity is not futile as it brings about manifestation of an unmanifest effect. But manifestation is a novel thing and if it is held to be identical with the thing manifested, there would be production of a novel effect. If it were different, the manifestation would not relate to the effect. So the pre-existence of the effect is to be understood as having a partial reference. The effect is pre-existent in so far as it is the same substance with the cause and pre-non-existent in so far as it is a new phenomenon. The identity again of the cause and the effect is not to be understood in all its aspects. In other words, the identity is limited in its reference. The effect is partially identical with the cause and different in other respects. This is the position maintained by the Jaina and it has been shown to be inescapable. The escape is possible only by having recourse to the heroic line of action adopted by the Vedāntist who repudiates causality as illusory appearance. An elaboration of the absurdities inherent in the absolutist stand adopted by the Sāṅkhya in respect of causality and by the Mīmāṁsist in respect of the eternity of word-essence is uncalled for. There is no via media between non-absolutist realism of the Jaina and the Vedāntist idealism. The Sāṅkhya and the Mīmāṁsist are only half-hearted realists. Whether they are conscious of the implications of their views is not a matter of importance in an objective study of philosophical problems. But the absolutist attitude taken with regard to causation or to the eternity of word is fraught with grave difficulties, which can be avoided either by the adoption of the non-absolutist standpoint of the Jaina philosophers or by unqualified repudiation of the phenomenal world as made by the Vedāntist.

The problem of the eternal existence of word has been alluded to by us. It is a pet theory of the Mīmaṁsist. The Mīmāṁsist believes that 'word' is eternal and ubiquitous. The exercise of the vocal organs is necessary only to make it articulate and amenable to perception. But the question can be decided by a dilemma. Is the quality of articulateness eternally existent in the word or not ? On the former alternative the activation of the vocal organ would be uncalled for and the occasional absence of perception of word would be unaccountable. It has been held that the vocal activity is needed to break the veil which prevents its cognition. But the hypothesis of veiling is understandable and may have justification only if it induces a state which is different from the state when the veil is removed. This means a difference either in the word or in the percipient consciousness or in the vocal organ. But all these three are eternal entities and veiling would be incompatible with the absence of change in them. The problem is entirely on a par with that of causation. It may not be inappropriate to remark that word according to the Jaina is a material stuff like earth. It exists even when it is not heard. The material stuff undergoes a change in order to become perceptible. So the Jaina is not in uncompromising opposition to the Mīmāṁsist view of the eternal existence of word, whether perceived or unperceived. But there is a vital difference in this that the Jaina does not maintain that the word-stuff is unchangingly real, which is the position of the Mīmāṁsist. But unchanging existence is a philosophical anomaly. That there is a change of character in a perceived word from the unperceived one is obvious. The only course open to the Mīmāṁsist is this; either he must surrender his theory of unchanging existence and qualify it in the manner of the Jaina, or declare the change and together with it the word, as the substrate of change, to be illusory appearance. As he cannot follow the latter course, he must frankly accept the non-absolutist position.

In the previous paragraph we have shown how the acceptance of non-existence as an element in the make-up of reals is inescapable in the philosophy of the Sāṅkhya and the Mīmāṁsist. But the problem cannot be regarded as solved unless the formidable array of arguments of the Cārvāka materialist, who denies the reality of non-existence on entirely different grounds, is disposed of. Non-existence as a separate objective category has been denied by the Jaina. It is believed to be an objective real, but only so far as it is an element in the constitution of a real. But hitherto no light has been thrown on the nature of non-existence as a positive fact. But unless we are enabled to form a clear conception of its nature and function the postulation of non-existence will remain a vague assertion. To get down to the brass tacks of philosophy, we propose to take up the question of pre-non-existence and post-non-existence. The constitution of entities is believed by the Jaina to be dynamic. It changes every moment. But change does not mean that one thing is succeeded by another *in toto.* In that case the concept of change would have no meaning. It is the presupposition of change that the identity of the thing undergoing change is maintained in spite of the change that happens to it. It changes and persists in the same act. Change has no meaning without persistence and the contradiction between change and persistence is only apparent. Let us apply the results attained to the consideration of the problem. Production of an effect implies that a change has taken place in the causal stuff. But the stuff has been undergoing change for all the time whether the effect in question was produced or not. So not mere change but change of a distinctive character can account for the production of a particular effect. To be explicit and precise, it must be held that for every different effect there is a corresponding differential change in the causal stuff, which is directly and unconditionally responsible for the emergence of the effect. If pre-non-existence be the cause of the effect, as admitted by the advocate of non-existence, then it is to be equated with the immediate antecedent phase of the causal stuff. But if the pre-non-existence of the effect consists in the immediate antecedent phase of the causal stuff, the absence of this particular phase in the infinite past history of the causal stuff would entail the existence of the effect in question even before its production. It is held that effect is the negation of its pre-non-existence. Now if the pre-non-existence of the effect is distinctively identified with the immediate antecedent phase of the causal stuff, there is no room for denying that such antecedent phase was not in existence before. And when the absence of pre-non-existence entails the existence of the effect, its existence during the infinite past career of the causal stuff cannot be prevented by any logic. The consequence is that the Jaina is confronted with the issue of the beginningless existence of the effect to prevent which he trotted out the theory of pre-non-existence. So the admission of pre-non-existence and its denial lead to the same consequence. It may be argued that though the series of antecedent phases prior to the immediate phase do not constitute the pre-non-existence of the effect, still the issue of the previous existence of the effect cannot materialize, because the antecedent phases are numerically different from the effect, and numerical difference is as much a bar to the production of the effect as pre-non-existence is. But in that case the postulation of pre-non-existence is superfluous, as the numerical difference of the series of antecedent phases would prevent the emergence of the effect before its time. One might reply that the postulation of pre-non-existence is made in deference to the dictum that the effect is the negation of pre-non-existence, But since the negation of such pre-non-existence is found in the whole antecedent history of the cause, the issue of the pre-existence of the effect is unavoidable. A different approach may be made to find a way out of the *cul de sac*. It might be maintained that the immediate antecedent phase may be regarded as the pre-non-existence of the effect and the effect may be regarded as the destruction of the pre-non-existence. As the phases previous to the phase called pre-non-existence do not constitute the destruction of the pre-non-existence, the question of the pre-existence of the effect does not arise. But the defence smacks of the Buddhist position which holds the destruction of the previous moment and the origination of the next moment as equivalent. The Jaina cannot consistently adopt this position as he maintains that pre-non-existence is devoid of a beginning. Being unbounded by a previous time-limit it cannot be identified with the immediate antecedent phase, which is bounded by all that goes before and comes after. If, in the alternative, it is held to be distinct from all the previous phases of the causal stuff as identification with any one phase would raise all the difficulties, the pre-non-existence would not be an element in the being of the cause, which is the Vaiśeṣika position, and it has been found to be unacceptable.

The beginningless existence of pre-non-existence may however be asserted to be a fact with reference to its identity with the causal substance, as the substance *quâ* substance exists from eternity. But this seems to be a poor defence. If pre-non-existence be given a beginningless status on the basis of its identity with beginningless substance, it would be regarded as destitute of end also, as substance, *quâ* substance has no end. But in the case of endless persistence of pre-non-existence there would be no occasion for the emergence of the effect, as the effect can come into existence only on the cessation of pre-non-existence. So pre-non-existence as a part of existent has no logical sanction. Nor can it be held to be an independent category, as there is no proof of it. It may be contended that such judgments as 'the jar was not existent before its origination' are cognisant of non-existence. But the contention falls through as judgments like 'There is no post-non-existence in pre-non-existence' have also reference to non-existence, but nobody believes in the existence of non-existence in another non-existence, as such belief would involve an infinite series of non-existences. If it is held that the series of non-existences are not numerically different, but one and the same, the four types of non-existence would become one indistinguishable fact — a consequence which cannot be accepted by the advocate of objective non-existence.

It has been urged by the Vaīśeṣika that the above criticism may be successful against those who believe non-existence to be identical with existence. But non-existence is a separate principle, as it is always determined by a positive entity. Non-existence is always understood as non-existence of positive reals, *e.g.*, the non-existence of pen or chair has chair and pen as its determinants. The determinatum is of a different order of being from the determinant and so non-existence as a different principle is to be admitted. But the argument has no cogency. A quality is a determinant of a substance, but the two are equally positive. It is thus not proved that the determinant and determinatum must be of different kinds of being. The objectivity of pre-non-existence will be exploded by the following dialectic. Pre-non-existence may be conceived to have both a beginning and an end; secondly, it may be conceived as having a beginning, but no end; thirdly, it may lack both the limits — that is to say, it may have neither beginning nor end; fourthly, it may have no beginning but may have an end. In the first alternative, the production of effect prior to pre-non-existence would not be barred out. In the second, there would be no subsequent production as pre-non-existence is without end. In the third, there would be no effect at any time as pre-non-existence is eternal. The fourth alternative is no doubt the accepted position. But the question may be pertinently raised whether pre-non-existence is one self-identical fact with reference to all effects or its number varies with the number of effects. If it be one, it would cease when even one effect is produced and there being no other pre-non-existence to preclude their production, all possible effects would emerge simultaneously at that moment. Of course the contingency does not arise if each effect is supposed to have a separate pre-non-existence corresponding to it. But it would occasion another difficulty. Let it be true that each effect has its own pre-non-existence, which ceases when the effect comes into being. But has the pre-non-existence in question an independent ontological status or is it dependent upon the positive real to which it relates? An independent pre-non-existence cannot be regarded as non-being, as non-being is by your very definition a determinant of being and an independent principle cannot be determinant of anything. Let it be supposed that it is dependent upon a positive real. But the only entity upon which it can be supposed to depend is its relative negatum. But the negatum is *non est* while pre-non-existence persists and the latter ceases to be when the negatum comes into being. So the relation of dependence or independence of pre-non-existence in regard to the negatum is unthinkable. But there is a third possibility which may avoid the alleged difficulties. Let pre-non-existence be one and its diversity be supposed to be a relational characteristic with no ontological status. So the contingency of simultaneous emergence of all possible effects on the cessation of pre-non-existence does not arise, for relational diversity will continue as effects will come into being in succession. But if the diversity of pre-non-existence be only relational and not real, then there would be no logical necessity for postulating four types of non-existence. One non-existence in relation to time-divisions, prior and posterior, may appear as pre-non-existence and post-non-existence. The same non-existence, again. as related to all the divisions of time, past, present and future, will assume the rôle of absolute non-existence and that of mutual non-existence with reference to the mutual relation of diverse reals. But if one non-existence may function as diverse types of non-existence, in spite of the lack of intrinsic diversity, why should not reality as such play the rôle of non-existence? The Jaina and the Mīmāṁsist have made out a plausible case for non-existence as a part of reality. But as there is no proof of the existence of non-being in all its varieties apart from reals, it stands to reason that positive reals alone should be supposed to account for the different concepts of non-existence. There is no necessity that all our concepts should be grounded in objective reality and as regards non-existence the opponent has been compelled to concede that varieties of non-existence are more or less unreal constructions. The Cārvāka would conclude that non-existence as such is a metaphysical fiction, uncritically hypostatized as an objective fact on the evidence of concepts, which do not stand the test of critical analysis. Non-existence, whether as a part of positive reals or an independent fact having no logical sanction, should be boldly asserted to be a fiction, pure and simple.

The Jaina does not believe that the Cārvāka has made out an unimpeachable case for the unreality of negation. The idea of negation is there, and there is no reason why it should be an ungrounded illusion. It is not an illusion, as it is not invalidated by the testimony of subsequent experience. Whether one may like the idea or not, one cannot get rid of it as much as one cannot get rid of the idea of existence. If non-existence be a metaphysical fiction, there is no reason for preferential treatment of existence. Both should be discarded or accepted without reservation. Of course the Vaiśeṣika view of independent non-existence is riddled with difficulties. But non-existence as an element in the make-up of positive existents should be regarded as factual. The objections of the Cārvāka are not insurmountable. Of course, the position would be hopeless if the sceptic's objections were backed by logic. Let us examine whether the difficulties are real or only conjured up by sophistry. Let it be granted that the immediate antecedent phase of the causal stuff constitutes the pre-non-existence of the relevant effect. Yet, the consequence alleged, that there would be continuous existence of the effect throughout the past except at the last moment when the immediate phase comes into being, would not arise. The difficulty raised by the Cārvāka, if sincere, is due to the oversight of the difference between post-non-existence and other types of non-existence. The effect is the negation of pre-non-existence, whereas the immediate antecedent phase of the cause is the pre-non-existence of the effect. It was not in evidence in the past and so the question of its post-non-existence before its emergence and consequently the emergence of the effect before its time have no *raison d'etre*. There is the absence of pre-non-existence and of the effect both in the past, and there is no incongruity in it. The effect is incompatible with the presence of pre-non-existence and not with its absence. The absence of the pre-non-existence in the past history of the cause is itself an instance of pre-non-existence and thus if the infinite past series of pre-non-existences be regarded as one whole, the continuity of pre-non-existence in the past, which is the import of the dictum that pre-non-existence is without beginning, is established. The same result is reached even if pre-non-existence be asserted to be identical with the causal substance. The causal substance is without beginning. The issue of endless continuity of pre-non-existence would not arise, since the identity of pre-non-existence is maintained with the causal substance only in so far as it is bereft of the effect. And as there is no time in the past when the causal substance is destitute of the absence of effect, the continuity of pre-non-existence in the infinite past is assured. Again as the substance qualified by the absence of the effect ceases to be when it comes to be vested with the effect, which is only a modification of the causal substance, the pre-non-existence *quâ* the qualified substance also ceases. The endless continuity of the effect would not therefore be possible. It is to be distinctly recognized that there is a vital difference between the causal stuff as qualified by the absence of the effect and the same as qualified by the presence of the effect. The absence of the effect previous to the emergence of the effect is of the nature of pre-non-existence and not numerical difference (*itaretar-ābhāva*), and the same again subsequent to the effect is of the nature of post-non-existence and not again numerical difference. The objections raised by the Cārvāka on the basis of numerical difference are therefore absolutely irrelevant. The pre-non-existence of the effect in the past and its post-non-existence in future are not jeopardized in any event whether the said pre-non-existence is regarded as identical with the immediate antecedent phase or with the causal substance as one whole.

We now propose to consider another problem raised as a side-issue in this connection. Let it be granted that the Jaina has succeeded in proving that pre-non-existence is continuous throughout the infinite past. But in that case it would not be liable to cessation, as a thing which is without a beginning is of necessity without an end also. Even if exception is made in the case of non-existence as done by the Vaiśeṣika, the rule is inflexible so far as existent things are concerned. The Jaina makes out both pre-non-existence and post-non-existence to be entitative in character and this exposes him to the charge advanced. But the Jaina does not believe in the universality of the rule that whatever is beginningless is also endless or vice versa. The Vaiśeṣika contention is not endorsed as non-existence apart from and independent of an entity is held to be a fiction. But everybody, who believes in the salvation of souls, must admit that the unblessed condition of the transmigratory soul is brought to an end on the cessation of bondage despite the fact that it is without a beginning. The converse of the proposition that whatever is endless is also without a beginning is also not true. Salvation is endless. Nobody believes that a saved soul again returns to the cycle of birth and death. But though endless it is not without a beginning. It is an event in the history of a soul and thus is a definite chronological fact. The rule breaks out in this instance again.

The conclusion is inevitable that pre-non-existence is a fact and a positive fact at that, the denial of which entails the absurdity of the continuous existence of the effect in the infinite past. There is no incongruity in the fact that though positive it should be construed in terms of negation. It is true that the negative judgment 'there was no jar in the past' arises only on the emergence of the jar. It is also true that the pre-non-existence of the jar is a positive real, being regarded as identical with the immediate antecedent phase of the causal stuff or the causal stuff as a whole. But it is not necessarily true that a positive fact is always interpreted by an affirmative judgment or that it is repugnant to a negative judgment. The vacant ground is referred to by the negative judgment *viz.*, 'There is no jar on the ground', although the content of the judgment is nothing more than the positive fact, the ground.

We shall conclude the present chapter by adverting to the problem of post-non-existence and happily it will prove a lighter task as all the formidable difficulties have been disposed of in the course of the dissertation on pre-non-existence. Post-non-existence is also a positive real. It is identical with the phase of the causal stuff which arises on the emergence of the effect.

The emergence of the effect implies the cessation of the previous phase. To take a concrete example. When a jar is shattered to pieces by the stroke of a club, it is replaced by potsherds. There is a change in the material cause, *viz.*, the clay-substance. It was previously of the shape of the jar and upon the destruction of the jar it assumes the shape of potsherds. The clay continues as a substance despite the change of shapes. Shapes are but passing phases and their appearance and disappearance do not affect the identity of the causal substance in which they occur. The disappearance of the previous phase does not imply that the cause ceases to exist—which is the position of the Buddhist fluxist. The appearance of the subsequent phase is construed as the disappearance of the previous phase. So post-non-existence is nothing but the immediate subsequent phase, just as pre-non-existence has been found to be identical with the immediate previous phase. The immediate previous phase *quâ* pre-non-existence is the cause of the subsequent phase *quâ* post-non-existence. And though post-non-existence as identical with the subsequent phase does not and cannot persist through the endless course of time and ceases to exist on the appearance of a third phase, still the cessation of post-non-existence would not entail the resurrection of the defunct negatum. This will be evident from a consideration of the relative character of cause and effect. The emergence of effect is possible only on the disappearance of the antecedent phase of the cause and so there is opposition between effect and cause. It is the effect which is hostile to the cause provided the cause and effect are understood as passing phases. But the cause even as the passing phase is not hostile to the effect, as the emergence of the cause is not in any way dependent upon the cessation of the effect. The cause, on the other hand, is conducive to the emergence of the effect. Since the emergence of the cause is not identical with the cessation of the effect, though the emergence of the effect is identical with the cessation of the cause, the cessation of the effect would not entail the re-emergence of the defunct cause. But what about the dictum that post-non-existence is endless? The dictum can be justified by the same line of argument as applied in the case of pre-non-existence. Though the particular non-existence as identical with a phase of the causal substance cannot continue in future, the post-non-existence of the first non-existence and that of the second and third and so on to infinity will continue unhampered. And the infinite chain of post-non-existences in future will each typify the non-existence of the defunct cause. Thus the endlessness of post-non-existence will be assured, even when the causal relation is understood to subsist between the passing phases. But if the whole causal substance irrespective of the passing phases is considered as one identity which it is in virtue of its character as substance, the problem of endless continuity of post-non-existence will find an easy solution. The substance continues as substance even after the disappearance of the passing phase known as post-non-existence.

An example may elucidate the point we are maintaining. The jar is transformed into potsherds and potsherds may again be transformed into a mass of powder. The potsherds represent the post-non-existence of the jar and the powder represents the post-non-existence of the potsherds. But the emergence of the mass of powder would not entail the revival of the jar on the ground that the potsherds constituted the post-non-existence of the jar. So though the clay-stuff will continue without end, it will never come to be re-invested with a defunct phase. It is a wholesome truth which it will be wise for us to remember that there is no revival in the scheme of things. There may be emergence of a similar phenomenon and this may be mistaken for the revival of the past event. What is past is irrevocably gone We may expect a better state of things or a worse state of things, but there is neither stagnation nor revival. This is a momentous truth, which has its value not only for the professional philosophers, but also for reformers and philanthropists. A correct realization of this philosophical truth will save much useless lamentation for the past and will put the reformer in a correct perspective. Instead of trying to restore the old order of things, the reformer should address himself to bring about a better and happier state of affairs. This does not mean that the past has no lesson for us. The laws of nature, spiritual and material alike, are eternal verities and the past will be a source of inspiration and enlightenment if it is studied as the field of verification of these laws. The study of history should enable us to avoid the mistakes and disappointments of our ancestors by understanding the root-causes of their failure. The past failure lay in the failure of understanding the laws of nature and the discovery of the truth will serve as a warning against the repetition of past errors. The knowledge of the achievements and glories of our ancestors should help us and inspire us with hope for the future, as by the pursuit of the same causes and effects, by observance of the same discipline and avoidance of past errors we may be enabled to achieve, though not a new heaven on earth, at least a better and worthier world. It is some comfort that philosophy in spite of its dry dialectic and forbidding use of logic is not without a lesson for the practical man of the world. The Jaina conception of the dynamic constitution of reality and the eternity of existence may be applied in the various fields of human activity to ensure our progress towards the *summum bonum*, which is the goal of our destiny.

CHAPTER III

NUMERICAL DIFFERENCE AND ABSOLUTE NON-EXISTENCE

In the last chapter we have endeavoured to establish that denial of pre-non-existence and post-non-existence as part of a real leads to absurdities — *viz.*, the impossibility of the law of causation and the consequential impossibility of all theoretical and practical activity. In the present chapter we shall try to show that the repudiation of the remaining two types of non-existence, *viz.*, (1) non-existence of mutual identity or what is called in modern philosophical terminology, numerical difference and (2) absolute non-existence, is also impossible in view of the disastrous consequences to which it inevitably leads. That things are numerically different presupposes that the identity of one is not the identity of another. If this mutual non-existence were repudiated there would be left no means of distinguishing one thing from another thing. In other words, every thing would be every thing else and one uniform and identical existence would have to be posited — a consequence which cannot be accepted by any philosopher other than a Vedāntist. The denial of absolute non-existence too would make confusion of all things inevitable, inasmuch as no definite affirmation of any one thing in one context in contradistinction to another context would be possible. That a table as a whole inheres in its members, exists in its own place and time and is existent in so far as it is a table, that is to say, in so far as it is itself, implies the negation of the contradictory determinations. But if the existence of the table in the rôle of a not-table is not denied, and its existence in a different spatio-temporal context is allowed, there would be no meaning in asserting that the table exists here and now and not elsewhere and elsewhen. The issue that emerges is a simple dilemma. Either there would be no logical predication possible or the affirmation of one undifferenced being — absolutely homogeneous and unvariant — would be the only legitimate consequence. If a philosopher is not prepared to accept this consequence as a satisfactory explanation of reality, he will have no alternative to the acceptance of diversity which presupposes the reality of the two types of non-existence mentioned above. So far as the Sāṅkhya who postulates twenty-five ontological principles and the materialist who believes in the variety of matter are concerned, the denial of non-existence inevitably lands them in a morass of self-contradiction. And as regards the Buddhist idealist, he too cannot deny the reality of numerical difference. The idealist denies the objectivity of the content of awareness apart from the act of awareness of which it is only a part; or to be precise, the content is identical with awareness. The content of awareness is however felt to be distinct from awareness. Awareness is always of something and not purely itself so far at least as the psychology of cognitive processes testifies. But this distinction of awareness from its content, whatever be the ontological status of the latter,[1] can be accounted for only on assumption of numerical difference. Awareness is a fact, which has an individuality of its own distinct from that of the content and also from that of another awareness. This is intelligible only if the individuality in question is regarded as possessed of a double facet, *viz.*, the capacity to assert its existence, which is the aspect of self-affirmation, and the capacity to exclude itself from others, which is the aspect of negation. The postulation of affirmative-cum-negative nature of a real is thus an inescapable conclusion even for the Buddhist idealist.

As regards the Buddhist who believes in the identity of a cognition, having a diversified content, for example, of a variegated carpet, he too will have to admit that the content is a diversity in unity. The patch of blue and the patch of red in a variegated carpet are different in identity. If these were not numerically different just as the blue is not different from itself, there would be one unvaried content. But the conclusion cannot be accepted by the Buddhist, as it takes away all logic from his assertion of the identity of the cognition in spite of the diversity

1. The Buddhist holds that the polarization of consciousness into subject and object is due to nescience. Whether the status of the content is co-ordinate with that of consciousness is a problem which is undecided more or less.

of contents. The logical consequence of the postulation of a numerically identical awareness in the presence of a multiplicity of contents is the inescapable proposition that the awareness in question is numerically different from the contents. Thus not only the difference of the contents from one another, but also that of the awareness from each one of these contents, is to be admitted on pain of self-contradiction. This result also undermines the assertion of the fundamental unity of awareness and its contents as advocated by the Buddhist idealist. The Jaina theory squares with the exigencies of the situation. The relation of awareness to its contents or the objective data is neither one of simple identity nor one of simple otherness, but one partaking of both the characteristics. There is no contradiction between identity and otherness, as they are not absolute characteristics. The contradiction would be insurmountable if awareness and its contents were affirmed to be identical in an absolute reference, that is to say, exclusive of the aspect of difference. But the identity and otherness asserted by the Jaina philosopher are only partial and limited and not complete and unqualified. The Vedāntist is correct, while refuting the Buddhist idealist in his assertion that the relation of cognition and cognitum is neither one of identity nor one of difference. But the Jaina joins issue with the Vedāntist when the latter asserts the relation in question to be a case of illusion on the ground of the incompatibility of identity and difference which are presupposed by the relation. The Jaina asserts that the contradiction would be undeniable if the two traits spoken of were absolute characteristics. But they are not absolute and so the reading of contradiction by the Vedāntist seems to be only a hasty conclusion in the view of the Jaina philosopher.

The unity of the cognition having diversified contents is also to be regarded as only a part-characteristic. The cognition is a unity as well as a plurality. The contents are not absolutely different and distinct. A relation presupposes that two terms which were once apart are now held together. The relation is the cementing bond between them. Things which are absolutely autonomous and independent of one another cannot be brought into relation, or to put it the other way round, the relata have to shed their exclusive autonomy and discreteness if they are to be bound by a relation. So the terms of a relation are neither absolutely identical nor absolutely different. Absolute identity of the relata would annul the duality of the terms, which is a necessary condition of relation. Absolute difference, on the other hand, would never allow the terms to come into a point of contact, which is again the presupposition of relation. Thus the affirmation of absolute unity of the cognition in spite of its relation to different contents is only an imperfect statement of a fact. It is one and many at the same time. The denial of unity on the ground of the incompatibility of its co-existence with diversity would, on the other hand, split up all unity into a multiplicity. And as multiplicity implies the existence of multiple unities, the unities in their turn would again be split up, if there be no unity anywhere. Apart from the consideration that entities are constantly undergoing change of attributes and aspects and thus there is no unity which is not related to a diversity, the epistemological diversity in respect of one and the same thing would also lead to the same result. A supposed self-identical object as viewed by a person from a distance presents a different picture from that which is obtained by the same person situated in close vicinity to it. The same diversity of presentation is also obtained by different persons placed in different positions. It is quite legitimate to argue that the object varies with its presentation, or to convert the proposition, that the variation of presentation is due to the variation of the object. The consequence would be unavoidable that there is no unity anywhere — either in the internal cognition or in the external object, as the unity in question is never found apart from variation and as variation is deemed, on the hypothesis under consideration, to be incompatible with unity. Even change in external relation entails change in the nature of an entity. External or internal, relation connotes the emergence of a novel quality in the relata, no matter that the quality is relational and not original. That a term stands in one relation to a second term and in another relation to a third implies that the term comes to have the quality of standing in those relations. Thus every change in relation or in the relata would bring about a qualitative change in the terms. In the example cited above, the supposed selfsame object, as viewed by different persons from different positions, undergoes qualitative change in consequence of the change of relations or change of the persons viewing it. If then the proposition that unity is inconsistent with variation were to be maintained the result would be the disappearance of unity altogether from the world. The Jaina solves the problem by his approach from the standpoint of non-absolutism. He asserts that neither unity nor diversity sums up the nature of a real, but both taken together do it. Unity is not exclusive of diversity or vice versa. The difficulty that is confronted is not grounded upon objective reality, but arises from a subjective aberration, which consists in the imagination of inconsistency between unity and diversity. But unity is associated with diversity and diversity is never found apart from unity, which is its very foundation. The Vedāntist, who is the paragon of absolutists, and the Śūnyavādin both avoid the difficulty by declaring all relations to be false creations of the intellect. Thus the diversity which originates relation or is originated by relation is asserted by them to be *non est*. We now propose to consider whether the repudiation of relation is a logically sound proposition or not.

It has been seriously contended that relations are intellectual constructions without any ontological status. If things are real in their own right, they should have independent status. Anything, which is supposed to depend for its existence upon another real and hence would cease to exist divorced from it, is certainly not real in its own right and on its own account. In that case it would not be real at all. Reality cannot be conferred upon anything which lacks it in its own right. The proposition is self-evident and does not require to be elucidated. Let us consider whether any relation is possible between such independent reals. Relation is a fact which concerns two terms. It further implies that the terms are no longer autonomous, as absolute autonomy will never allow the terms to come together. To put the positive side of it, it must be admitted that relation is possible only if the terms are dependent upon one another, or at least if one of them is dependent upon the other. If we look deeper, it will transpire that dependence is always mutual, though the subject or the predicate, as the case may be, may have a superior status to that of the other. Take any proposition for example and the truth of the statement will be borne out. The table is round. The table is the subject of which roundness is predicated. The table as the substantive term may be looked upon as the principal element and the quality of roundness as an adjunct to it. But it will be a mistake to argue from this felt superiority of the subject that it is not dependent upon the predicate in the sense in which the predicate is dependent. The 'table' would not be a subject unless it were related to roundness and vice versa. Thus in all relations the terms are no longer in indifferent isolation, but each depends upon the other. This is certainly the implication of all judgments and the epistemology of relations involves mutual surrender of independence on the part of the terms. But is this surrender of independent being and status possible? If things are not dependent for their being upon any extraneous condition they cannot come into relation which presupposes the surrender of independence on the part of the terms. So there can be no relations between things which are independently and intrinsically real. The relation of terms as understood from a proposition is only possible, if the terms signify things which are mutually dependent. But dependent things cannot be real, as reality is an intrinsic and independent characteristic of things. The terms of a relation are therefore unreal symbols — at most they stand for ideal constructions, which are ontologically speaking nothing but fictions. Relations are therefore *a priori* ideal constructs.[1]

The arguments adduced in the preceding paragraph are really formidable. But the Jaina philosopher, who is noted for his firmness and sobriety of outlook, is not perturbed by them. The Jaina maintains that if the nature of things is allowed to be determined by *a priori* logic in defiance of experience, the results would be even more fatal. Certainly logic is incompetent to tell us whether anything exists at all. It is only perception which can assure us that anything exists. Even the doubt and the denial of the sceptic cannot be proved to exist except on the evidence of introspection. "We can have no reason for believing

1. pāratantryaṁ hi sambandhaḥ siddhe kā paratantratā. tasmāt sarvasya bhāvasya sambandho nāsti tattvatah. As., p. 111.

X to exist, unless we either directly perceive X itself, or else perceive Y, whose existence involves the existence of X. Thus our belief in the proposition "something exists" depends upon "perception." "No proposition is true" is a self-contradictory proposition, for, if it were true, then it, together with all other propositions, would not be true. But the truth of "nothing exists" is not inconsistent with itself, though it is inconsistent with the assertion of itself, or even the contemplation of itself, by any person. Thus "something exists" is not a proposition of which we can be certain by pure logic, as we are of the proposition 'something is true."[1] The sceptic may insist that though the existence of something may be conceded, this will not afford any proof of the reality of relation. But we shall show that the admission of existence perforce involves the existence of qualities. "For existence is not a term which has no reference beyond itself, so that it would be sufficient to say that the nature of that which exists is that it is existent. To say that something exists inevitably raises the question what this something is. And that question must be answered by asserting something of it other than its existence." "It remains true that something exists, but of that something, something besides its existence must be true. Now that which is true of something is a quality of that something. And therefore whatever is existent must have some quality besides existence, which is itself a quality."[2] The denial of quality and so also of relation is self-contradictory. "Not only the possession of this or that quality but the non-possession of these qualities would give the existent a nature beyond its existence. ... If we stop with existence, and refuse to go any further, the existent is a perfect and absolute blank, and to say that only this exists is equivalent to saying that nothing exists. We should thus be involved in a contradiction, since starting with the premise that something existed, we should arrive at the conclusion that nothing exists."[3] Now what is true of quality is also true of relation. If we deny that anything stands in a relation to some-

1. The *Nature of Existence* by McTaggart, Vol. I, p. 59.
2. The *Nature of Existence* by McTaggart, Vol. I, pp. 60-61.
3. *Ibid.*

thing else, we should at the same time affirm that it is unrelated. But unrelatedness can be predicated only if there is a relation between the predicate and the subject. The admission of quality involves the admission of a relation between the quality and the substance to which the quality belongs. So relation is undeniable. The same result is attained from a consideration of the fact that a plurality of substances exists. If the existence of something cannot be proved or denied by pure logic, and if the proposition "something exists" is to be accepted only on the evidence of perception, by a parity of reasoning the existence of other substances, which is asserted by perception, cannot be denied. "Unless it is the case either that solipsism is true, or that I myself have no reality, it must be the case that both I and something else exist,"[1] and this would prove that there is a plurality of substances. The admission of a plurality of substances will make the admission of relations inevitable. "All substances will be similar to one another, for they are all substances. And all substances will be diverse from one another, since they are separate substances. ... And substances, which are similar to each other or diverse from one another, stand to each other in the relations of similarity and diversity."[2]

We have seen that relations are not capable of being denied without denial of all existents. The denial of existents as such is self-contradictory. The existence of denial at any rate is to be maintained as real. If it is maintained that the denial is as illusory as the thing denied, the existence of the illusion must be a fact. The argument finally rests on propositions taken as ultimately certain, which if challenged cannot be proved by further arguments. "If, for example, anyone should assert that his belief that nothing existed was only an illusion, and should then deny that this explanation involved that an illusion existed, I do not see how he could be refuted." The absolute and uncompromising sceptic, who is prepared to carry his scepticism to any limit, cannot be refuted by arguments, which he may doubt or deny with equal vehemence. But for a person, whose scepticism is inspired by sincere doubt and who is open to conviction,

1. The *Nature of Existence* by McTaggart, Vol. I, pp 60-61.
2. Op.cit., p. 79.

our arguments may not be entirely fruitless. We have shown that the acceptance of the existence of a plurality of substances makes the acceptance of relations inevitable. We have also shown that the existence of quality and, by similar logic, the existence of states and modes also make the admission of relations unavoidable. The denial of relations would, on the contrary, reduce all things to nullity. The proposition "things cannot be real if relations are unreal" is not of course self-evident. But it follows from the consideration of the propositions which are ultimately certain. If there were no relation between a quality and a substance, or between a substance and its modes, the quality and the mode would be unreal, as they cannot exist independently of and apart from a substance to which they belong. A mode, which is not a mode of anything, and a quality, which is not a quality of anything, is neither a mode nor a quality. And a quality which is not a quality is nothing. The same is true of the mode. But if modes and qualities are unreal, substance too cannot be real. A substance without a quality and a mode is not a substance. And if a substance cannot be a substance, it will be nothing. The denial of relations between a substance and a quality thus makes both of them unreal fictions. The denial of the relation of coinherence in a substance between the several qualities would again make them cease to be qualities of the same substance. So much about the relation between a quality and a substance, which may be regarded as internal relation. With regard to external relations, too, their denial will be seen to lead to equally fatal consequences. No sense-perception would arise if there were no relation, however indirect, between the senses and the objects of perception. In the absence of sense-perception the existence of senses would also be robbed of all means of proof and similarly the existence of material objects cannot be asserted. The existence of sense-organs is inferred from the very fact that sense-perception is not possible without an instrument. The existence of matter is asserted also on the evidence of sense-perception, as it is believed to be directly perceived. But the denial of relation, direct or indirect, physical or quasi-physical, between an organ of sense and the sensed object makes sense-perception impossible and the latter makes the denial of sense-organs and material objects inevitable. There would be no causation either, if the relation of temporal sequence between cause and effect were denied. Inference again would be impossible if the invariable relation between the probans and the probandum were not real. This is not again the only consequence.

No knowledge would be possible if relations were unreal. Knowledge presupposes that something is known. There must be an object to be known and a consciousness to be aware of it — in the common philosophical terminology, there must be a content and an awareness of it. The existence of two things, namely awareness and content, perforce involves the reality of a relation between them, without which there would be no knowledge. The very possibility of knowledge thus involves that there must be a relation and a real relation at that between consciousness and a content. The existence of relation, once admitted, entails the mutual dependence of the relata. If a content were not dependent upon consciousness, it would exist independently of consciousness, and if consciousness in its turn were not dependent upon a content, it would become contentless. But the Buddhist cannot endorse this proposition. Even the philosophers, who believe in a contentless cognition, must believe that there is a relation between consciousness and its object and this belief would necessitate the further belief that consciousness in its relation to the object is dependent upon its difference from the object. Whatever be the character of the relation between awareness and its object, it is obvious that awareness is not pure awareness, but that of an object. And this shows that awareness is dependent upon its object and the object *quâ* object is dependent upon awareness.

What is true of relation is also true of absence of relation. If absence of relation is not dependent upon an entity, that is to say, if it were absolutely independent in being, it would be indistinguishable from being, the characteristic of which is, according to the opponent's hypothesis, complete independence. The issue can be made clear by a dilemma. Is absence of relation predicable of a term or not? If predicable, it is not absolutely independent. On the second alternative, it is not intelligible. It may be the case that everything is not predicable of everything. Between any two things one may exist independently of and out of relation with the other and thus in the absence of a recognizable relation they may be regarded as independent. But to make a generalization on the basis of such independence to the effect that all reals must be independent and unrelated will involve the fallacy of analogical extension. It is a fact that oil is not causally dependent upon sand, as sand never produces oil. But that does not make the conclusion legitimate that oil is causally dependent upon nothing else. If, however, we look deeper into the problem, it will transpire that nothing exists which is independent of the rest of reals. Even between oil and sand it is not a fact that there is no relation. The absence of causal relation itself constitutes a relation. The proposition that oil does not stand in causal relation to sand involves the proposition 'oil stands in the relation of not being causally related to sand.' Of course it would be a cumbrous proposition to state it. But the truth that the absence of relation between any two terms itself generates a relation cannot be denied by a philosopher. A denial of this truth would be tantamount to denial of negative propositions. The proposition 'A is B' states that A stands in the relation of identity to B. The proposition 'A is not B' states that it does not stand in that relation. But that it is a proposition implies, equally with the affirmative proposition, that there is a relation between A and B. As the relation is not identity it must be other than identity. So there is no escape from relation if one is to make any assertion. The denial of relation is thus found to be contradicted by the assertion of such denial. Even the contemplation of the denial will be self-contradictory, as contemplation as well as assertion envisages a relation even in the denial of it. All activity, mental, verbal and practical, would be tabooed, if relation were denied a status and a real status at that, since it is possible only on the basis of such relation. A judgment is possible if it judges a relation between two concepts, and a verbal proposition is only a judgment externalized. The validity of judgment has been challenged by philosophers. But it is easy to see that the whole system of thought that is built by the Śūnyavādin would fall to pieces if there were no judgment. The sceptic may retort that he does not make out a constructive system. The sum-total of his speculations consists in the destruction of systems that are built by others and so the denial of judgment does not affect him. But this defence is not honest. Unless he imposes upon himself the vow of eternal silence, nay, unless he stifles all thought-movement in his mind and thus commits physical and intellectual suicide, the sceptic cannot contemplate, much less assert, the invalidity of judgments including his own. Certainly a philosophy which leads to the abrogation of all thought is an abnormality. But for the people who decline to enter into the peace of death that absolute scepticism holds out as its temptation this negative philosophy will have no charm and no appeal.

The Jaina is not however prepared to let down the sceptic on such easy terms. He would challenge the sceptic to justify his position. The sceptic does not believe causation to be veridical, since he does not believe in the reality of relation. He argues 'Relation is between two terms. And if these terms are real in their own right, neither of them depends upon the other for its existence. In the absence of dependence there can be no relation, which is possible only if there is dependence. If there can be no relation between reals, much less can there be any between a real and an unreal or between two unreals. The effect is not real before its existence and as such it is unreal. How can there be a relation then between a cause, which is a real, and an effect, which is unreal ?' To this argument the Jaina would make the following reply. The argument of the sceptic is an instance of logic moving *in vacuo*. He assumes that there can be no relation between reals or unreals, because a real is not dependent upon another real for its being. And what is unreal is *non est* and as such cannot be conceived to be dependent upon anything. But the assumption, which gives the major premise, is not true. Of course between two independent reals there can be no relation of causality. But there is no logical incompatibility for other relations, which actually do exist. And as regards causality, it is possible only between a real and an unreal, as the sceptic puts it. If the effect, which is not, strictly speaking, as real as the cause in the sense of being an accomplished fact like the cause, were not dependent upon the cause, the effect could come into existence even when the cause was absent. The fact remains that a particular effect comes out of a particular cause. It is a fact that oil is produced by pressing oil-seeds and not sands. How can the situation be met except on the hypothesis that oil depends upon oil-seeds and not upon sands? If nothing were produced, then everything would be either eternal like space that is unproduced or a fiction like a square circle. But effects belong to neither of the kinds. An explanation must be offered. The difficulty is solved by positing the dependence of the effect upon the cause. The effect is not a nonentity though it is unreal before its origination. It is not, however, absolutely unreal as a chimera. It is real in so far as it is identical with the causal substance, of which it is a modification. But it is unreal also in so far as it is an unprecedented phenomenon. If this explanation be accepted, the problem of causality is solved. The truth of this explanation is proved by the *reductio ad absurdum* of any other theory, *e.g.*, the theory of emergence of an absolutely pre-non-existent effect held by the Nyāya-Vaiśeṣika school or the theory of manifestation of an absolutely existent effect. It has been irrefutably shown by Nāgārjuna, the pattern and paragon of sceptics, that an existent effect has no necessity for a cause and a non-existent also cannot be made existent. A combination of existence and non-existence is logically incompatible and exclusion of both is rejected by the Law of Excluded Middle. Nāgārjuna concludes that causation is only an appearance of which no rational explanation is possible. It is alogical in character and so cannot be real, as reality must not contradict the laws of thought which are also the laws of being.

The Jaina would agree with Nāgārjuna subject to a qualification. Nāgārjuna is right in his criticism of the Sāṅkhya and Nyāya theories, but he has taken the formulation of these theories at their face value. He has read contradiction in the theories and his criticism is, no doubt, correct, and it is fully deserved because these philosophers have been hasty in their evaluation of the nature of reality and because also their representation is not wholly correct. These philosophers have failed to notice that existence is not exclusive of non-existence. Existence is only a part-characteristic and so also is non-existence. The Naiyāyika errs by emphasizing one or the other as the exclusive characteristic. But the nature of reals, as has been sufficiently proved by the Jaina, is not exclusive or extremistic. It is existent-cum-non-existent. The charge of contradiction, as pointed out by Nāgārjuna, holds unassailable against those who regard existence and non-existence as absolute and exclusive characteristics. But absolutism is due to abstractionist tendency of our thought, which requires to be checked and revised in consonance with experience, which is the ultimate source of knowledge of the existence of things and of their relations. Experience does not warrant such extremistic characterization of reality and so the finding of contradiction is based upon a hasty study of facts. The fault and fallacy of Nāgārjuna and his followers lie in their acquiescence in the interpretation of reality by those very philosophers whom they criticized. Instead of taking their interpretation of the nature of things on trust they should have gone into the original field. Nāgārjuna also has not succeeded in preventing himself from falling a prey to the facile observation and superficial exposition of the professional philosophers who held the field. The antinomies, which are inherent in the professional orthodox theories, did not escape his vigilant logical vision. But this should have given him a reason for pause and impressed upon him the necessity of fresh thinking on the nature of reality. Nāgārjuna failed to do this and transferred the antinomies, which are inherent in the traditional theories, to the nature of things. The result is unrelieved scepticism, which gloats over the failure of professional philosophers. He was not serious enough to contemplate whether an alternative explanation was possible.

The Jaina begins from where the sceptic stopped. Instead of being satisfied with the finding of antinomies in the current theories, the Jaina directs his attention to the fresh study of reals. The result is the discovery of *anekāntavāda*, the law of the multiple nature of reality. It corrects the partiality of philosophers by supplementing the other side of reality, which escaped them. The effect is both pre-existent and non-existent. So far as it is a passing phase of the causal substance and so far as it is a novel emergence it is pre-non-existent. But so far as it is a continuation of the causal substance it is pre-existent. The same is true of identity and difference. The effect and the cause are identical and different both. There is no contradiction, as identity *quâ* substance and difference *quâ* modes are attested by indubitable experience. The contradiction would be insuperable if both identity and difference *quâ* substance were maintained. But the Jaina never does this. It is a pity that rival philosophers, instead of profiting by the wisdom of the Jaina philosopher, have maligned him without trying to understand his real import. The Jaina is reproached with maintaining that cause and effect are identical in the same reference and in all its implications. He is criticized on the ground of advocating the identity and difference of the cause and effect both as substance. But this has never been done by the Jaina and so the criticism is based upon a hasty interpretation. The philosophers have been hasty in their interpretation of reality and also in their interpretation of the Jaina view.

We began the present chapter with the consideration of the reality of numerical difference and this led us to the consideration of relations. We endeavoured to establish that the reality of these concepts is to be admitted on pain of absurdities. And once their reality is conceded the multiple nature of reals follows with irresistible logic. Incidentally we dealt with the problem of causation and gave the views of the Masters on the supposed antinomies. If the discussion of these problems, which raised themselves in connection with the enquiry into the reality of negation, be looked upon as a digression, our apology is that it was neither irrelevant nor unnecessary. The problems of philosophy are inter-connected and our understanding of one makes the examination of others necessary. The central thesis of the Jaina is that there is not only diversity of reals, but each real is equally diversified. Diversification as induced by relations has been explained. The conclusion is legitimate that each real is possessed of an infinite number of modes at every moment. The number of reals is infinite and consequently their relations with one another are infinite. We have shown that all things are related in one way or the other and that relations induce relational qualities in the relata, which accordingly become infinitely diversified at each moment and throughout their career, which is unbounded both by past and by future limits. Things are neither momentary nor uniform, which is respectively the position of the fluxist and of the Vedāntist. A real changes every moment and at the same time continues. The continuity never breaks down. The Vaiśeṣika maintains that when things perish, they irrevocably disappear from the world. But the Jaina in agreement with the Sāṅkhya maintains that cessation is not absolute. If absolute cessation of the cause were the indispensable condition of the emergence of the effect, the mutual dependence of cause and effect would not be intelligible. The cause would not be of service to the effect, if it were defunct at the time the effect emerges into being. In other words, the cause would not be cause of the effect and the effect would not be affiliated to the cause. The cause continues while it is changed into the effect. The cause is independent of the auxiliaries so far as its natural change is concerned. Because the cause is dynamic and changing by its very nature it is self-sufficient with reference to its constitutional change. The modes are transitory by their nature. Change means the emergence of modes which were not in evidence before. And unless the modes *per se* are perishable, there would not be new modes and consequently no change. The services of external causes are not superfluous, as they are responsible for the speciality of the modes. What is maintained is that things are dynamic by their nature and so their changefulness is spontaneous. But that the change should assume this or that shape depends upon the presence of other factors which are in operation.

The Jaina has no hesitation in accepting the Sautrāntika's position of causal efficiency as the criterion of reality. Being dynamic in constitution every real is the cause of its own change. We have seen that change is inexplicable if an absolutist standpoint is adopted. Vedānta is obliged to declare it to be an appearance. The fluxist who swears by change ultimately ends in denying it in effect. In the philosophy of flux each entity exists for a moment and perishes at the next moment *in toto*. So there is no change in any existent. It has a definite assignable place in the time-continuum, but it is there unchanged and unmodified. Change implies that the thing should become different from what it is. This is possible if an entity persists at any rate for more than a moment. It comes into being and it is what it is at the moment of its origin. It could change only if it were vested with a novel attribute at the next moment. But if it had no continuity beyond the first moment, it would have no scope for change of attributes. The fluxist, in spite of all appearances to the contrary has to conclude that things are static and unchanging and to declare all change to be an unmitigated appearance. He proceeds from the datum of change and comes to a conclusion which denies it. This is self-contradictory. Then again he starts with causal efficiency as the equivalent of existence and comes to a conclusion which makes causal efficiency impossible. We have proved in Chapter II that there can be no causal relation between momentary existents. This is another contradiction in the fluxist position. The Jaina conception of reality avoids the Scylla of fluxism and the Charybdis of illusionism. I cannot conceive of any other philosophy which can maintain realism against the onslaughts of idealists without endorsing the Jaina conception. A real is that which not only originates, but is also liable to cease and at the same time capable of persisting. Existence, cessation and persistence are the fundamental characteristics of all that is real. To a person trained in the school of *a priori* logic the proposition may sound paradoxical and even self-contradictory. But we have taken sufficient pains to demonstrate that the reading of contradiction in it is due to preconceptions fostered by *a priori* logic. This concept of reality is the only one which can avoid the conclusion that the world of plurality, which is the world of experience, is an illusion. Either the world is to be accepted as real or dismissed as an unreal appearance. The latter conclusion is drawn by the Vedāntist. But if realism is to be maintained it can only be done by means of Jaina logic and Jaina conception of reality. We have shown how Nyāya and Sāṅkhya have failed to explain causation and change. A system of philosophy which fails to account for these two fundamental problems cannot lay claim to unqualified allegiance.

The affirmation of origination, cessation and persistence as elements in the constitution of reals has to be substantiated. We have shown that a real is always changing and the change of attributes, that occurs at every moment, is due both to its internal dynamic constitution and to its relation with the infinite plurality of reals. We have seen that change presupposes the persistence of an underlying stuff. So persistence is to be accounted as an element in a real together with change. But change means the cessation of a previous mode or attribute and the coming into being of a new mode. As modes and attributes are identical with the causal stuff in which they occur, the birth and cessation of modes are to be regarded as the birth and cessation of the causal stuff *quâ* the modes and attributes. That a thing changes means that it has ceased to be what it was and comes to be what it was not. Cessation and birth are thus the invariable concomitants of change and thus should be predicated of the changing stuff. A real then has birth and cessation as its elements and the element of persistence also is to be affirmed as it is the very presupposition of change. The affirmation of origination, cessation and persistence as elements of the constitution of a reality has therefore nothing paradoxical about it. The three elements are a natural deduction from the reality of change. The Jaina believes in the dynamic nature of reals and, in deference to the demands of reason and experience alike, he sums up the three elements mentioned above as the component factors of the constitution of reality. One can avoid this triple characteristic only by the declaration of change as appearance, which is the position of Vedānta. One must offer one's allegiance either to Vedāntic monism or affirm the multiple nature of reality, which is the teaching of Jaina *anekāntavāda*.

Viewed from the Jaina standpoint a real is a continuum through the infinite variation of its modes at every moment of its being. The continuum is a reality as much as the variation. Thus there is unity as well as multiplicity in perfect harmony. The real viewed as identical with the changing modes is thus coming into being every moment and perishing every moment. That it comes to evolve a new mode implies that the previous mode has ceased to exist. So a real *quâ* its modes is becoming something new by ceasing to be its old self. The birth of the new is thus the logical concomitant of the death of the old. Let us illustrate it by an example. A self which was feeling unhappy is now feeling happy. Strictly analysed it comes to mean that the unhappy self is no more at once the happy self comes into being. So a real in undergoing change both ceases and comes to be. That it persists through both the acts is evident, since birth and cessation as the concomitants of change are predicable only of a continuity. The affirmation of the three apparently incompatible elements as making up the constitution of a real is thus the result of a logical analysis of a real as it is. If one is not prepared to believe in this triple affirmation one has to assert that things are not real at all. Either pure negation or pure affirmation are the only alternatives left for acceptance. The former is the position of the Śūnyavādin and the latter is of Vedānta. Is the paradox greater in the Jaina view than in the two other systems? Is the Śūnyavādin, who dismisses the whole world of experience as an unfounded illusion, less paradoxical ? Is the Vedāntic view, which endorses the Śūnyavādin's repudiation of the whole world of pluralities, calculated to satisfy the abhorrence of paradox in a more satisfying manner ? The paradox is only apparent as it alone provides a satisfactory explanation of experience and thought. The criterion should be whether or not it succeeds to explain the world as we know it.

But a difficulty has been raised with reference to the triple character enunciated as the universal feature of reality. If persistence, cessation and birth were each of them identical with the substance of which they are predicated, then being identical with the same substance, all of them would be identical with one another. Thus persistence would be the same thing as cessation and birth, cessation would be identical with persistence and birth, and birth would be identical with cessation and persistence. So the triple character is reduced to an identical single mode. And if each of these modes were regarded as numerically different from the substance and also from one another, and if each of them were believed to be real, then again each of these modes would have triple character. An infinite vicious series would be inevitable as each of the triple modes would have another triple character and so on to infinity, unless the triple mode were severally and jointly asserted to be unreal characterization. Either a single mode in the place of the triple character, or an infinite series, or its unreality, is to be asserted. But the Jaina answers the critic by asserting the non-absolutistic position. So far as persistence etc. are regarded as identical with the substance, it is legitimate that persistence and cessation and birth should be regarded as identical. And if attention is concentrated on the aspect of difference of these modes from the substance and from one another, then each of them would have a triple character. There is no reason for the infinite series, as difference is not absolute. The modes are identical with the substance only so far as the substance is focused in the modes. The modes are not absolutely different from substance, as in that case the modes would not belong to the substance. The mode is a mode of the substance because the identity of substance is focused in it and is not annulled. So a mode is identical with substance in that respect. To take an example, clay is transformed into a jar, and so the former is regarded as the cause of the latter. The jar is different from clay no doubt, but the jar could not be a jar unless it were the same substance as clay. So difference and identity both being inseparable moments in the relation, a mode as identical with the substance may have the same predicates with the substance and as different from the substance may each of them behave as an independent reality and as such may have the triple characteristic. The reduction of the triple character to a unitary character is also a matter of point of view. The mode and the substance may be viewed as identical and also as different, as they are both in one. Thus the consequences, alleged to be inevitable by the opponent, are not inevitable, as they are based upon exclusive identity and exclusive difference. But the identity is not exclusive of difference and vice versa, as both are the attested traits of reality. A mode and a substance are different because they are two, and they are identical because one is not independent of the other. If identity is to be asserted on the evidence of experience, difference also should equally be asserted on the strength of the same evidence. The compartmental way of looking at things leads to the affirmation of one and to the negation of the other, since it concentrates on one and ignores the other. The besetting sin of philosophers has been the habit to put the telescope upon the blind eye and then to deduce that the other aspect is not real. The Jaina philosopher voices the necessity of using both the eyes and of seeing the obverse and reverse of the coin of reality.

The triple mode of origination, cessation and persistence as the necessary presupposition of change gives out the internal constitution of reality. A real is undergoing change *for all time* and change connotes these three characteristics. Time is understood as comprising three determinations, *viz.*, past, present and future. A real persists through time and thus has these three temporal determinations. That a real embraces the three time-determinations is again a necessary deduction from its possession of causal efficiency, which is the criterion of existence according to the fluxist. The Jaina endorses the Buddhist affirmation of causal efficiency as the criterion of existence. But whereas the Buddhist deduces from this premise the conclusion that everything is momentary, the Jaina affirms that things, because of their causal efficiency, must have the three temporal determinations. Causal efficiency is not predicable of a momentary in the same way as it is not competent to an unchanging unity. If a real were not amenable to change, it would not be the cause of an effect, as we have seen that the concepts of eternal cause and eternal effect are self-contradictory.[1] Exercise of causal efficiency is possible in time and is thus possible in that which is temporal. An unchanging eternal has no temporal character and so cannot be a cause. The momentary has been found to be equally unchanging and so cannot have causal efficiency.[2] Causal efficiency presupposes change and change presupposes persistence through time-divisions. So a real, which is dynamic by its nature, must have a history, that is to say, it must have a past and a future in addition to its being present. The Jaina, in agreement with the Sāṅkhya, holds that a non-entity cannot become an entity and vice versa. Such being the case a real is real for all time. It was real in the past, is real in the present and will be real in future. A 'real' which has no past and no future is a fiction and a non-entity. It is obvious that it was not an entity before and will cease to be an entity after. But if a thing must be real in its own right, it cannot be unreal at any time. The fluxist fails to take note of this necessary truth when he denies past and future history of a real. The fluxist was misled by his dialectic that things must be perishable or not by their very constitution. He accepted that things were perishable on the evidence of experience, and discarded their continuation though it was equally attested by experience. The Jaina shows the fluxist

1. *Vide* Chapter II.
2. *ibid.*

to be in the wrong. He is disloyal to experience and to logic alike, as experience shows the persistence of things and logic proves that change, which is also the premise from which the fluxist starts, is impossible without persistence. The Vedāntist accepts the continuity of things and dismisses change. The Buddhist accepts change without continuity, though experience, unsophisticated by considerations of pure logic, attests both to be actual. The Jaina accepts both continuity and change on the evidence of experience and maintains that there is no logical contradiction between them. The Vedāntist is consistent in that he does not abandon pure logic. Pure logic demands that a real is real for all time, and as change connotes the emergence of a novel attribute, which was not in existence before at least in its present form, the Vedāntist discards change as contradictory to the inherent reality of a thing. The Vedāntist is loyal to logic, though he is disloyal to experience, which he asserts to be illusory. The fluxist accepts change as the very essence of reality in adherence to the verdict of experience. He is not deterred by the considerations of pure logic that a real is real for all time and in its own right and so cannot be unreal. Had he been loyal to pure logic, he ought to have held that things were imperishable and were real for all time and in their own right. He discarded logic and accepted experience as the authority. But in the course of his development of his philosophy he allowed himself to be swayed by considerations of pure logic. He argued that as change was contradictorily opposed to not-change, not-change was unreal. The fluxist here proves disloyal to experience in deference to pure logic. The result has been that he has not been loyal either to pure logic or to experience and in this his philosophy is less satisfactory than Vedānta.

The position that is adopted by the Jaina is this: Pure logic, prior to and independent of experience, is a blind guide to the determination of truth. Logic is to rationalize and systematize what experience offers. All our knowledge is ultimately derived from experience. Even lhe knowledge that something exists is not capable of being derived from any other source. The existence and behavior of things and their mutual relationship can be ascertained only on the basis of experience and the function of reason or pure logic is only to reduce the data of experience to order and system To allow logic to work *in vacuo* and to dictate term to the data of experience to behave in a way different from their own is neither a sound philosophical procedure nor a safe course of thought. The unfettered exercise of logic, in defiance of and in opposition to the testimony of experience, has been responsible for the hopelessly chaotic results achieved by metaphysical speculations. That philosophy has not made progress commensurate with the progress of science is due to the illegitimate freedom usurped by reason by deposition of empirical evidence. The laws of thought, if they are to be the laws of being, must be propounded in a fashion that they may be really helpful to the progress of knowledge. We have already seen how the application of these laws to the data of experience, unhampered by considerations of loyalty to experience, has worked. The law of causation, which is so necessary for reducing a major part of experience to order, has been declared to be false. Change has been declared by the Vedāntist to be an illusion, although the fluxist, who swears by logic with as much verve and gusto as the Vedāntist, asserts it to be the only truth. Nāgārjuna and his followers, if the interpretation of Candrakīrti and the representation of their critics are to be believed, came to the conclusion that no affirmation was possible. The Vedāntist by the pursuit of rigorous logic comes to the finding that the world of plurality as experienced by us is only an illusion, and only one reality which is consciousness-cum-existence, exists. The Jaina insists that our method of philosophical enquiry should be loyalty to experience and also to logic in so far as it does not outstrip the authority of experience and in so far as it helps us to explain and to rationalize the data of experience. Logic is to be applied to experience and never allowed to do away with it. In one word, logic must be empirical logic and not abstract or *a priori*. As we discussed in the very first chapter the scope and character of the Laws of Thought, we do not propose to carry our examination of them to any further length. It is necessary to observe in this connection that the Jaina is loyal to logic and experience alike when he asserts that change and continuity are both essential notes in the constitution of reality. The Vedāntist also has ultimately to rely upon experience in order to be able to assert that consciousness is the only reality. The existence of consciousness is proved by intuition, and not by logic. The contradiction that is involved in the denial of consciousness is to be known also by means of experience. When one denies that consciousness exists, the denial is found to be self contradictory because the denial itself is a case of consciousness. The denial of consciousness is thus an affirmation of consciousness and as such is a case of self-contradiction. The Jaina philosophers only affirm this truth when they assert that the nature of reality is to be determined by the evidence of experience and thus endorse the fundamental position of the Vedāntist. But his loyatly to experience is not half-hearted. He maintains that when experience is the source of knowledge of existence including the existence of our own selves, why should it be discarded when it testifies to the existence of so many selves and things ? We have seen how the Laws of Thought have been given a new orientation by the Jaina philosopher, and how these laws, as reoriented by him, enable him to arrive at the conclusion of the multiple nature of reality.

Chapter IV

ABSOLUTE NEGATIVISM AND ABSOLUTE PARTICULARISM

We have found that existence of things cannot be denied and that existence is only a part-characteristic which is not exclusive of non-existence as another element in the make-up of real. Non-existence as a characteristic is as much real and objective as existence is. But the objectivity of non-existence has been denied by some philosophers. The fluxist believes that non-existence is only an ideal construction. But if non-existence were not real, how would the Fluxist account for the non-existence of consciousness in matter and of colour and extension and shape in consciousness ? A thing is possessed of its own nature and not of the nature of another. This makes it possible for us to assert negative propositions. We assert 'A chair is not conscious' and 'consciousness is not extended.' The non-existence of consciousness in chairs is true for all times and for all places, and similarly the non-existence of extension in consciousness is true irrespective of time and place. The denial of non-existence would make these assertions false and unmeaning. But we see no logical ground to condemn these negative judgments as false, which the denial of non-existence would involve. The Fluxist contends that 'non-existence is not competent to perception' as it has no causal efficiency, which is the distinctive criterion of existence. The object of perception is that which is the cause of it, and since non-existence cannot be the cause of anything, it cannot be the cause of perception. It is further denied that non-existence can be inferred. Inference is based either on causal relation or on identity of nature between the probans and the probandum. But non-existence has neither causal efficiency nor a nature of its own. So nothing can be its effect or its correlate having identity of nature with it, on the basis of which non-existence could be inferred. Thus, there is not a single proof to establish the reality of non-existence. This argument of the Fluxist, however, affords another illustration of the unreliability of abstract logic as an instrument for the determination of reality. It also involves self-contradiction as it is admitted even by the Buddhist that non-perception of a perceivable entity in spite of the presence of all the conditions of perception thereof (*yogyānupalabdhi*) is the ground of inferring the non-existence of the unperceived thing. But the Buddhist has contended that this admission is not inconsistent with his denial of non-existence as an objective fact. The 'non-perception of a perceivable' does not mean absence of perception, but perception of a positive datum, with which the negatum would be perceived if it were present upon it. For example, the non-perception of the pen upon the table is nothing but perception of the table. An assertion of non-existence of the pen is thus only another way of asserting the existence of the table and nothing more. But the Jaina maintains that this is an argument of the escapist, who would not boldly face a difficulty. It is ignored that the table could be responsible for the negative judgment, only if non-existence of the pen were a part and parcel of the being of the table. Unless the table were recognized to be existent and non-existent both, existent in so far as it is itself and non-existent in so far as it is not anything other than a table, the emergence of the negative judgment, 'There is no pen upon the table', would be unaccountable. If, however, the denial of non-existence were interpreted to be the denial of an independent non-existence, which was in perpetual opposition to existence, the Jaina would have no reason to take exception to it. But the Buddhist does not assert that non-existence is an aspect of a real complementary to the aspect of existence, which is the Jaina position. So his denial of non-existence is only tantamount to the assertion that it is a fiction. We have shown in the preceding chapter the absurd consequences which inevitably arise on the denial of the reality of non-existence and this constitutes the *reductio ad absurdum* of the Fluxist position.

The result which we have attained so far is that non-existence as an element in the constitution of a real has to be accepted as a verity. But it is real only as an element in a real and is not again the exclusive character of it. If non-existence were to be the sole and sufficient character of things, nothing would be existent and, consequently, neither affirmation nor negation of anything would be possible. Paradoxical as it may appear, this is, however, the position seriously maintained by the Voidist (*Śūnyavādin*), if we are to believe that the interpretation of Candrakīrti, the commentator of Nāgārjuna, and the criticism of the rival philosophers constitute a faithful representation of the position of Nāgārjuna. Stcherbatsky and the Japanese exponents of Nāgārjuna would, however, have us believe that Nāgārjuna's philosophy is not absolute negativism. Whichever may be the correct position, the problem appears to be one which concerns the historian of Indian philosophy. So far as pure philosophy is concerned, it cannot be disinterested in such a doctrine, which is a possibility, though its historical authenticity may be problematic. The Jaina philosopher seeks to establish that absolutism in philosophical speculation is only the outcome of abstractionist tendency of thought, against which philosophers have not sufficiently been on their guard. Absolute affirmation of being is the conclusion reached by the Vedāntist. Absolute negation of being as its direct antithesis is the result attained by others. The difficulties raised by the former position have been discussed by us. We now propose to consider whether the opposite position of absolute non-being is tenable.

The Voidist asserts that things are supposed to be determined by characteristics. A thing is asserted to be one or many, constant or changing. But these determinations, unity or plurality, uniformity or variation, which are supposed to give real insight into the nature of existence, are unreal and so existents are also unreal. An existent having no determination is a fiction and so the unreality of determinations proves the unreality of things determined. The unreality of determinations is proved by the impossibility of a relation between the determination and the thing determined. The determination is not identical with the existent, as identity would make them one, and in the absence of the two terms, determination and determinatum, there would be no relation, which is possible only between two terms. Let again the relation be supposed to be one of difference. But this is also impossible. If the determination were different and aloof from the determinatum, the latter would not be determined and so would not have a definitive its own. That a thing is what it is and is different from what it is not is due to the fact that it has a definitive nature which is not shared by others. But the nature of a thing consists of determinations. If a determination were found to be impossible, things would have no nature and thus no reality. So there is no reality anywhere. It is only a false appearance that things are perceived by us. The data of our wakeful experience are as unreal as those of dream-experience. The Voidist would in this way apply his dialectic of the impossibility of relations to all the categories and concepts and prove them to be impossible. We have shown in the preceding chapter that relations are real and it is the abstract logic of the sceptic, based upon incomplete observation and unwarranted generalisation, that is in fault. But the Voidist, who triumphs in the repudiation of all reality and all system and structure of thought, would not be abashed into silence or confession of failure if the impossibility of theoretical or practical activity is alleged to be the consequence of his dialectics. He would only maintain that this is the position which he is interested in. The whole world is an unmitigated illusion and if the conclusion hurts the feelings of the realist, it is the latter who is responsible for the consequences of his illogically hugging this illusion as truth. So all our previous efforts to determine the nature of reality would be robbed of all their value, since the absurdities, shown by us to follow from the denial of the nature of reality, would have no influence upon the Voidist, who would construe these absurdities as proof of his position. But the Jaina is not alone in his fight against the sceptic. He is in the respectable company of all the philosophers, who have any constructive scheme to offer.

The Jaina would pose a simple question to the Voidist. What is the motive of the sceptic in elaborating such destructive dialectic? Does he do so for his own conviction or for the conviction of others who hold the opposite view ? So far as the Voidist may be concerned for the sake of his own conviction, he must rely upon the truth of his own findings. He must accept that his own realization of the unreality of thought and things is a fact. He must be at least conscious of his own conviction that everything is an illusion, otherwise he cannot think or assert that it is an illusion. He must again admit that his thought of illusion at any rate is real. And if his mission is to correct the illusion of others, he can achieve his objective only by adducing reasons in support of his position and in refutation of the opposite position held by others. If he does not believe in the truth of the arguments he employs for the conviction of others he cannot be sincere to himself or to others. So his conviction would be unreal and insincere as he has no logic in his support; and a realization of the absurdity should convince the Voidist of the impossibility of his philosophy. The Voidist, however, is not prepared to take such an easy defeat. He has argued that this accusation is unfair, as the logical apparatus, he has to employ not for his subjective satisfaction but for the conviction of erring humanity, does not prove his faith in its absolute reality. He has to follow the logical convention that is in currency among philosophers and if these philosophers are sincere in their conviction of the truth of their logical canons, that should be enough. The question whether the Voidist believes in the logic which he employs is irrelevant. His mission is satisfied if he can produce conviction of the self-contradictory nature of things and beliefs held to be veridical by others. The Voidist does not really believe in the reality and truth of the canons of logic. But his want of faith does not detract from their probative value for those who believe in their truth and efficacy. The opponent could find fault in the arguments of the sceptic and then assert that the conclusion did not follow from the premises. If there is no logical flaw in the arguments of the sceptic, the opponent who believes in the validity of logic, should accept the conclusion which is irresistible. It would not help his cause to complain that the sceptic does not believe in the validity of his own argument and, so, he cannot accept it as valid. The sceptic has his own reasons to call in question the validity of logic, but as these reasons are not shared by the believer in logic, there is no ground of complaint by the latter.

But this disclaimer of the sceptic of all responsibility does not absolve him from the charge of self-contradiction. He may satisfy himself with exposing self-contradiction in all our concepts. The question whether and how far he is successful in his task apart, he must frankly accept the consequences of his own thought. He must admit that the world of experience and thought is an illusion. The question can be posed to the sceptic whether he accepts his conclusion to be true or not. If his conclusion is true, then illusion must be a fact and a reality. If illusion be itself an illusion, that is to say, if the conclusion that everything is an illusion be itself an illusion, the reality of the world of experience and thought would remain unimpeached. But the Voidist has argued that his recourse to logic is rendered necessary to remove doubt and error on the part of the opponent and not for proving that everything is void. It is self-evident that our consciousness bereft of subject-object polarisation, which has been shown to be impossible by the proof of the unreality of relations, is not a fact, since all our experience of consciousness finds it to be polarized. Polarized consciousness cannot be real, because it presupposes relation between the subjective and the objective pole and because relations as such are unreal. There is no evidence of unpolarized consciousness and so also it cannot be accepted as real. But this defence seems to be a deception. He must accept his awareness of the unreality of polarized consciousness to be real, otherwise he would not be in a position to assert the unreality. In that case the awareness in question cannot be an illusion. An illusion is corrected only if something is the basis of this correction: that is to say, there must be a real substance which is to appear as what it is not. A false judgment or a false assertion means that the predicate is falsely attributed to a subject. The *that* of the judgment has a *what* which is false. But though the *what* may be false, the *that* must be real. If both *that* and *what* are believed to be false, there is no meaning in correction or removal of errors. To take an instance the judgment 'It is silver' is false, as the predicate is not truly affirmed. The correction of the false judgment presupposes a true judgment, *viz.*, 'It is a shell.' But if the result of the corrected false judgment is no true judgment, and the implication of the correction is not the assertion of a real datum, we cannot conceive how the correction is possible at all. If the correction is not real, in other words, if the correction of a judgment is itself an illusion, the original judgment must be true. At any rate, the reality of a datum, upon which the illusion is centred, must be true in the ultimate analysis. The charge of insincerity and want of seriousness of outlook that has been levelled against the Voidist by Akalaṅkadeva does not seem to lack a substantial foundation.[1]

The defensive plea of the Voidist that the denial of existence and affirmation of non-existence are rendered possible by the sanction of conventional thought (*saṃvṛti*) stands in need of critical analysis. If the affirmation of existence in deference to convention means the affirmation that the thing in question exists in its own character *quâ* substance, in its own time, in its own place and in reference to its specific functional character (*dravyakṣetrakālabhāvātmanā*), the Jaina would accept his position as correct. If again the negation of existence has reference to the opposite characteristics, that is to say, if a thing is denied to have existence in respect of the character of another thing having a different identity, a different spatio-temporal setting and functional character, the Jaina would also accept this predication of non-existence as correct. The assertion of existence in reference to its own context and denial of existence in reference to a different context, severally and in combination, are also admitted to be factual characterization of reals. If this be the real import of the Voidist's assertion of unreality of all things, there would be no ground to call in question the justice of his position. But the term, 'conventional thought' (*saṃvṛti*) has been given a different meaning. It is construed as thought which does not stand critical examination. The metaphysical speculations of philosophers have been subjected to a searching analysis by Nāgārjuna and his followers, and self-contradictions have been discovered in them. The world of experience and the metaphysical systems that have been built upon the data of experience are, according to the Voidist, as unsubstantial and hollow as dream-experience is illusory, because like dream experience they do not stand the test of logical examination. But this plea of the Voidist also is to be condemned on the

1. parapratipādanārthaṁ śāstram upadeṣṭāraṁ vā varṇayan sarvaṁ pratikṣipatī 'ti katham anunmattaḥ ? tatra Śauddhodaner eva kathaṁ prajñā 'parādhinī. babhūve 'ti vayaṁ tāvad bahuvismayam āsmahe'.

As., pp. 116-17.

charge of self-contradiction. If normal experience and the interpretation thereof are to be condemned on the ground of their incompatibility with the requirements of logic, then consistency demands that the canons of logic and the examination based upon these canons must be valid. If so, the assertion of invalidity of thought cannot be universal. But the Voidist, who asserts that all that appears to have existence including logical thought is an unsubstantial appearance, evidently contradicts himself. If there be no truth in thought and if even the act of discovery of this want of truth would also lack truth, we do not see any possibility of success in proving or disproving anything. Even the assertions 'experience is false' and 'the proof of this falsity is also false' are propositions which lay claim to truth. Unless the aforesaid propositions be true, the unreality of experience and thought cannot be established. So the truth of the proposition, by means of which the alleged unreality is proved, must be accepted. The universal denial of truth of all thought and experience would thus involve the sceptic in hopeless self-contradiction.

Let us sum up the results of our investigation into the nature of reality. The Jaina philosopher has proved that absolute unqualified affirmation of existence is not in conformity with the nature of reality. He has also proved that absolute negation of existence is self-contradictory. He has further proved that fidelity to experience and thought demands that existence and non-existence both are to be accepted as equally valid traits in the make-up of a real. We now propose to consider whether the simultaneous assertions of existence and non-existence can be accepted by the exponents of absolutistic logic. If existence were contradictorily opposed to non-existence, which is the position maintained by professional logic, then the whole range of reality as envisaged by our experience and thought has to be declared to be an unmitigated illusion. We have shown that the Voidist, who does not believe in the reality of anything including the reality of his belief that it is so and who condemns all beliefs as false including the belief which enables him to make this assertion, hopelessly contradicts himself. Of course, the Vedāntist, in spite of his agreement with the Voidist so far as the denial of validity of all judgments is concerned, stands in a different position. The Vedāntist is not a universal sceptic. He believes that the finding of the truth that the world is an appearance is true and real, as it is based upon the intuition of One Reality, *viz.*, one pure consciousness bereft of subject-object polarization, which is the only reality. But though the Vedāntist cannot be convicted of self-contradiction in so far as he adheres to his fundamental assertion of the reality of One Absolute Consciousness and his denial only has reference to anything which is in excess of this unity, it has been shown to lead to consequences which have not commended themselves to the majority of thinkers. But leaving the Vadāntist severely alone, we must address ourselves to other philosophers, who believe in a plurality of ontological reals. The Sāṅkhya-Yoga school believes in the reality of a plurality of facts. We have shown that the reality of plurality presupposes the reality of numerical difference and also non-existence of one in the other. We have also shown that the reality of causation involves that the effect is both real and unreal. The effect was not existent before and is made existent after. The Sāṅkhya theory of pre-existence of effect has been shown to be self-contradictory. So existence and non-existence both are to be predicated of all effects unless the law of causation be unceremoniously dismissed as an illusion which has been done by the Voidist and the Vedāntist alike. But the Sāṅkhya holds causation to be real. He also believes that things are numerically different. And, as we have shown, numerical difference presupposes that things have different identities, the implication of which again is the assertion of existence and non-existence as concomitant features in a real. 'A is numerically different from B' means that A is A and is not B. So A both is and is not. As this point has been elaborately discussed by us in the last chapter, we need not repeat the arguments which led us to the conclusion we are stating here.

It is undeniable for the Sāṅkhya that existence and non-existence are equally true of a real. But how can he maintain the reality of both if he does not shed his belief that existence and non-existence are contradictorily opposed ? If existence and non-existence were two wholes mutually exclusive of each other, there could not be coexistence of the two in any one real. To be further explicit, if existence were believed to be a whole-characteristic, possessing the whole extent of a real and thus leaving no room for the other characteristics, which are not involved by existence, we cannot see any reason how the Sāṅkhya can justify his belief in the reality of change and causation and also numerical difference. If a thing were existent in every respect and in every reference, irrespective of time and place and individuality, it is inconceivable how it could be characterized as non-existent. If existence again be a whole-characteristic and non-existence be again another whole-characteristic, the two cannot be the characteristics of one and the same thing. The Sāṅkhya has to accept the truth that existence and non-existence as concomitant traits in the being of a single real are only part-characteristics, which is the position of the Jaina Non-absolutist. The Sāṅkhya has unconsciously, as it were, adopted the non-absolutist logic and metaphysics, which the Jaina philosopher propounds. Consistency would require a thorough reformulation of the categories from the Sāṅkhya philosopher. The *Pradhāna* (Primordial Matter), which is held to contain all the future evolutes in its being in implicit state, cannot be categorically asserted to be a unitary principle. It must be asserted to be one and many, identical and different, existent and non-existent both. It is one in so far as it runs as an underlying unity in and through all the forms which are evolved from it; and it is many in so far as it is identical with the changing forms. It is existent in so far as it is one principle embracing the whole extent of evolution, but non-existent so far as the evolutes are non-existent *quâ* finished evolutes. As for identity and difference, both are true of it. It is identical in so far it is the same causal stuff which changes into the different evolutes and is different in so far as the unfolding evolutes are the different manifestations of it, which cannot but vary with the varying forms. It is an obvious deduction from the Sāṅkhya postulates that this philosophy is justifiable only by the canons of non-absolutist logic, and it is necessary both in the interests of clarity of thought and expression and as a safeguard against prevailing misconception that this truth should find ample handsome recognition and unhesitating formulation in the hands of the orthodox exponents of Sāṅkhya-Yoga Philosophy. All pretence of loyalty to Pure logic must be unhesitatingly surrendered.

The results we have reached from the analysis of the concept of reality are that a real has three characteristics which can be stated in three distinct propositions, *viz.*, 'A is,' 'A is not' and 'A is and is not.' In order to guard against the absolutist habit of believing existence and non-existence as whole-characteristics excluding each other from their respective orbit, the Jaina philosopher prefaces each proposition by the limiting phrase 'in some respect' or 'in one particular aspect' (*syāt*). The insertion of this phrase is a warning against reading an absolutist sense into the predicates. There are philosophers, who having recognized the necessity of the compresence of the three characteristics in a real, would prefer to characterize it as 'inexpressible' or indeterminate' (*avācya*). It is true that the three characteristics, or rather the first two characteristics — 'is' and 'is not' — are not capable of being expressed by one word at a time. The co-existence of these two predicables is sought to be implied by the phrase 'inexpressible' (*avācya*). But this is again a new predicable and if a real were absolutely unamenable to description, the assertion of 'inexpressible' as a predicate would be impossible. The word 'inexpressible used as a predicate asserts a real characteristic of a real subject and the possibility of such predication means that a real is not entirely incapable of being described. So the predicate 'inexpressible' cannot be taken in its literal absolute sense. 'In some respect, a real is inexpressible' is the correct proposition. If things were absolutely incapable of being expressed, the assertion of the proposition would be a case of self-contradiction. The Buddhist Fluxist, however, holds a different view according to which a real is a distinctive particular having a peculiar nature which it shares with none else and which distinguishes it from all other reals. Reals are thus self-distinguished (*svalakṣaṇa*). The predicate is always a generic attribute, and such being the case, no predicate is capable of being affirmed of such a real. A real is thus inexpressible in an absolute sense. Even it cannot be described as a self-distinguished particular. No predicate, however it may be hedged round by qualifications, can give insight into the peculiar nature of a real, which must be known by intuition alone. Even the word 'inexpressible' has a generic reference, which is evidenced by the fact that it can be predicated of several reals. A real being absolutely incapable of being expressed cannot be described even as 'indescribable' or 'inexpressible'. A real is untouched by a word. A word is neither identical with a real, nor has it any necessary relation to it. There is no necessity, logical or epistemological, that a real when cognized in its true nature should be cognized along with a name. What language enables us to know is only an ideal construction and not a real entity. A term can express only a general concept and not an individual. So the very nature of reality forbids the association of linguistic symbols with it, as in its true nature uncoloured by conceptual constructions, it is absolutely devoid of association with a verbal expression.

The Jaina is not satisfied with this evaluation of reality. If association with a verbal expression on the part of a real is denied on the ground that there is no necessary relation either of identity or of container and content between a real and a verbal expression, the same lack of necessary relation between consciousness and objects would make knowledge impossible. The argument may be put in the following syllogism:

All that, which is not a content of anything or identical with it, is not perceived when the latter is perceived.

A word is not a content of a perceptual cognition or identical with the latter.

∴ A word is not perceived when the latter is perceived![1]

But the major premise is not regarded as true by the Jaina. If it were true, no cognition, perceptual or otherwise, would be possible. It might be argued that as the particular object is neither identical with, nor a content of, a cognition, it would not be cognized when the latter were cognized. It may, however, be contended that the relation of container and content is not necessary, but the relation of causality is. Since a perceptual cognition is the effect of the object, the latter is necessarily associated with the former. But even this amendment of the major premise is not free from difficulties. If causality were the

1. na hy arthe śabdāḥ santi tadātmāno vā yena tasmin bhāsamāne te 'pi pratibhāseran. As., p. 118.

determinant of the co-perception of a perceptual cognition and its object, then there would be no ground for preventing the perception of the sense-organ or its causal efficiency, which are also the cause of the perceptual cognition. It is held in defence that though the sense-organ and its causal efficiency are also the cause of the sense-perception, there is difference between an object and a sense-organ. The cognition emerges with an image of the object and not of the organ. Therefore the object is perceived along with the cognition and the sense-organ is not. Not every cause, but the cause that imprints its likeness upon perceptual cognition, is capable of being perceived when the cognition is perceived. But we do not see any logical necessity that causality should be so circumscribed with restrictions. Besides, the question would arise, why does perception take the likeness of the object and not of the sense-organ, though both are equally the causes of perception? Again, a further problem would be raised, why should the perceptual cognition copy the object, and not the previous cognition, which is also the cause of the former ? The perceptual cognition is supposed to be produced by the object, the sense-organ and the previous consciousness-unit. The last-mentioned cause is called homogeneous-antecedent cause (*samanantara-pratyaya*) from which the perceptual cognition is supposed to derive its conscient character. It has not been satisfactorily explained why perceptual cognition should receive the image of the object, and not of any other cause. It is no solution of the problem to say that the reflective judgment, that arises in the trail of sense-perception, has reference to the object and not to the sense-organ or any other cause, and that, therefore, the object is the only cause which should impart its likeness to the perception. The solution begs the question. The question, why the reflective judgment (*adhyavasāya*), that follows a sense-intuition, should not have reference to the sense-organ or any other cause, is not answered. The Buddhist attempts an impossible task. He seeks to determine by *a priori* logic what should be perceived and what should not be perceived. He argues that as words do not stand in the relation of causality or of identity to the objects of perception, words should not form contents of perception. What is perceived and what is not perceived, what should be the contents of perception and what not — these are questions which cannot be answered by *a priori* logic. If you accept perception to be a fact, you must accept together with it all that is felt as its content without question. One might as well argue that there should be no knowledge of an object, as the object in question is not necessarily related to consciousness. The relation of object to consciousness is neither one of identity nor one of difference which are the only kinds of relation possible. In the absence of a real relation, consciousness and object must remain unrelated and hence knowledge of an object is an impossibility. Indeed, this line of argument has been adopted by the Vedāntist to deny the possibility of knowledge. The Jaina submits that these are matters wherein logic has no justification. The existence of knowledge and the nature of its contents are facts which can be determined on the verdict of experience alone. When experience testifies to the existence of knowledge and its contents, it does not lie in us to question the possibility of knowledge and the reality of its contents. Knowledge is a fact which must be accepted as a whole together with its contents. Either you must accept it as it is or dismiss it as a whole, which latter is done by the Vedāntist.

As the problem under consideration is intimately and inseparably connected with the epistemology of perceptual knowledge, we have to embark upon this epistemological discourse, although the task we have set to ourselves is only the evaluation of the metaphysical problem of non-absolutism (*anekāntavāda*). We cannot help making this digression, as the thesis of the Fluxist 'A real is inexpressible' is based on his theory of perception and can be evaluated only by means of a critical analysis of the nature and conditions of perceptual cognition. The attempt at explaining the relation of sense-intuition with the object by reference to the law of causality is bound to fail. No explanation has been offered as to why perceptual cognition should receive the likeness of the object and not of any other causal factor and also why the perceptual judgment should have reference only to one of its causes *viz* , the object and not any other. Again, the Sautrāntika has grievously failed to explain why the objective datum should not directly and in its own right give rise to the perceptual judgment (*adhyavasāya*), and how, again, the perceptual cognition can generate the judgment in question. A judgment, it is urged, deals with concepts, and concepts having a generic reference are unrelated to the objective datum, which is a particular, discrete and different from everything else. But the question cannot be evaded as to how an indeterminate perceptual cognition can be responsible for conceptual thought (*savikalpaka*). The Buddhist maintains that a real is inexpressible because a word can express only a concept and not an individual and the criterion of conceptual thought is the association of verbal expressions. As the individuals are alone real, no real can be expressed by a word. The conceptual thought which arises in the trail of perception is, thus, a construction of the intellect. But why and how should the perceptual cognition give rise to conceptual thought associated with verbal expressions ? If perception, though bereft of verbal expression, can give rise to conceptual thought of which verbal expression is the very essential factor, it passes our understanding why should a real again fail to produce such a conceptual thought. If lack of verbal expression as an element in the real be the reason for assertion of its failure, the same reason is also present in perceptual cognition, which being a real itself cannot have a verbal expression as an element, and so should not generate a conceptual thought. It is propounded that cause and effect are homogeneous, and so the effect should be like the cause. If the law of homogeneity be accepted, perceptual cognition cannot produce a conceptual thought, as they differ in fundamental respects, the former being cognisant of an individual and the latter of a universal. It has been maintained by the Buddhist that sense-object contact cannot give rise to a conceptual thought, which is possible on the cognisance of the individual and its relation to a universal. Certainly all this complicated process cannot be supposed to be accomplished by unreflective perception. But if *a priori* considerations can determine what is possible and what is not possible for perception to apprehend, we cannot understand how can any subsequent cognition generated by perception should transcend the limitation of perception. The universal, if not apprehended in perception. will remain uncognized by any cognition which is generated by perception — a natural deduction from the homogeneity of cause and effect as propounded by the Buddhist.

A later Buddhist exponent has tried to meet the afore-mentioned criticism by his assertion that perceptual cognition alone is not the cause of the conceptual thought that arises in its trail. Perception together with the latent traces of previous conceptual thoughts, which are the legacy of similar previous experience, is responsible for the emergence of conceptual thought. So there is no departure from the law of homogeneity of cause and effect and the criticism of the Jaina philosopher does not invalidate the Buddhist's position. But if conceptual thought be the effect of like conceptual thought in the past psychological history of an individual and if there be no such thing as a first beginning in his career, the difficulty in the homogeneity of causation is avoided, no doubt; but it is not explained how such concepts, which have no connection with sense-intuition or with the objective datum which gives rise to such sense-intuition, can come to have any bearing upon perceptual experience. It is certainly held that these concepts are not generated by things-in-themselves (*svalakṣaṇa*). Whether these concepts are acquired from undated past experience, as the Buddhist would have us believe, or be immanent in our understanding as Kant maintains, it is left an inexplicable mystery how our perceptual judgments (*adhyavasāya*), to be more precise, the judgments generated by perceptual intuitions, should have a direct reference to external objects and to their mutual relationships. It is undeniable that these judgments are not like imaginary concepts unfounded on reality. The indeterminate simple intuition, which is truly cognisant of a real according to the Buddhist, is of no use unless it is determined by conceptual thought. The intuition of a chair, unless it is interpreted as intuition of a chair as an individual belonging to a class, does not enable us to affirm either the existence of the chair as a fact or of the intuition itself as the proof of it. The Jaina emphatically asserts that these concepts and conceptual thoughts are not in opposition either to the objective datum or to sense-intuition. If sense-intuition can be determined as having reference to an external datum only when clarified by concepts and conceptual thoughts, it is exceedingly difficult to understand why these concepts should not be of service in the emergence of perceptual intuition. The Jaina maintains that there is no logical cogency in the contention of the Buddhist that perceptual judgments are not founded upon reality. It is admitted that consciousness, as influenced by a sense-organ, is capable of cognizing a real. This truth is certainly not discovered by pure logic. It is only a deduction from sense-experience itself. Parity of reasoning requires that we should maintain that consciousness, with the aid of sense-organs and concepts, can give us the full knowledge of reality as it is. The Jaina does not impugn the existence of concepts in their latent form as the Buddhist asserts and Kant maintains, but he differs from both the Buddhist and Kant in this that he does not regard the concepts as antagonistic to reality. The concepts are as much the means as the sense-organs and consciousness are of gaining an insight into the nature of reality. The necessary result of such an epistemological evaluation is his metaphysical doctrine that a real is not a particular alone, but particular-cum-universal, the universal as embodied in the particular. The real is, thus, amenable to verbal communication and to judgment alike.

The Jaina philosophers do not rest satisfied with the suggestion of the possibility of conceptual thought being directly occasioned by the objective datum. The Jaina of course believes that all valid knowledge is of the nature of certitude and, hence, conceptual. But he justifies his belief by proving the impossibility of indeterminate simple intuition, which is held to be the only authentic knowledge by the Buddhist. The Buddhist believes that the primal sense-intuition directly envisages the real and is free from verbal association, since it is non-conceptual. If it be so, the original intuition cannot enable a percipient to recollect a similar object previously perceived. The recollection of a similar object is possible only through recollection of the name of the thing. But the thing perceived in the first intuition is held to be felt without a name and this want of perception of the name would make recollection impossible. If there be no recollection of the name there would be no conception and, hence, no certitude. Certitude is possible only if the intuition is felt as intuition of some object, which is possible only through the use of a name or concept. The point at issue can be made clear by the recognition of the fact that the Buddhist cannot afford to deny the direct cognition of the name of the thing when the latter is perceived. If he denies this, he cannot explain the recollection of such names, which is possible only on the basis of experience. Only that is recollected which has been previously perceived. But all perception being of a thing unattached to a name, the perception of name is ruled out as an impossibility. Nor can a name be perceived independently because that would also be a nameless intuition. The same argument would make the intuition of concepts impossible, as concepts and names go together. The difficulty here is only a restatement of the difficulty of causation discussed in the preceding paragraph. How can a nameless non-conceptual intuition give rise to conceptual thought invariably associated with names ? A defence has been made against this charge of impossibility. It is asserted that the recollection of the name and of the thing having the name takes place at one and the same time. The intuition of a thing acts as the stimulant of the memory-traces of the two together and so the difficulty does not arise at all. But even if the simultaneous recollection of the name and the thing named is conceded for the sake of argument, the problem of the original perception is not solved. Names and concepts are psychical facts, even if objective universals, for which they are supposed to stand as witness, may be denied. The existence of these concepts can be proved only by perception which, as we have shown, is the only proof of the existence of anything. But if the perception of these concepts be non-conceptual and non-verbal, that will not give certitude of their reality. If the ensuing reflective judgment required other concepts and other names, the result would be a *regressus ad infinitum*. The absurdity of simple non-conceptual intuition is further demonstrated by the consequences which arise from the consideration of the perception of names. Names, like concepts, must be perceived. It is only on the basis of their perception that they can be judged to exist. But if judgment of names required the association of other names, the result would be a vicious infinite series. If concepts and names, on the other hand, be admitted to be perceived and judged independently of other names and concepts, the Jaina would ask the Buddhist to admit the validity of perceptual judgment in other cases alike. If names can be perceived and judged without the help of further names, there is no reason why things cannot be judged without the help of names in the first cognition.

The whole difficulty springs from the Buddhist's assumption that only particulars are real and universals are ideal constructs. But the difficulty disappears if a real is taken to be universal-cum-particular. The test of causal efficiency is applicable to both the universal and the particular. The universal has a distinctive nature of its own as much as the particular has. The universal has its own causal efficiency. The universal gives rise to a concept and a common name, which apply to several members of a class. The particular has its particularistic effects in the shape of particular cognitions. The function of one is not discharged by the other. So they are both real. But in spite of their distinctive functions they are not absolutely different entities. They are also identical, as they are inseparable. If the particular were absolutely different from the universal, there would be no relation between them. The fact that they are related shows the two to be identical and different both — a truth which has been proved by our discussion of the nature of relations. If the identity of the universal and the particular were not admitted, the recollection of the pre-perceived universal on the perception of the particular would not be possible. Furthermore, how could the intuition of the particular, which is held to be inexpressible, generate a recollection of the universal, which is expressible ? Certainly the perception of a cow does not necessarily occasion the recollection of the hill. It must, therefore, be admitted that they are related and relation presupposes the identity in difference of the relata. The Buddhist avers that the perceptual judgment that arises in the trail of perception comprehends the particular and the universal as identical and so the perception of the particular occasions the recollection of the universal.[1] This is a significant statement of the Buddhist and an analysis of its implication will yield important results. If the Buddhist theory be accepted,

1. viśeṣasāmānyayor ekatvādhyavasāyād viśeṣasyā 'nubhave sāmānye smṛtir yuktā. As., p. 122.

a perceptual judgment cannot be supposed to comprehend the universal and the particular as identical, as it has no jurisdiction over the particular, which is the province of perception according to the Buddhist. Perceptual cognition, too, is not competent for the task, as the universal does not fall within its ken. The identification of the particular with the universal is, however, a felt fact and the Buddhist is correct in referring to this. But he fails to explain its origination. The situation admits of an easy explanation if it is held that both the elements are perceived in the sense intuition and the synthesis of the perceived datum with the unperceived data is possible, as both the perceived and the unperceived are recognised to possess the same universal.

There is another problem which the Buddhist takes for granted, but does not solve. He asserts that when the percipient perceives a thing, he happens to recollect its name. But what can make this possible? If a name is not related to a thing by a natural bond of relation, the recollection of the name on the perception of the thing would not be possible. It is not a satisfactory hypothesis that names are associated with concepts and concepts being identified with perceived data, the association of names with reals is falsely understood. It has been shown that the identification of the universal and the particular and, implicitly, the identification of a concept with a perceptum are not possible. It seems legitimate to conclude that no line of demarcation can be drawn between the universal and the particular in the objective datum and, consequently, no line of cleavage is justifiable between a concept and a percept. Unless the concept is founded upon a percept, there would be no relation between them; and the logic of relation proves that the two are not absolutely different and distinct. Every perception contains an element of conception and is, thus, cognisant of the real, which is a unity of particular and universal. Even if the relation between a name and a real be supposed to be instituted by convention (*saṅketa*), it must be admitted that convention is not entirely arbitrary or factitious. In any event, it remains true that the relation between names and things is not capable of being altered or abolished by us. Whether the relation in question is natural, as the Mīmāṁsist holds, or conventional and covenantal, as the

Naiyāyika asserts the fact is undeniable that names and nameables are bound together by a nexus, which are, to all intents and purposes, given as accomplished facts and not created by us. That the name stands for the real and not for a subjective idea is, we hope a conclusion which the Buddhist has not succeeded in demolishing.

We have not dealt with another objection of the Buddhist which seems to possess a good deal of plausibility. It is urged that the sensuous intuition, which is generated by direct contact with the objective real, can take cognisance of the real as it is in itself. In other words, only particular as a particular can be cognised by sense-perception. If sense-perception were to cognise the particular as belonging to a class, that is to say, if it were conceptual in character, it could do so only by recalling the name of the object. But the recollection of the name would detach the sense-perception from the object. So sense-perception must be regarded as non-reflective and non-conceptual. But this argument does not care to consult the psychology of perception. It is incontestable that the perceptual judgment is felt to be cognisant of the real object. To deny its perceptual character on the ground of *a priori* considerations does not seem to be a sound procedure, logically or psychologically. Moreover, the argument is suicidal even to the Buddhist. Perceptual judgment is believed by the Buddhist to be conditioned by sense-perception. But sense-perception can give rise to the perceptual judgment only if there be a recollection of the name of the thing perceived. The recollection of the name, standing ,as it does, between the sense-perception and the perceptual judgment, would cut off the latter from the former. That being so, perceptual judgment would not be conditioned by sense-perception — a position which the Buddhist cannot endorse.

The Jaina thinks that all knowledge including perceptual knowledge is of a determinate nature which is opposed to doubt. The Buddhist hypothesis of indeterminate cognition is not supported by experience. Only doubt can be indeterminate. The Jaina does not also admit that determinate knowledge is always dependent upon verbal association. Verbal association is only an accident due to knowledge of language. In adult psychology conceptual thought is always seen to be mixed with sub-vocal speech-forms and it is true that language helps the development of thought. But that does not mean that thought is absolutely impossible without the knowledge of language. The Buddhist also admits this when he defines conceptual knowledge to be such as is competent to be associated with linguistic symbols. But it may still be contended that sense-perception cannot give full conceptual knowledge, which presupposes a synthesis of the presented datum with the past data. The knowledge of a pen as a pen presupposes the synthesis of the particular pen with a whole class of pens, and this identification with unpresented data cannot be effected by sense-perception which is concerned with the presented datum. But we have seen that the postulation of indeterminate perception, which cannot be asserted even as perception of a pen or of any other thing, is not free from difficulty. The question, how the 'indeterminate' can be made 'determinate' or, in other words the non-conceptual cognition be replaced by a conceptual cognition, has been found to be unanswerable. Instead of supposing that concepts are unfounded subjective constructions, it is quite legitimate to maintain that the percipient has the capacity to interpret the presented data with the aid of these concepts which are evolved from its own nature.[1] Kant has put forward a similar theory and the Jaina thinks in the same strain. But the latter differs from Kant and the Buddhist both in maintaining that these concepts are necessary instruments for the knowledge of reality as it is and that they are not obtruded as alien elements upon the objective data. The Jaina does not make this assertion as a possible explanation of experience. He insists that his interpretation is the only legitimate explanation because there is absolutely not a shred of evidence to condemn conceptual knowledge as untrue or unobjective. On the contrary the following weighty considerations tend to prove the validity of the Jaina position: firstly, conceptual knowledge is verified by experience; secondly, it is the only instrument of knowledge of reality; thirdly, it helps us to make indefinite knowledge definite, and fourthly, it is the only knowledge that is required by the

1. ātmaivā 'hampratyaprasiddhaḥ pratibandhakāpāye 'bhyāsādyapekṣo vikalpotpādako 'stu. kimadṛṣṭaparikalpanayā. PKM, p. 36.

subject for his conviction and progress of thought. There is no reason to think that concepts are untrue since they have reference to facts which may not be existent.[1] The concept of humanity applies even to men who are dead and who are not yet born. But this should not make a concept invalid. The dead men were existent once and unborn men will also one day be existent. So concepts are never without their bearing upon existent facts.[2] The denial of validity to conceptual thought would make nonsense of all our theoretical and practical activity.

Let us sum up the results of the epistemological enquiry. The Buddhist contention is based on the assumption that reals are particulars and universals are ideal constructs. In conformity with this assumption the Buddhist further assumes that sense-perception is non-conceptual. It is deduced from these two premises that words have no relation to reals, since words have a necessary reference to universals, which, according to the Buddhist, cannot be real either independently or as elements in reals. The third assumption made by the Buddhist is that conceptual knowledge is made possible only by recollection of names and of their relations to things. Fourthly, it is assumed that the recollection of names cannot occur before the sense-perception, since in that case it would make sense-perception independent of the objective datum. The Jaina denies all these assumptions and has exposed the flaws inherent in the Buddhist position. It is, in any event, incontestable that the Jaina's evaluation of perceptual knowledge does not make it necessary to sacrifice any one of our cherished beliefs and convictions. Perceptual judgment, which is felt to be directly conversant with reality by all of us, is not condemned. The Jaina interpretation of sense-experience squares with our beliefs and thus psychologically speaking, seems to be more faithful. The Jaina has also

1. tato vikalpaḥ pramāṇaṁ saṁvādakatvāt, arthaparicchittau sādhakatamatvāt, aniścitārthaniścāyakatvāt, pratipattrapekṣaṇīyaivāc ca . . . na tu nirvikalpakaṁ tadviparītatvāt. ibid.

2. nāpy asati pravartanāt, atītānāgatayor vikalpakāle 'sattve 'pi svakāle sattvāt. ibid, p. 37.

shown that the difficulties alleged by the Buddhist are all creations of abstract *a priori* logical thought and that they are not insurmountable. We shall return to the consideration of the metaphysical problem of inexpressibility of reality in the next chapter, and the epistemological enquiries we have conducted in this chapter and the results attained by such enquiries will facilitate the evaluation of this metaphysical problem.

CHAPTER V

THE INEXPRESSIBLE OR THE INDEFINITE

We have discussed the reasons which the Buddhist Fluxist put forward to support his position that reality in and by itself is not capable of being expressed by words. Words, it has been asserted, deal with concepts and that reals being particulars, distinct and different from one another, have nothing to do with concepts. But we have shown that the Buddhist theory raises difficulties which are insoluble for pure logic, upon which he banks. The Jaina philosopher maintains that reals are not particulars alone, but particulars having universals as elements. The universal is not an independent entity, but is realised in so far as it is an element in the particular. The particular is, thus, a concrete entity having the universal for its content or filling. The Jaina also maintains that being and non-being are equally predicable of a real and, as such, they are elements in its constitution. We have made out that being and non-being are not whole-characteristics which are mutually exclusive. We have further shown that there is no contradiction in the fact that a real is existent in one context and non-existent in another context and how the denial of this truth lands the Buddhist in a hopeless self-contradiction. Absolutist logic has been shown to be grievously inadequate to impart insight into the nature of reality and the difficulties of the Buddhist philosophers have been shown to be their own creations arising out of love for absolutist ways of thinking in utter disregard of experience.

We now propose to consider the consequences of absolutism in another school of thought. The Mīmāṁsist's view of reality is closely analogous to the Jaina conception.[1] The former believes in the dual nature of reals. A real is always both existent and non-existent, as both the characteristics are attested by experience, which is not contradicted. But this formulation suffers from a vital defect in that it does not set forth the limitations, subject to which the predication of existence or non-existence is logically possible. It cannot be a fact that a thing is existent in the same

1. As. p. 129.

reference and context in which it is non-existent. That would be a case of self-contradiction. For instance, a pen is existent in so far as it is a pen-substance and is non-existent in so far as it is not a chair. It exists as a pen and not as a chair. If a pen were existent both as a pen and as a chair and non-existent both as a chair and as a pen, it would be an unreal fiction, being riddled by hopeless contradiction. The Jaina believes that a real cannot be self-contradictory and he is sò far in agreement with the Buddhist and the idealists. But we have shown in the first chapter that the grounds of his disagreement with the advocates of *a priori* logic are fundamental.

The Jaina insists that the Mīmāṁsist should take care to make his formulation precise, as lack of precision here may be responsible for an erroneous conception of reality, which is certainly not contemplated, far less endorsed, by him. A thing is existent in one aspect and non-existent in another aspect. The difference of aspects cannot be slurred over in any philosophical estimation of reality. The results we have attained so far can be summed up as follows. A thing is existent, is non-existent and is both existent and non-existent, but always subject to limitations imposed by objective differences of substance, time, space and attributes (*dravyakṣetra-kālabhāvāpekṣayā*). The differences in predication are not due to our subjective contemplation from different angles of vision, but are founded upon objectively real attributes. They are facts irrespective of the consideration whether we contemplate them or not. This is a truth which has not been adequately appreciated by exponents of other philosophies. Even the modern exponents of Jaina thought have not been sufficiently on their guard against the possibility of misconception, to which their exposition may be exposed.

Is it possible to view a real as of a kind different from both existent and non-existent ? The Jaina would accept the position subject to a reservation, which is necessitated by the verdict of experience. If a real were regarded as of a type absolutely different from existent and non-existent, the predication of either in regard to a subject would be false. If existence and non-existence were not elements of a real, then the apprehension of these two traits would have no *raison d'etre*. But they are equally felt in and along with the real. So, if a real is to be of a separate type from existence and non-existence both, it can be so only in so far as it embodies these two characteristics within its fold. It would be equally a perversion of truth to regard these two elements as exhausting the nature of a real between themselves. The real is a unity with existence and non-existence severally and jointly forming its content. If the elements were separate facts, the synthetic unity of a real would not be true. But there is no reason why it should be repudiated. The real is, thus, existent, non-existent, and both existent and non-existent. The third predication is not a mere reduplication or restatement of the first two predicates. The synthesis of the two is not a mere aggregate, but something more than this. To take a concrete example, a beverage is composed of several elements, curd, sugar, spices, and so on. It is undeniable that the beverage, in spite of its composite character, is a unity. It is the beverage that is sweet, fragrant and refreshing. It is no doubt *non est* outside and independently of its elements. But that it is a unitary whole cannot be gainsaid without violently twisting the verdict of experience. Likewise, a real, though composed of existence and non-existence as its elements, is not a mere aggregate, but a synthetic unity also. It is analysable into its elements no doubt, but the analysis does not, and cannot, abolish the unity which the compresence of the elements entails. It is this truth which is stated by the third predication. The real is, thus, a unity, though a composite unity. It is identical with its elements and also different from them. Neither identity nor difference is absolute. Absolute identity with the elements would annul the unity and absolute difference would make the real independent of its elements.[1] As the unity of the whole and the plurality of the elements are equally felt facts, the two must be accepted without differential treatment.

The Jaina is a scrupulous stickler for precision of thought and speech and so always qualifies his statements by a restrictive expression *syāt*. The expression *syāt* has been a source of confusion. We shall dwell at length upon the significance of this expression and the reasons for its insertion as a preface to every proposition in our treatment of the Doctrine of Sevenfold

1. As. p. 129.

Predication, which demands a separate chapter by reason of its extraordinary importance. Suffice it to say here that this insertion is a safeguard against the consequences which the absolutist reading of the import of proposition involves. It emphasises the fact that a real is only a part of a system knitted together by a network of relations, from which it cannot be divorced. Abstract ways of thinking, indulged in by professional adherents of *a priori* logic, have been responsible for the hopelessly discordant conclusions of philosophers and their lack of unanimity. The Jaina has succeeded in evolving a philosophy in which the results are synthesised and the differences have been adjusted by allotting each a distinctive place in a synthetic view. It has made agnosticism impossible and reconciled the claims of idealism and realism. But a detailed working out of these results has to be postponed to a subsequent chapter, and we beg to proceed with our examination of the nature of reality.

It is incontestable that the synthesis of existence and non-existence is not capable of being expressed by a whole word. The limitations of human language make it impossible for us to express the synthesis of the two characteristics by means of one word. We have to assert that a real is existent and non-existent. The two predicates, because they are two, can be asserted in succession and not simultaneously. This necessitates the recognition of the fact that a real is inexpressible by a unitary predicate in so far as it is a synthesis of the two characteristics. In fact the two predicates together give us a completer picture of a real than each of them does. It gives us a better insight into the nature of the individual. While the assertion of existence takes cognisance of a fundamental characteristic, it fails to represent the distinctive individuality of a real, which is made up by the negative element. But this failure of human language should not be regarded as warrant for agnosticism. As a matter of fact there is a class of thinkers who made philosophical capital out of this limitation of language. These philosophers maintained that we should not assert that a thing exists, nor even that it does not exist, nor even should we assert that we assert anything. In fact no assertion is possible or meaningful. But this unqualified agnosticism leads nowhere. If a thing cannot be asserted to exist or not to exist, the result will be an unrelieved dumbness. But humanity has refused to put a gag upon their tongue or to suspend their thought. If things were absolutely inexpressible, they could not be thought of. In the absence of thought, nothing could be judged to be apprehended. But unless the sceptic were convinced of the truth of his finding that no assertion is true of a real, he could not make even such a statement. He cannot plead that his knowledge of the truth is derived from an unanalysable simple indeterminate perception. Indeterminate perception, which cannot be determined as perception of any thing, is only a fiction of logic, for which there is not a single shred of evidence from psychology. And we have shown that there is not an iota of logical necessity for its assumption, which, on the contrary, makes the emergence of perceptual judgment impossible. And even if its possibility were conceded, the denial of the validity of perceptual judgment would make the indeterminate cognition absolutely useless just like the consciousness of a man in swoon. An indeterminate cognition uninterpreted by conceptual thought is as good as non-existent, as it does not enable anybody to judge even that it exists.[1]

Bhartṛhari, the author of the *Vākyapadīya*, an extraordinary work on the philosophy of language, has advanced an elaborate plea that the whole order of reality, subjective and objective, is but the manifestation of word. It is familiar to students of philosophy that idealists have endeavoured to deduce both the subjective and the objective orders of reality from consciousness. The Vedāntist, the Buddhist Yogācāra and Hegel in Germany have endeavoured, each in his own way, to explain the world of matter in terms of thought or consciousness. The deduction of the world from word is, however, a novelty in philosophical speculation. But the transition from thought to language is quite natural. Bhartṛhari first equated all thought with language and then his deduction of objective categories from word-essence was a comparatively easy procedure. He asserts 'There is no cognition

1. tarhy astī 'ti na bhaṇāmi, nāstī 'ti ca na bhaṇāmi, yad api ca bhaṇāmi tad api na bhaṇāmī 'ti darśanam astv iti kaścit, so 'pi pāpīyān. tathāhi, sadbhāvetarābhyām anabhilāpe vastunaḥ kevalaṁ mūkatvaṁ jagataḥ syāt, vidhipratiṣedha-vyavahārāyogāt. na hi sarvātmanā 'nabhilapyasvabhāvaṁ buddhir adhyavasyati. na cā 'nadhyavaseyaṁ pramitaṁ nāma, gṛhītasyā 'py agṛhītakalpatvāt, mūrchācaitanyavat. As. p. 129.

which is not interpenetrated with word. Thought is impossible without verbal expression. It is language that makes cognition illuminative of its objects'. This equation of thought with language makes all objects of thought objects of verbal expression. Thus, this philosophy is the very antithesis of the sceptic's position which we have just passed under review. The latter makes all objects of thought free from verbal association. According to the sceptic, reality is absolutely inexpressible; but, according to Bhartṛhari expression is the very essence of consciousness and, hence, of all that exist. So whatever exists and whatever is thought of is completely expressible. The Jaina holds the scales between the two extremes. He has refuted the Buddhist position that reality is untouchable by language. And he now proceeds to check the extremism of the grammarian by drawing his attention to the qualitative difference of perceptual cognition from non-perceptual cognition. If words could express the full nature of reals, there would be no difference in verbal cognition from perceptual cognition. Certainly the difference is not due to the difference of the conditions of cognition. It is a truism that sense-organs are in request in perceptual cognition, whereas the instrument of verbal knowledge is language. But this can make no difference, if language is capable of giving a full insight into a reality. The difference can be explained if it is supposed that the individuality of a real is envisaged in perception and not in any other species of knowledge. But this supposition would make an element in a real unamenable to verbal cognition. It has been asserted that cognition and word being identical, the object of perceptual cognition is also the object of word. So there is no element in a real which is not expressed by a word. But this assumption would raise another difficulty. If word is cognition and cognition is word, and if there is no difference, qualitative or otherwise, between them, it passes one's comprehension how can there be a qualitative difference in different cognitions. An attempt has been made to explain the difference as due to external conditions. In perceptual cognition word *quâ* consciousness operates subject to the presence of sense-organs, whereas in non-perceptual cognition word-consciousness has to operate subject to the services of other instruments, and this makes difference in the quality. But this seems to be an argument of despair of a philosopher brought to bay. Apart from the fact that this admission is tantamount to a confession that a real with its full individuality is not amenable to what is admittedly a non-perceptual cognition, the position advocated involves the grammarian in self-contradiction. He starts with the premise that all that exists is word or a manifestation of word and word is consciousness. If that be the case the mutual difference of conditions cannot be maintained as real. And if these conditions be unreal, they cannot account for the difference in quality between perceptual and non-perceptual cognition. The conclusion is inescapable that a real, in so far as it is an individual, is not expressed by a word.[1]

The Buddhist position that a real is absolutely inexpressible will be examined at length and we shall find reasons to reject it. The principal defect of this theory is that it entails consequences fatal to logical thought and expression. If verbal expressions are without a bearing upon reality, then all propositions would be false. There would be no difference between a true and a false proposition. The result is the repudiation of the validity of philosophical discourse and, thus, the Buddhist stultifies himself when he repudiates philosophical discourse by means of such a discourse. So, the true position can be stated as follows: A real is not entirely expressible in all its aspects and modes. But it is not inexpressible altogether. A real being a multiple entity is expressible and inexpressible both in reference to different aspects; it is expressible in so far as it partakes of a universal and is inexpressible so far as it is a unique individual. The unique individual is known by direct intuition alone.

The Jaina avoids the extremism of Bhartṛhari and the Buddhist, and asserts that reals are expressible and inexpressible both and there is no contradiction in it. Reals are concrete embodiments of being and non-being, of being in so far as they are determined by their intrinsic determinations and of non-being in so far as they are distinguished from others by the corresponding extrinsic determinations. A pen has its intrinsic

1. sarvātmanā 'bhidheyatve pratyakṣetaraviśeṣāprasaṅgāt *et seq.* ibid., p. 130.

determinations in the shape of its inalienable individuality (*svarūpa*), constituted by the specific attributes, which distinguish it from other reals, and by the generic attributes, which affiliate it to other pens. The specific nature is constituted by the individualistic and generic attributes, which mark it out both as a type and as a unique individual. Besides, time, place and constitutive substance of the real form a system or context or universe of discourse, in which the real lives, moves and has its being. But the individuality or distinctive character of the real can have its meaning only in so far as it negates its opposite. It exists in its own context or system and not in another system. Every real is thus hedged round by a network of relations and attributes, which we propose to call its system or context or universe of discourse, which demarcates it from others. A real is thus a focal unity of being and non-being, which cannot be reached by logical thought. Language deals with concepts and logical thoughts and, thus, has no competency with regard to the unique individual. This truth has been emphasised by the Buddhist, but he ignored that language and conceptual thought took stock of the generic attributes which are part of the real and constitute its being. The absurdities of the Buddhist position have been discussed and the grammarian has been found to be equally guilty of dogmatism. The Jaina accepts the results of their speculations and synthesizes them in his theory. The Jaina theory effects the reconciliation of the opposing findings not in a syncretic spirit, but by going deeper into the nature of reality. The concrete unification of being and non-being is not a mere mechanical juxtaposition, but a transformation of the two with their individualities unannulled. The Jaina does not find a logical contradiction in this act of synthesis, since he does not take it to be a logical process, but as an ontological fact, which can be realised by intuition alone. How are two extremes, being and non-being, appropriated as elements into a concrete synthetic unity ? This is not regarded as a logical surd by the Jaina, as formal logic is out of place here. That it is a fact cannot be denied without contradicting the plain and unmistakable verdict of intuition. The Jaina does not again condemn logical thought as false, but recognises its incompetency with regard to the nature of reality. The reading of contradiction in it involves a higher and a wider contradiction that it makes knowledge impossible. So the Jaina does not hesitate to recognize the limitations of pure logic.

The Jaina goes further than this. Not only are the objects of cognition concrete embodiments of being and non-being, but even cognition itself partakes of this dual character. The duality does not annul the unity, and the unity does not cancel the duality, but exists in and through them. The position will be made clear from the examination of the nature of cognition. It is not necessary to dilate upon the dual nature of judgmental knowledge, which is a unification of the subject and the predicate through a relation. The three elements, the subject, the predicate and the relation, are distinguishable in the judgment, but that they are unified in one unit, which a judgment unmistakably is, proves that the three are transformed into a whole, though the transformation is not destructive of the individuality of the elements. It must be confessed that the unity is inaccessible to logical thought. . It is immanent in the elements, but at the same time transcends them in that it is not analysable into elements. The elements by themselves, that is to say, as out of relation or in a different relation, do not make the unity. It is idle to raise questions of chronological status as to whether the unity is prior to the elements or the elements are prior to the unity. In the concrete real at any rate they are co-ordinate. This unity of being and non-being, or rather of self-being and negation of other-being, is beyond the reach of logical concepts, and, hence, of linguistic symbols, which are but the vehicles of such concepts. The Jaina in recognition of this inalienable character of reals declares them to be inexpressible. The inexpressible may be called indefinite from the standpoint of formal logic. But this is not the whole character of a real. It is also expressible and logically definable as existent, as non-existent, as pen, chair or table, and the like. These expressions and concepts are not unrelated to reals, since by following their guidance we reach the unique reals, which embody the attributes which are signified by the former. That words and concepts cannot envisage the concrete reals can be established by logical considerations also. Things are known as what they are and what they are not by intuition. But even perceptual intuition cannot take in one sweep the whole individuality of a real. A pen is perceived with all its intrinsic determinations as an individual. The perception is of the positive aspect and also of the negative aspect, but not at the same time. The pen is a pen only because it has an individuality which is not the individuality of the table. The pen is perceived as pen and also as not not-pen. The not-pen is an indefinite periphery of the pen. But are the two elements perceived together in one simultaneous act ? Most probably not. The perception of the pen, again, is a real in so far as it is the perception of pen and the non-perception of not-pen. It is not a verbal quibble, though it has an awkward look. The perception of the pen is the perception of just what it is and *not* the perception of the table. Thus both perception and perceptum have a positive-cum-negative character. But the two characters can be conceived only alternately. It is problematic whether perception also can take note of the two characters both in itself and in the perceptum at one and the same time, though it is indisputable that the unique individual is realized by perception.

The Jaina is emphatic that a real is a synthetic unity of being and non-being, being as it is and non-being as it is not. This unity is unreachable by a logical concept and, hence, by a verbal expression. Concepts and verbal expressions can give us either being or non-being in alternation, and not simultaneously. Let us examine the expressive capacity of words, and the position we are maintaining will be apparent. There is not a single word which can express both being and non-being as co-equal elements of a real. One word can express one concept and, hence, one truth. The word being or existence does not express non-being or non-existence. Likewise the word non-being or non-existence does not express being or existence. Such words have a determinate significance and the positive and the negative terms cannot interchange their functions. If the term 'non-being' could express being and non-being as well, the employment of the two terms would not be necessary. But both being and non-being are co-equal factors of the individuality of a real and a word being incompetent to take stock of both the factors, it cannot express a real as it is. The position stands that a real is inexpressible. But are there not terms which express more than one thing ? Are homonyms recognized by lexicographers impossible fictions ? With due deference to the lexicographers the

Jaina maintains, and in this he is fully endorsed by the Mīmāṁsist, that each word has a definite meaning which cannot be the meaning of another word. As regards the so-called homonyms, they are numerically different terms and it is by reason of their phonological similarity that they are regarded as one word. The term '*gau*' is said to mean 'heaven,' 'a point of compass,' 'a cow,' 'a word,' 'a ray of light,' and so on. But the terms are not the same, though similar. Each term varies with each meaning. The unity is only a pseudo-unity due to similarity. If a single individual word could signify many things, there would be no logical impossibility for one word to signify all things. If the possibility of one word signifying more than one were conceded, the determinate relation of word and its import would not be capable of being logically justified.

This demonstration of the incapacity of the individual terms for more than one meaning constitutes a refutation of propositions yielding more than one judgment. The third proposition in the chain of sevenfold predication,[1] which predicates existence and non-existence of the same subject, is not, strictly speaking, one proposition, but two propositions. It is due to the similarity of order and phonetic similarity that the two propositions are treated as one. The numerical difference of the proposition will be apparent from the consideration that the predicates are communicated in succession and not at a time to our consciousness. If, however, the import of the third proposition is considered to be the co-equality of the two attributes successively understood, the proposition may be regarded as one in point of fact. The unity or multiplicity of a proposition can be determined by the unity or multiplicity of the predicate, and if the predicate of the third proposition be the co-equality of existence and non-existence and not the two distinct attributes, the proposition under consideration should be regarded as a factually unitary proposition.

But why should not a word signify more than one thing ? It is a question of fact and not of logic. We can only appeal to experience for the determination of the problem. Words signify things by virtue of possessing a capacity for signifying or suggesting these facts. What power is possessed by what word is a

1. SBT, p. 32.

question of fact and, as such, can be decided by evidence of experience. It is a matter of fact that the word 'blue' signifies that very colour and not any other. The answer to the question why should it not signify 'red' will be that it does not do so in point of fact, and that shows that it has not the expressive power in that respect. The word 'exists' signifies existence and not non-existence. Even in the case of suggestive symbols, they, too, cannot transcend the limitation of one power for one meaning. The relation of word and meaning, and consequently the nature of the expressive or suggestive power, can be determined only by convention and practice. But is not convention ultimately reducible to an act of will, corporate or individual ? The Naiyāyika, who does not believe in the existence of power in words beyond this convention, has repudiated the view that the relation of word and import is natural, and not factitious. The Jaina does not go the whole extent with the Mīmāṁsist in maintaining that the relation in question is entirely natural, nor does he subscribe to the Naiyāyika's position that it is purely factitious and conventional, reducible to an act of volition. He thinks it to be natural and conventional both. The power is natural, but it is made effective only by convention. We have to learn the relation of words to facts and this shows that knowledge of convention is necessary for understanding the meaning of words.

But the knowledge of convention is only a means to the discovery of the power of the word and does not make the postulation of power unnecessary or redundant. It is by a laborious research that we have to discover the powers of things and not all at once. The cognition of a piece of iron or of wood does not all at once give insight into their powers, which lie unsuspected and undetected until by a series of observations and experiments we come to discover them one by one. The necessity of investigation or learning from the funded experience of mankind does not annul the existence of natural powers. So with regard to words. It is by an arduous process of learning that we acquire the knowledge of a language, but this process of slow learning is nothing but a process of discovery. If a weapon of steel cannot operate upon a diamond, but does operate upon a piece of wood, that proves that steel has the capacity for operating only upon wood and the latter has the capacity of being so operated upon. Similarly, if a word signifies one thing and not another, that should be interpreted as evidence of the definite significative power of the word and of the power of the thing to be so signified. If the meaning of a word is not known, the power is not discovered. But that does not argue that the power is absent or non-existent. It will not serve the purpose we have in view to enter into the discussion of the metaphysical necessity of powers as objective facts. Even leaving aside the discourse on the objective existence of powers, it can be maintained with the support of experience that a word cannot be made to signify more than one thing. Take the case of homonyms. Certainly the word 'pole' cannot mean 'a pole of the earth' and 'a staff' at one and the same time. The word is to be uttered or thought twice to give the two meanings. The necessity of repetition is proof enough that a word cannot signify two things, and the word repeated a second time is as good as a new word. The rule holds good of even those newly coined words which are made to stand for more than one thing. Thus, the word *saṃyama* is used by Patañjali in his *Yogasūtra* as the symbol for three distinct acts, *viz.*, fixation of thought, meditation and ecstatic absorption. He might as well have used an unmeaning symbol 'X'. The crucial point is, firstly, whether the word yields one concept or more than one; and, secondly, whether the concepts two, three or any number as the case may be, arise in our consciousness simultaneously or in succession. Certainly, they occur in succession, and the word is to be recalled each time. This should clinch the issue that for each meaning we should have a different word, no matter whether the second word is ontologically the same with the first or not. The balance of reasons, however, seems to preponderate on the side of the Jaina and the Mīmāṁsist. The Jaina position will be established if one word cannot be found for signifying being and non-being at one and the same time.

The law enunciated above that one word conveys one meaning is not found to break down even in the case of collective names, *e.g.*, crowd, army, forest, village etc., which seem to signify many things at a time. The word 'crowd' denotes *a collection* of men, a unitary fact, and not the individuals costituting it; an 'army' stands for the collection of soldiers; a forest for the trees taken together as a unit; a village is the collective name for number of inhabited houses which has a distinctive individuality in contradistinction to another village. So, all these words are individualistic in their signification. None of them denotes a plurality in the sense of many. A difficulty has been raised with regard to inflected words signifying 'two' or more than two things. The word 'trees' signifies two or more trees in English. The words '*vṛkṣau*' and *vṛkṣāḥ*' in Sanskrit respectively signify two and more than two trees. How can the situation be explained? There are two theories regarding the problem — the theory of Pāṇini and that of the Jaina grammarians. According to Pāṇini, the word *vṛkṣau* is not one word but two words, *vṛkṣa* and *vṛkṣa*, of which one word is suppressed as a matter of convention. And the word in the plural number symbolically represents as many individuals as are meant in the case. So the number of the words is equivalent to the number of individuals denoted. And as regards the Jaina theory which holds that the word with the dual or plural inflection denotes things (a tree in the present instance) as endowed with the number two or more, there is no breach of the rule. The base *vṛkṣa* or tree stands for the entities which possess the class character *vṛkṣatva* (treehood or tree-universal), and the inflection denotes the number. The two together denote 'tree-as qualified by that number.' Though from the point of view of denotation, one word 'trees' stands for many things, still the law of one word for one meaning does not suffer. For though the individuals are many, the connotation of the word, which is the class-character of the trees, is one self-identical attribute. The word 'one meaning' in the proposition is to be understood as having one connotation. In the proposition 'It exists and does not exist' the predicates are two and, so, the two attributes are understood in succession. The point at issue is that no single word can express the two attributes, existence and non-existence, as co-equal facts, and, hence, the subject, of which these attributes are predicated, is inexpressible as having such attributes. The terms 'exists' and 'does not exist' stand for two different attributes. 'Exists' connotes existence and not non-existence. The position maintained is that one word conveys one principal meaning, and this is substantiated by showing that no single word can be found to express the two attributes, existence and non-existence, as co-equal facts. It is proved by irrefutable logic that being and non-being are the attributes of all entities, and that being so, the conclusion is inevitable that all entities are inexpressible by a single expression, which we have found no reason to repudiate by our examination of the nature and powers of words. We shall discuss the concept of inexpressibility further in Chapter VI and there we will show that the concept is not a mere logical or verbal characteristic, but an ontological attribute, which is different and distinct from existence and non-existence severally and jointly.

Let us examine the meaning of the term 'inexpressible,' which is the predicate of the fourth proposition. It cannot be maintained that the term signifies a real determined by the two co-equal attributes, existence and non-existence, as simultaneously present in it. For the assertion would be tantamount to the repudiation of the Jaina position that such a real is not capable of being expressed by single word or a single concept. But if the word 'inexpressible' could express this very attribute, there would be no sense in the advocacy of the concept. Moreover, if the word 'inexpressible' could express the compresence of the positive and negative attributes with co-equal status, the thing would not be inexpressible. And if the word inexpressible could be invested with such a power by a fiat of will, we do not see any logic in the denial of this prerogative to any other word. If it is admitted that any other word would only express the two attributes in succession owing to the limitation of human language and logical thought alike, we cannot conceive how the word 'inexpressible, can be in a privileged position in this regard. If the word be regarded as an abbreviated formula for the two attributes having a co-ordinate status, it must be admitted that it can convey the two attributes as two and at two moments. In that case there would be no necessity for the fourth predication, since its purpose would be served by the third predication, as will be demonstrated in the next chapter. But the word 'inexpresssible' is not an unmeaning juxtaposition of syllables like abracadabra. It has a meaning, else it would not be used as a separate predicate in a separate proposition. Vimaladāsa, the author of the *Saptabhaṅgītaraṅgiṇī*, here offers a solution, which, though it departs from the traditional interpretation, seems to be the most reasonable of all. The word is a negative term and has no positive significance. It simply asserts that the real *quâ* possessed of existence and non-existence as co-equal attributes is not capable of being expressed by a word, as no word can have such a double sense. The negation of expressibility is an attribute by itself, which is different from the unique inexpressible attribute resulting from the compresence of existence and non-existence.

But does not the absolute denial of expressibility contradict the Jaina position that all predicates are concomitant with their opposites?[1] Is it not further in flagrant opposition to the explicit assertion of Samantabhadra, a great authority on Jaina philosophy, that the affirmation of the predicate 'inexpressible' would be illogical if the subject were absolutely incapable of being expressed ?[2] The import of the proposition seems to be as follows: "If a real as endowed with existence and non-existence were inexpressible by all words, it could not be so expressed even by the term 'inexpressible'." But this cannot be the interpretation since it involves a contradiction. It is the position of the Jaina that a real cannot be expressed by language as possessed of both being and non-being. Now, if it be the truth that the word 'inexpressible' could express this very attribute, how can it be said to be inexpressible? It involves a contradiction in terms to assert that a thing is inexpressible as both being and non-being and in the same breath to affirm that it is expressible in respect of both these attributes by the term 'inexpressible'. The contradiction is on all fours with the contradiction that is involved in asserting that the pen exists *quâ* pen and does not exist *quâ* pen. The interpretation propounded above is wrong. The real interpretation of the proposition should be as follows: "A real is certainly capable of being affirmed as existent or non-existent each at a time, but it is not capable of being affirmed as existent and non-existent both at the same time and by a single word. If, however, a real were inexpressible even as existent or non-existent, as the Buddhist holds, then assertion

1. The proposition will be elucidated in the next chapter.
2. avācyataikānte 'py uktir nā 'vācyam 'iti yujyate. AM, I, Ch, II. 32.

of inexpressibility would also not be possible. To assert that a real is inexpressible is to assert a negative attribute of it. A real has at any rate the attribute of being not expressible. But if the negative attribute can be predicated of a real, it ceases to be absolutely inexpressible." This should certainly be accepted as the meaning of Samantabhadra. There is no contradiction in the proposition 'An assertion is impossible' as there is in the proposition 'A square is a circle.' But the contradiction arises as soon as the proposition is asserted for the conviction of the opponent.

The Buddhist fluxist maintains that words cannot express individuals, as individuals are infinite in number. A word can express the thing to which it is known to stand in a relation. The relation is one of expressive and expressed and is called convention. If a word were related to one individual, it would not express another individual, which it is found to do. The word 'cow,' for instance, is found to express not this or that cow, but any and every cow that is, that was, and that will be. But how can it express all these individuals in the absence of the knowledge of convention with all of them ? It is humanly impossible to get in touch with all these individuals distributed through all the divisions of time and to cognise the relation with them. If a word could denote an individual without a relation or without the knowledge of the relation, it could denote anything. A determinate relation is, therefore, the necessary condition of the use of a word in a determinate sense. But even if such relation were factual, there is no instrument available to us to be sure of this relation. Moreover, the individual is never presented in verbal knowledge, which is independent of such individuals. It is a truism that verbal cognition does not take stock of the individual with all its features which constitute its individuality. It is only perceptual cognition that gives us the full picture of the individual, and non-perceptual cognition only presents a blurred picture, which fits in with all individuals. Perceptual cognition is determined by the real and is in touch with it, whereas non-perceptual cognition occurs even in the absence of such reals. A word, for instance, signifies also a past and a future real, which is not in existence at the time. A word then can give us a concept. The Jaina replies that this denial of objective touch to non-perceptual cognition is suicidal. If language cannot communicate reality, why should the Buddhist make use of it for proving his contention and for disproving the position of others ? All philosophical arguments, which are necessarily conducted by means of language, would have to be condemned as false. Why should not again the word 'cow' denote a horse, when words are absolutely ungrounded in reality ? As regards the lucidity of perceptual cognition, that alone does not give it the stamp of authenticity. Even erroneous perception possesses this lucidity, but that does not make it veridical. So the test of authenticity of cognitions must be found in verification or non-contradiction, and if this be available, there is no reason to call in question the truth of verbal inferential knowledge. Both perceptual and non-perceptual cognition must then be believed to be founded upon objective reality though perceptual cognition makes us acquainted with all the distinctive features of the real. A word may give us only a concept, but why should concepts be condemned as devoid of objective affiliation ? And as regards indeterminate perception it is as good as non-existent, until it is interpreted by concepts. Further, if concepts have no bearing upon reality and, hence, have no place in perceptual cognition, how can they convert such intuition into knowledge ? Indeterminate perception cannot determine itself as perception of this or that. It is concepts which make it determinate. We have fully discussed the relation of concepts to reality and their status in perceptual cognition in Chapter IV and the reader will do well to read the present discourse in connexion with what has been said therein.

As regards the absolute sceptic who condemns all knowledge as false, it should suffice to observe that apart from the self-contradiction in which he involves himself when he makes such assertions,[1] the position is absurd on the face of it. A cognition is false when it is contradicted by a veridical cognition, but a veridical cognition must have a veridical standard in comparison with which its truth can be ascertained. But the sceptic cannot appeal to any such standard or criterion when he condemns all cognitions as false. How does he again convince himself of the errors in the positions of other thinkers ? If his conviction be also false,

1. Vide Chapter IV.

he cannot make any assertion either by way of affirmation or by way of negation. It is self-evident that falsity is a relative concept which can be ascertained only with the help of truth, as falsity is nothing but a perception of partial truth. Śaṅkara is right when he makes the false the co-associate of the true.[1]

To sum up the results, the Jaina admits the partial truth of the conclusions of the grammarians, who believe that language has the capacity to express everything that is real, and of the opposite position of the Buddhist who places all reals beyond the range of linguistic and conceptual thought. The position of the absolute sceptic is rejected without reservation and the Jaina has adduced convincing reasons why such a suicidal and self-contradictory position cannot be entertained as a serious account of reality. Reals are certainly expressible, and words and concepts are derived from reality and their reference to reals cannot be impugned without contradiction. But he recognizes the qualitative difference between perceptual and non-perceptual cognition, and this qualitative difference is accounted for by the consideration that the full individuality of a real is envisaged in perception alone. But non-perceptual cognitions are also veridical, though they do not give us the unique individuality of the real, but only those attributes which it shares with other individuals of the class. In support of this position he adduces the consideration that the constitution of reals is made of both these kinds of attributes. He also points out that being and non-being are equally real factors of reals, and the compresence of the two elements in the unique individual, though it can be envisaged only in intuition, is logically justifiable by the *reductio ad absurdum* of all theories which purport to repudiate this truth. The unique individuality of a real is not accessible to conceptual thought and, hence, to language, but it is reached by an analysis of the nature of reality as it is apprehended in perception. If we are to survey the results of our investigation of the nature of reality, which has been attempted in these five chapters, we can assert that we have tried to prove, following the guidance of the Jaina philosophers, that

1. satyānṛte mithunīkṛtya . . . lokavyavahāraḥ, *Adhyāsabhāṣya*, BSU.

the nature of reals, on analysis, has been found to exhibit the following traits, *viz.*, existence, non-existence and inexpressibility. The results achieved will be helpful to the complete determination of reality as unfolded in sevenfold predication, which will be treated in the next chapter.

CHAPTER VI

THE DIALECTIC OF SEVENFOLD PREDICATION

(*Saptabhaṅgīnaya*)

SECTION I

The Jaina affirms that an existent is possessed of an infinite number of attributes, and though the knowledge of infinite attributes is not attainable on this side of omniscience, the affirmation or negation of a predicate is not untrue. The affirmation or negation gives only a slice of the existent, but that does not afford a reason to doubt its authenticity. The most characteristic contribution of Jaina thinkers lies in their formulation of the theory of sevenfold predication, which for its originality and novelty roused the philosophical conscience of India at the time of its promulgation. We do not undertake the baffling task of tracing the chronological landmarks in the evolution of this theory and we deliberately address ourselves to the purely philosophical interest and value that this theory possesses in so far as it has been interpreted by philosophers of the Jaina school from the medieval ages down to very recent times. Our interest is purely philosophical and we leave the historical problem to be tackled by other scholars. The Jaina asserts that even the knowledge of a single attribute in respect of a substance must assume the form of seven modes, if it is to be free from obscurity and inadequacy. The sevenfold predication is, thus, a representation of this sevenfold conception and is expressed in a set of seven distinct propositions from which the knowledge of mutually consistent predicates, affirmative or negative, in respect of one subject is derived. The full predication of an attribute, it is asserted, requires seven distinct propositions and an additional proposition is superfluous and the suppression of any one results in incomplete knowledge. But why should the number be seven, neither more nor less ? The answer is that each proposition is an answer to a question, possible or actual. And only sevenfold query is possible with regard to a thing. The questions are seven because our desire of knowledge with regard to any subject assumes seven forms in answer to our doubts, which are also seven. Doubts are seven because the attributes, which are the objects of doubt, are only of seven kinds.[1] So, the sevenfold assertion is not the result of a mere subjective necessity, which has nothing to do with the objective status of attributes. All assertions are in the last resort traceable to an objective situation, which actually possesses seven modes or attributes as an ontological truth.

The seven attributes are, thus, real properties in a subject and they are stated as predicates in seven different propositions (*bhaṅgas*). The assertions derive their genesis from an initial doubt which is occasioned by the *prima facie* opposition of the positive and negative attributes. Take a concrete example of the attribute of existence, and we can illustrate the sevenfold proposition. Does a pen exist or not ? This is an instance of doubt, since the opposition of existence and non-existence is self-evident. The predicates, it should be remembered, are but the expressions of real attributes. The full formulation of the predicates will assume the form as follows : (1) existence (in a specific context); (2) non-existence (in another specific context); (3) successive occurrence of both the attributes; (4) inexpressibility; (5) inexpressibility as qualified by the first predicate: (6) inexpressibility as qualified by the second; (7) inexpressibility as qualified by the third. These are seven attributes which are expressed by seven propositions. The same rule holds good of any other attribute. The seven propositions distinctly stated will be as follows: (1) The pen exists (in a certain context); (2) the pen does not exist (in another context); (3) the pen exists and does not exist (respectively in its own context and in a different context); (4) the pen is inexpressible (*quâ* having both existence and non-existence as its attributes at the same time); (5) the pen exists (in its own context) and is inexpressible; (6) the pen does not exist (in other than its own context) and is inexpressible; (7) the pen exists and does not exist and is inexpressible. All these assertions are to be understood as subject to the conditions which objectively demarcate the attributes. Thus, existence can

1. bhaṅgāḥ sattādayaḥ sapta, saṁśayāḥ sapta tadgatāḥ. jijñāsāḥ sapta, sapta syuḥ praśnāḥ, saptottaraṇy api. SBHT, p. 5.

be predicated of the pen only in relation to a definite context. The pen exists in so far as it is a substance and a specific substance at that, that is to say, in so far as it is a pen. Thus, existence can be predicated of it conformably to reality only by qualifying it by a necessary proviso indicated above. Again, the pen exists in its own space which it occupies and in the time in which it is known to endure. Further, the pen has a particular size, colour and shape and so on. The pen is not the pen if it is abstracted from these attributes which give it a definitive individuality. Thus, substance (*dravya*), attribute (*bhäva*), time (*kāla*) and space (*kṣetra*), form the context, in relation to which an attribute, existence etc. can be predicated. As has been observed more than once, the affirmation of an attribute necessarily involves the negation of its opposite, and, thus, the predication of the opposite attribute is also a logical necessity. The existence of a pen is necessarily bound up with its non-existence in another context. So both are to be predicated. But a question naturally arises. If existence and non-existence are understood in relation to definite contexts, then there is not only no opposition between them, but one is the necessary concomitant of the other. Such being the case, there is no possibility of a doubt regarding them, and in the absence of doubt, no enquiry is felt and, consequently, no answer is necessary. Where then is the psychological necessity which was propounded as the basis and occasion of the sevenfold predication ? The answer is that the opposition in question is not between existence and non-existence as part-characteristics, but between unqualified existence and qualified existence. The affirmation of existence is, thus, necessary in order to rebut the possibility of unqualified existence irrespective of time, place, substance and attribute, which give the predicate a determinate reference. Thus, the assertion of the first proposition is logically necessary and significant. And if, again, we are to take the opposition to refer to the opposite of existence, *viz.*, non-existence, there would not be any difficulty either, as non-existence, too, is to be understood in an unrestricted reference. The assertion of determinate existence in the first proposition, thus, rebuts the possibility of absolute non-existence or absolute existence.

The second proposition is also significant as there is opposition between determinate non-existence and absolute non-existence or absolu'e existence. It can be shown in this way that each predicate is asserted in response to a logical necessity, *viz.*, the exclusion of its opposite. It may be contended that the opposites under consideration. *viz.*, absolute existence or absolute non-existence, are not objective facts, as no existent is known to have absolute existence or absolute non-existence as its characteristic. Thus, the opposite in question is unreal and the exclusion of an unreal opposite is not necessary, as an unreal fact cannot be the object of doubt. But the contention is not true to psychology. Though absolute existence or non-existence be not real facts, it cannot be denied that a thing may be conceived as existent or non-existent without reference to their ontological context. Though not ontologically real, absolute existence or non-existence is conceivable, and doubt as a psychical fact has reference to this conception. So, the charge of lack of logical necessity for the sevenfold proposition is not founded upon a fact. The opposition is a logical relation and it is not necessary that the opposite must be of the same ontological status. The very fact, that absolute existence is opposed to even limited non-existence, and absolute non-existence is not compatible even with limited existence, shows that the relation is true, though as a matter of fact, absolute existence and absolute non-existence are not ontologically real.

The Vedāntist, who holds absolute existence to be the only reality, cannot believe in the reality of non-existence, absolute or qualified. Similarly the *Śūnyavādin* who does not believe in any existence, absolute or limited, cannot but regard absolute non-existence as standing in opposition to existence. The opposition between existence and non-existence has, thus, a logical or psychological value and does not involve the reality of the terms in opposition. It is enough if the other opposite is conceivable. In point of fact, opposition may hold between two ontological facts or between an ontological fact and an unreal fiction, provided it is psychologically conceivable. The first two propositions in the sevenfold chain of predication are, thus, logically valid and psychologically necessary inasmuch as they serve to exclude absolute existence or absolute non-existence from their respective loci. The insertion of the qualifying phrase '*syāt*,' which emphasises the relative truth of the predication, is dictated by a twofold necessity of, firstly, furnishing a necessary proviso and, secondly, a corrective against the absolutist ways of thought and evaluation of reality.

In the evaluation of the necessity and justice to the assertions in the chain of sevenfold predication, which the Jaina thinks to be the universally valid form, whatever be the predicates, we shall have to take into consideration two facts, one logical and another ontological. The logical criterion is satisfied by considering whether the assertion is in response to a genuine desire for knowledge of a fact and the ontological criterion is the consideration whether the assertion is true of the fact. The word fact is to be understood in the present context as standing for anything possessed of a characteristic. In the first proposition 'the pen exists,' existence is predicated of the pen. The existence is a determinate characteristic having reference to a definite context. But is there any necessity for this assertion ? Does not the factuality of the pen carry the assurance of existence by itself ? The answer is simple. The proposition in question may be viewed as analytical and synthetical according to our intellectual equipment and psychological interest. If perfect knowledge were possible, the assertion would be redundant for such a person, as nothing is unknown to such an omniscient person; but philosophical enquiry is instituted only for the benefit of persons who are aspirant for perfect knowledge, but have not reached the level. A perfect man, who knows all things and each thing as possessed of characteristics which follow from the very nature of each, will regard all assertions as analytical. But the consummation is not the possession of imperfect human beings like us, for whom the growth of knowledge is a slow process proceeding by stages, and for such each stage is a discovery attained after a laborious investigation of the nature of reality. It is not necessarily true that existence is understood only as a part of the connotation of the subject, since there has been a class of thinkers who call in question the reality of all things in an unrestricted reference. Again, 'existence' by itself is not capable of being understood in a uniform sense. Existence may be absolute or relative and, as such, there is room for misconception.

Moreover, the assertion of all predicates is subjected to a question, which has been made a peg upon which the idealist and the sceptic hang their respective theories. Is the predicate a real characteristic of the subject, which belongs to it in its own right, or a characteristic which is foisted upon it from outside ? In the first alternative, the predicate is useless as it does not assert anything new. In the second alternative, it is false as it does not belong to the subject of which it is affirmed. But the question is neither fair nor sincere. The necessity of predication lies in the subjective necessity of attaining knowledge of an objectively real characteristic. The very fact that there has been a difference of views among philosophers about the authenticity of the predication shows that the problem is not so simple as the question seems to indicate. The predicate 'existence' may be a part of the connotation of the subject, but it is discovered only after the meaning of the assertion is understood and verified. So the proposition is synthetic before it is ascertained and verified, and is analytic after such discovery. The sceptic ought to be satisfied by the answer that all propositions are analytical to an omniscient soul, but synthetical to an enquirer of truth, who has his doubts and difficulties about everything.

The Jaina asserts that unguarded predications have been a source of confusion and misconception in the history of philosophical speculations; and in the interests of precision of thought and clarity of our conception it is imperative that the predicates should be so asserted that the chances of misconception are eliminated as far as possible. It is for this reason that he adds the corrective proviso *syāt* to every assertion, which serves as a warning-post. But it is certain that whatever attribute may be predicated, it must not be understood to exclude the other attributes. Every predicate involves the concomitance of its opposite, and we shall see that the compresence of the two gives rise to a different attribute. Each predicate in the sevenfold proposition is distinct and different from the rest and so none of the propositions is superfluous. That the first predicate is different from the second is obvious. 'Existence' and 'non-existence' are not the same attribute. The combination of the two, successive or synchronous, gives rise to a distinct attribute and so also the combination of these derivative attributes with the original attributes of the first two modes is the occasion for the emergence of novel attributes. But however much we may vary the combination, the number of attributes and consequently the number of propositions will neither be more nor less than seven. It is to be remembered that the seven attributes stated as seven predicates in the seven propositions are numerically different from one another, and, secondly, that whatever ways of permutation and combination may be resorted to, the number of the attributes and of the consequential modes will remain constant. We now propose to substantiate the thesis stated here in dogmatic form by arguments.

Assuming for the present that the seven propositions state seven numerically different attributes, it may be questioned why the combination of the first and the third, and of the second and the third, modes should not give rise to different attributes in their turn. The successive occurrence of the first two attributes, positive and negative, is believed to evolve the third attribute, and it is quite conceivable that the same law of synthesis should operate in the combination of the first and second attributes respectively with the third, which is believed to be distinct and different from the first and second. If this possibility is conceded, we should have two other additional attributes and, consequently, two other additional modes and propositions. In answer to this question the Jaina avers, that the assertion of the first and third attributes, either successive or synchronous, does not evolve a novel attribute is obvious from the consideration that the combination of the first and third attributes involves false tautology. The first proposition states existence as the predicate and the third asserts a combination of existence and non-existence as two distinct individuals. The combination would imply the addition of another 'existence.' But neither experience nor reflection reveals the reality of two existences in the subject. The combination may result in such a proposition as 'The pen exists and exists and does not exist.' But the assertion of existence twice is useless, as the pen does not appear to have more than one existence. It may be contended that the existence of the pen, as qualified by the pen-character, and the existence of the pen, as qualified by the character of the stuff of which it is made, are different and so the assertion of the two existences is neither illegitimate nor unnecessary. But the contention is hollow. Granted that the existence of the pen *quâ* pen and its existence *quâ* 'wood' are different, the latter existence as contrasted with its non-existence *quâ* earthy substance would necessitate another sevenfold proposition. The upshot is that the predication of double existence in the same reference is logically impossible as it is ontologically false. It is maintained that the sevenfold predication as generated by a psychological and a logical necessity, which are based upon an ontological situation, and further that the predicates, in their different combinations, are to be understood in reference to the same context and not different contexts. The apparently 'identical pen' in reference to different material, as *e.g.*, the pen made of wood and the pen made of steel, is only identical in one reference, but as concrete existents they are not absolutely the same. In the sevenfold predication, the subject and the predicate are to be understood as standing for the same ontological facts, subject to the same universe of discourse. The subject 'pen' in all the seven propositions is the same pen, of the same material, and not of different material. The combination of the first and third propositions is, thus, not logically factual. The combination of the second and third modes is equally a logical impossibility. The non-existence of the pen as other than pen is one identical attribute and the addition of another non-existence is logically false and ontologically unreal. It follows that the emergence of two other additional modes as the result of the synthesis of the first and second modes with the third alternately is not possible, logically and ontologically, and, consequently, the number of propositions cannot be multiplied.

But a difficulty may be raised with regard to the last three modes, which arise from the synthesis of the first three modes consecutively with the fourth mode. The fourth predicate is inexpressibility, which is but the abbreviated formula for the simultaneous co-existence of the positive and the negative attributes asserted in the first two propositions. 'The pen is inexpressible' is but an abbreviated assertion of the attributes of existence and non-existence at the same time in the same subject. Such being the case, the combination of the first and the fourth modes is not any more possible than in the case of the first and the third modes. The fifth mode is but the synthesis of the first and the fourth, but this should be impossible in view of the impossibility of the coincidence of two existences. The sixth mode should also be regarded as an impossibility, as the coincidence of two non-existences in the same reference is ontologically impossible and logically absurd. The seventh, again, being a combination of the first, second, third and fourth modes is vitiated by the same defect. But the difficulty raised is unreal. The simultaneous compresence of the positive and negative attributes, *e.g.*, of existence and non-existence, is not a mere summation of the two attributes, existence plus non-existence, nor is the expression, 'inexpressibility' only an abbreviated formula for the combination of such attributes. The compresence of the two opposite attributes is no doubt a fact, but the very compresence of the two attributes engenders a novel attribute, which is incapable of being expressed by human language. The inexpressibility is a synthetic attribute, different from its elements, and, so, the combination of the first, second and third attributes is neither ontologically impossible nor logically absurd. We shall subject the concept of inexpressibility to a further scrutiny when we shall discuss its difference from the third attribute.

To be brief, the import of the seven propositions may be asserted as follows. The first proposition asserts 'existence' as the principal predicate, the second asserts 'non-existence'; the third both existence and non-existence in succession, the fourth 'inexpressibility'; the fifth inexpressibility as qualified by 'existence', the sixth affirms the same as qualified by non-existence; and the seventh asserts inexpressibility as qualified by the successively occurring existence and non-existence. The assertion of the predicates only serves to emphasise the prominence of the attributes as psychologically felt. It is a matter of attention and interest that stress is laid upon one, but it never means that the precedence accorded to it excludes the other attribute. The affirmation of existence in the first proposition does not exclude 'non-existence', which is stated in the second proposition, but implies it. We shall deal with the matter at greater length later on.

A question may be raised. If 'inexpressibility' be a distinct attribute, why should not 'expressibility' be considered another different attribute, being its opposite ? If so, the assertion that attributes are of seven kinds only falls to the ground and, consequently, there should be eight modes of predication. But the Jaina does not think that expressibility is a novel attribute. That a thing is expressible as existent or non-existent is implied in the first two propositions, and, so, the predication of expressibility would not serve an additional purpose. And if for the sake of argument 'expressibility' be regarded as a novel attribute different from existence and non-existence and so on, still this would not cause a difficulty, as the attribute 'expressibility' together with its opposite 'inexpressibility' would give rise to a new sevenfold predication, as was seen to be the case with the attributes of existence and non-existence.

We have seen that the number of propositions cannot be multiplied further than seven. But is it not possible to reduce the number ? Are the attributes, whatever be their logical status, ontologically different ? But the attributes, existence and non-existence, are not ontologically different. A pen is existent *quâ* pen and non-existent *quâ* not-pen. But ontologically the existence of the pen is not different from its non-existence as not-pen. The difference is only relative and as such is only an intellectual construction. The difference, though psychologically necessary, does not argue the ontological reality of two attributes. So, the first two propositions are not logically necessary, since either of them is adequate to account for the other. With the collapse of the first two propositions as logically superfluous, the rest of the propositions will fall to the ground automatically as they are founded upon the former in the ultimate analysis. It is submitted in reply that the position, no doubt, follows from the denial of negation as a factual characteristic, but the denial of the factuality of negation has been shown to lead to absurdities. It will suffice to observe that 'existence' is always determined by the self-identity of an entity and non-existence has reference to another entity in respect of another identity. So, the determinants of existence and non-existence are different and, consequently, the determined should also be held to be different. Existence, undetermined by reference to the individuality of different entities, is only a blank abstraction. The existence of the pen is determined by its self-identity, and the self-identity in the very act of determining its existence implies its non-existence in the rôle of another entity possessing an identity different from it. Thus, it is the self-identity of an entity that determines its existence and the non-existence is determined by other-identity. Without these determinants, existence and non-existence are but nonsensical terms. It is the diversity of determinants which constitutes the diversity of the entities and the difference of existence and non-existence as ontological facts. If existence and non-existence were not ontologically different, a pen should be existent as not-pen as it is *quâ* pen and should be non-existent *quâ* pen as it is non-existent *quâ* not-pen. That the difference between existence and non-existence, as entailed by the difference of determinants (*avacchedaka*), is real and factual difference can also be deduced from an analysis of the import of the positive and negative propositions. There is a material difference between the propositions 'The jar exists on the ground' and 'the jar does not exist on the ground.' The first proposition asserts the presence of the jar and the second asserts the absence of the jar, on the ground. If there were no difference between presence and absence, absence of the jar could be asserted even when the jar was present. But this is not possible and this is proof of the difference of existence and non-existence. The Buddhist insists on the triple characteristic of a logical probans as the ground for inferring the probandum. The probans, *e.g.*, smoke, must be shown to exist in the subject (minor term) and in the homologue (*sapakṣa*) and to be absent from the heterologue. If there were no difference between existence and non-existence, the triple character would be impossible.

The result may be summed up as follows. The first two propositions are significant and neither is a reduplication of the other. But what is the *raison d' etre* of the third proposition ? The third proposition only states the successive occurrence of the two predicates noticed above. Suppose that a jar and a chair are successively perceived in a room and we assert the existence of the two entities therein. But the two are not different from each one of them. If 'two' is but a summation of the units, the third proposition is nothing but a summation of the first two. But the Jaina here would appeal to experience. That the combination of two units gives rise to a separate entity is a matter of experience. Take for instance the word 'go'. It is nothing but the successive occurrence of two letters 'g' and 'o'. That the word 'go' is different from both 'g' or 'o' is a matter of perception. If the distinctive unity of the word 'go' were not a fact, and it were identical with the constituent letters, the pronunciation of 'g' or 'o' would be sufficient for communicating the meaning of 'go'. It cannot be, therefore, denied that the successive presence of two things gives rise to a third thing, which has a distinctive individuality from the constituent elements. We can elucidate the matter by adding further examples. A garland of flowers has no existence outside the flower-units, no doubt. But it cannot be denied that the garland is different from the flower-units, as the latter, outside the juxtaposition that gives rise to a garland, do not serve the purpose of a garland. It is a matter of experience, and not of pure logic, that the combination of two units gives rise to a distinctive third, which is both different and non-different from the constituent units. The Jaina is emphatically empiricist here as elsewhere, when the nature of existence of an entity becomes the object of a doubt. The Buddhist and other idealistic logicians would scent a contradiction in such cases, but this is only another instance of the incompetency of pure logic to deal with the nature of existents *a priori* and independently of experience.

The third proposition, it has been seen, is not a mere reduplication of the first two. That the combination of the predicates of the first two propositions is a different predicate is, we trust, not open to sincere doubt. Let us now consider whether the fourth proposition is logically necessary. The logical necessity of the fourth proposition can be established if the simultaneous presence of two attributes can be shown to evolve an attribute distinct from the attributes predicated in the third proposition. The fourth predicate 'inexpressibility', it is urged, is but the abbreviated formula for occurrence of the positive and nagative attributes. The third predicate also states the presence of these two. The difference between the third and fourth predicates consists in the difference of time of their occurrence. But is the difference of time a proof of an ontological difference ? Let us consider the proposition, 'There are pen and paper on the table.' Our knowledge of the presence of pen and paper, in so far as it is derived from the knowledge of the proposition, is no doubt derived in succession. But this is due to the exigency of articulation, which cannot take place in one and the same time. It is obvious that the difference in the time of our cognitions cannot argue an ontological difference. The presence of the two in one substratum is a fact which does not admit of a difference in the nature of their existence, though there may be a difference in the time-order of their cognition. The difference is at most subjective. Some exponents of the Jaina dialectic have tried to meet the objection on logical grounds. They assert that though there may be no ontological difference between the third and the fourth predicates, the logical difference between them cannot be denied. The difference is a matter of formal logic, and this is not incompatible with the lack of objective material difference. After all, the sevenfold predication is only a series of formal predications, the validity of which is to be determined by canons of formal consistency. The demands of formal consistency can be satisfied by the application of the test of redundance. The fourth proposition would be redundant, if its import were self-identical with that of the third in form. But the identity of formal import is not present in these two propositions. This will be apparent from the consideration of the import of the two propositions we have given in the beginning of the present chapter. 'The pen exists and does not exist' is the third proposition and 'the pen is inexpressible' is the fourth proposition. The predicate 'inexpressible' is but the abbreviated formula for the simultaneous presence of 'existence and non-existence' in the subject, 'pen'. Even admitting that there is no material difference between the successive presentation and the simultaneous presentation of the two attributes in the selfsame substratum, the difference in the formal import of the two propositions is not liable to doubt. In the third proposition, the principal predicate is non-existence, and existence is only its adjectival adjunct. In the fourth proposition the predicate consists of both existence and non-existence having co-equal status and prominence. In the latter proposition 'existence' is not a mere appendix to non-existence, which is the case in the third proposition. Thus there is no logical redundancy and this is the logical warrant for their separate assertion.

But this defence of the fourth proposition on grounds of formal logic has not commended itself to all. The difference must be ontological and objective, otherwise the sevenfold predication would be only a matter of subjective necessity, which should not have validity apart from its foundation in objective truth. Moreover, this formal defence would not preclude the admission of two other propositions in addition to the seven. The order of predication may be reversed in the third and seventh propositions, and this should occasion two other propositions, the predicates having different formal import. Thus instead of asserting existence and non-existence in the order noted above, one may assert non-existence first and existence next, *e.g.*, the proposition may be stated as "The pen does not exist and exists.' Here the element of non-existence is given the formal status of an adjective to 'existence', and, so, its logical import is different from that of the third. In the seventh proposition the same reversal of the order of the two elements, existence and non-existence, would yield a different formal import. If formal logic were the determinant of the sevenfold predication, the introduction of the two additional propositions resulting from the admitted formal difference of import cannot be debarred by any logic. The difference of the predicates in the third and fourth propositions must be shown to be based upon a material difference, or either of them has to be expunged. Later exponents of the sevenfold dialectic are emphatically of the opinion that the difference is material and objective and not formal or subjective. The third predicate asserts the co-equal primacy of the two predicates taken together and the fourth predicate stands for a new attribute different from both. Let us examine the import of the predicates of the seven propositions *seriatim,* and the material difference of the attributes will become apparent.

The first predicate 'existence' is true, as the reality of the subject in its own context cannot be denied. The pen is really existent in so far as it is its own self. But this does not give us full insight into the nature of the pen. The pen is pen only because it is not not-pen. It can have a determinate existence only by virtue of its non-existence as anything else than pen. This attribute is asserted in the second proposition. Thus, each of the two attributes belongs to the pen. But each by itself does not lay bare the individuality, but the two together do. The compresence of the two, again, does not exhaust the nature of the pen. It is equally a felt fact that the compresence gives rise to a novel attribute, which derives from the two and at the same time is different from both of them. The attribute, engendered by the synthesis of the two attributes, is different inasmuch as it not only contains the two elements but transforms them. The synthesis of the opposite attributes, existence and non-existence, stated in the third proposition, is only a synthesis of togetherness. But the fourth predicate goes further than this togetherness, inasmuch as it asserts an attribute which not only is a compresence of the two, but a novel attribute in which the two attributes are dissolved into one. A concrete example may illustrate the truth of our contention. A beverage is made of several ingredients, sugar, curd, spices, and so on. It is a matter of perception that the beverage has a self-identity of its own different from that of the ingredients. The beverage is a unit — an organic whole. Likewise the synthesis of the two attributes, existence and non-existence, gives rise to a novel attribute, which transcends the two and at the same time comprises them as distinct elements in its being. It would be a mistake to suppose that this novel attribute, which cannot be grasped by a definite concept and, so, inexpressible by a definite linguistic symbol, is the exclusive characteristic of a real. That inexpressibility or indefiniteness is a factual characteristic, and that it emerges on the synthesis of the opposites is a truth which cannot be denied without stultifying experience. But this does not mean that the 'indefinite' or the 'inexpressible' (*avaktavya*) annuls the distinctive individuality of the elemental attributes, existence and non-existence. We must appeal to experience to determine the nature of existents; and, as has been set forth in the first chapter, reliance on abstract logic in this matter is more often than not a source of error and positive misconception. The indefinite or inexpressible is felt together with the definites, existence and non-existence. The pen is indefinite, but is felt as definite *quâ* existent and non-existent at the same time. The fifth proposition asserts the compresence of 'existence' with the indefinite, the sixth affirms the compresence of non-existence, and the seventh completes the modes by affirming the consecutive presence of the two, with the 'indefinite.'

The indefinite or the unspeakable is a characteristic concept of Jaina philosophy. The Vedāntist has proved that the nature of existents, as revealed to empirical knowledge, is a complex indefinite, which cannot be characterized either as real, or unreal, or both, or neither. By reality the Vedāntist understands logical being, which does not admit of lapse or negation in time, space and its uniformity. Phenomenal reals have reality in their own context and are *non est* outside this context. So, they cannot be regarded as having reality in their own right. In the ultimate analysis, phenomenal objects are unspeakable as real or as unreal, since reality, absolute and unconditioned, is lacking in them. The very fact that they are non-existent elsewhere and elsewhen is proof of their lack of reality in their own nature and right. But they are not unreal fictions, as they are objects of experience while fictions are not. Thus, they are unspeakable and indefinable as real or unreal. The Vedāntist concludes from these premises that the phenomenal objects are the creations of ignorance, cosmic or individual, and are unreal in the absolute sense. The Jaina admits the truth of the premises, but does not think that the Vedāntist conclusion is inevitable. The Jaina does not admit that reality is free from determinations. It is experience alone that can give us insight into the nature of reality, and experience acquaints us with determinate existents. Indeterminate or universal existence is only a matter of abstract thought. It has been said in the beginning of this chapter that the opposition of determinate being with indeterminate being is the starting point of the sevenfold dialectic. It has also been made clear that indeterminate being is only a logical thought and not an ontological fact, and that the relation of opposition does not presuppose the co-ordinate status of the opposites in the ontological order. The Jaina agrees with the Vedāntist that reals are indefinites, but this does not afford a logical warrant according to the Jaina for declaring them to be unreal appearance, engendered by ignorance. It is not untrue because it cannot be expressed by a single positive concept. We have to take it as it is, although it refuses to fit in with the logical apparatus, as employed by traditional philosophy. I take the liberty of quoting the pregnant observations of Prof. K. C. Bhattacharya and present them in spite of their difficulty to the reader without any comments. Prof. Bhattacharya with his microscopic vision has seized hold of the secret of Jaina thought and no better elucidation seems possible. "The determinate existent is ... being and negation as distinguishably together, together by what the *Jaina* calls *kramārpaṇa*. The given indefinite — the 'unspeakable' or *avaktavya* as it has been called as distinct from the definite existent, presents something other than consecutive togetherness;[1] it implies *sahārpaṇa* or co-presentation which amounts to non-distinction or indeterminate distinction of being and negation. ...It is objective as given, it cannot be said to be not a particular position nor to be non-existent. At the same time it is not the definite distinction of position and existence, it represents a category by itself. *The common sense principle implied in its recognition is that what is given cannot be rejected simply because it is inexpressible by a single positive concept. A truth has to be admitted if it cannot be got rid of even if is not understood.*"[2]

Section II

We now propose to discuss the import of each term of the propositions. Each term is logically significant and the significance of the terms contributes to the significance of the proposition as a whole. Let us consider the first two propositions. The first proposition is: 'The jar exists certainly in a context (*syād asty eva ghaṭaḥ*). The formal definition of the first proposition may be propounded in the following terms. It is an affirmative proposition which asserts a positive fact without negating other characteristics in respect of a subject. In the example given the jar is the subject and 'exists' is the predicate, which is a property of the jar. The second proposition may be formally defined as follows: 'It is a negative proposition importing negation of a certain property without negating other characteristics.' 'The jar

1. The matter of predication of the third proposition.
2. *The Jaina theory of Anekānta-Vāda* by Prof. K.C. Bhattacharya, p. 13. (The italics are mine.)

does not certainly exist in another context'. In the original proposition in Sanskrit two qualifying prepositions, *viz.*, *syāt* and *eva* are employed. It is difficult to find exact equivalents of these two terms in English. We have tentatively rendered *syāt* as 'in a context' and *eva* as 'certainly.' We are conscious of the inadequacy of the English terms to connote the sense that the original terms signify. But the elucidation of the meaning of the terms will serve to preclude misconception and so we do not wait for exact equivalents. In our opinion the term *syāt* is untranslatable. Let us examine the logical value of the terms of the first proposition. The particle 'certainly' (*eva*) is logically necessary inasmuch as it serves to exclude an undesirable consequence. The existence of the jar is to be understood as existence in reference to its own context constituted by its own individuality and specific spatio-temporal setting, and not in reference to a different context. The particle 'certainly' (*eva*) is calculated to exclude this contingency. It helps to clarify the import of the predicate that it relates to the subject in reference to a particular context and not in a different reference. The negative implication is derived from the use of the particle *eva*, which we have tentatively translated as 'certainly.' It has a restrictive force and this should be understood as the meaning of the English equivalent. The exact implication of *eva* in the proposition is the exclusion of the negation of 'existence'. The predicate 'existence' is affirmed of the subject, and this affirmation can be significant, only if the predicate belongs as a matter of necessity to the subject. The element of necessity is indicated by the adverb 'certainly' (*eva*). It means that the predicate is a necessary concomitant of the connotation of the subject, though not a part of it. It may be a synthetic proposition and the predicate may be a new attribute. But the very fact of predication implies that the attribute is not absent in the subject. The adverb 'certainly' implies that the attribute predicated is a necessary concomitant of the connotation of the subject, though not a part of the implication of the term, and the negation of the opposite follows from the necessity of the relation that is emphasised by it (*eva*).

The term *syāt* is untranslatable. It means that the subject possesses a manifold of attributes. In the proposition *syād ghaṭo 'sty eva* the particle *syāt* implies that the subject is a manifold of attributes of which the predicate is one as a matter of fact. That the predicate is one of the attributes possessed by the subject and that as a matter of necessity is implied by the term 'certainly' (*eva*). The full meaning of the first proposition may thus be stated as follows : "The jar is a substance of which 'existence' is one attribute as a matter of necessity among the plurality of attributes that belongs to it." The phrase 'as a matter of necessity' implies that the predicate is never absent in the subject. It may be urged that the element of necessity is falsely introduced inasmuch as the opposite of existence, *viz.*, non-existence, is also predicated of it in the second proposition. And the form of the proposition being the same, existence and non-existence, both being predicates, would belong to the subject as a matter of necessity. This seems to be a case of self-contradiction. But the Jaina does not find any contradiction in the two predicates belonging to the same subject, as existence and non-existence are determinate. If they were indeterminate, the contradiction would be inevitable. And the contradiction would again be irresistible if existence and non-existence were affirmed of the subject in the same reference. The jar is existent as a jar and non-existent as other-than-jar. There is no contradiction here. But if the jar were affirmed to be existent and non-existent both as a jar, the contradiction would be apparent. As in the first two propositions existence and non-existence are predicated in a determinate sense, there is no contradiction between them.

It is worthy of remark that the qualifying phrases *syāt* and *eva* are not absolutely indispensable for logical precision. It is necessary for those who have not realized the indeterminate nature of reality. Reals are indeterminate in the sense that they cannot be determined as possessing only such and such attributes and not the rest. The particle *syāt* is employed only to emphasise this truth. But it is not necessary for a person who is aware of the manifoldness of reals. Similarly the particle '*eva*' is redundant. They are employed only to guard against a customary misconception, and if such misconception be not present, they are not logically necessary. But a logical discourse is always aimed at persons, who are in doubt, but inquisitive for truth, and with regard to such persons the logical form has its significance and necessity.

Let us now sum up the results of the analysis of the import of the individual terms and determine the total import of the propositions. The import of the first proposition is thus to be stated as follows : "The jar is possessed of existence as determined by its own nature and so on." The second proposition means 'The jar is possessed of non-existence as determined by other individuality and so on.' The existence and non-existence that are predicated of the subject are determinate. 'The jar used as the subject in the proposition is only illustrative. We can substitute any existent for it and the predicate will relate to it. And as regards the predicates, 'existence' or 'non-existence,' they are also specific instances and can be replaced by any other attribute. The principle governing predication is that an attribute is necessarily concomitant with its negative. Whatever attribute, quality or action, may be predicated, it can be true of a subject only in reference to a context. The jar, for instance, exists in so far as it possesses the nature of jar and does not exist in the nature of a pen. Existence is determined by non-existence and vice versa. We have seen in the second chapter that non-existence is a case of other-existence. The jar is the non-existence of the pen and vice versa. Existence without reference to and independent of individual entities is only an abstraction of thought. 'A' can have existence because it has not existence as 'B.' Existence is always concrete and as such is defined and determined by other concrete existence. In other words, existence cannot be separated from what exists, though it is distinguishable in thought. What is said of existence also holds good of other attributes. A real is possessed of infinite attributes and these cannot be separated from the real. They are one with the real in the sense that they have no existence apart from and independent of the real, in which they are embodied. Thus all attributes are determinate in the sense of having determinate being. And determinate being means being in a particular reference outside which it is simply *non est*. So being and non-being are correlates and the predication of one implies the predication of the other.

It follows then that the negative proposition is as much true as the affirmative one. It has been contended by others that being or existence[1] constitutes the nature of a real and non-being only relates to another real. The import of the predicate in the proposition 'The jar exists' is that existence is a part and parcel of the reality of the jar. 'The jar does not exist' is really an apparent proposition, having only a formal similarity with the affirmative proposition. The predicate 'non-existence' does not in reality belong to the jar as a jar, but to what is not jar. The Jaina is also agreed that the negation of the attribute has reference to something else. The jar really exists as jar and *not as pen*. So negation of existence can have reference to the pen and other things which are not jar. If the non-existence of pen were an attribute of the jar, the colour, shape and other characteristics of the pen should also be the attributes of the jar. But this is absurd. The Jaina, however, does not think that the two cases are similar or that the contention is tenable. The colour, shape and other qualities of the pen are the exclusive properties of the pen and so cannot be predicated of any thing else. But non-existence-as-pen is an attribute of the jar. The jar has a self-existence and a self-identity which is inseparable from its non-existence-as-pen. As has been said above, existence has no objective status apart from the concrete real, and since one real is distinguished from another real, the existence of one is *ipso facto* distinguished from that of others. That one existence is distinct from another existence means that the two are not identical, that is to say, each has an identity of its own, which can be understood fully in reference to another existence. To know is to distinguish. A thing can be known fully as it is in itself only when it is known to be what it is not. It is really difficult to determine the status of the element of negation in the knowledge of a real — whether it is antecedent or consequent to the knowledge of the positive aspect. But the question of precedence is not material. It is undeniable that conception of a real is a complex of a positive and a negative aspect. The Jaina does not seem to be wrong when he insists that the determinate

1. The Jaina does not distinguish between being and existence, which are always concrete.

cognition of a real as what it is and as what it is not is a matter of intuition, sensuous or non-sensuous according to the nature of the object. It has been said in the fourth chapter that conceptual knowledge according to the Jaina is as much derived from objective reality as sense-intuition is.

Another consideration may be put forward in favour of the Jaina contention. 'The jar does not exist' is a proposition which has the same formal consistency as the affirmative proposition has. If non-existence be a characteristic, it must have a substratum of its own. The Naiyāyika would have us believe that it belongs to what is not-jar, since existence as pen and the like is denied of the jar, and the jar's non-existence is equivalent to the negation of existence as pen. But that only shifts the difficulty and does not solve it. The coincidence of non-existence and existence in the pen again would raise the same difficulty. The pen is a pen because it is not not-pen, that is to say, jar and the like. The negation of not-pen is thus as much an element of its being as the pen-character is. The Jaina again substantiates his position by a different line of approach. He examines the implication of the substantive-adjective relation and arrives at the same result. 'Whatever is an adjectival determination is necessarily concomitant with its opposite. The predicate is an adjectival determination. The predicate is concomitant with its opposite.' This is a perfect syllogistic argument and is also materially true. Take any proposition and the truth will be obvious. 'The pen is red' is a proposition with 'red' as the predicate. Now, the predicate 'red' has significance only, because it is a determinate attribute, which it is by virtue of its negation of the opposite, not-red. Many things may be not-red, but the negation of not-red would apply only to what is red. The implication of the proposition 'the pen is red' is that 'the pen is not not-red as distinguished from diamond.' Not only is the law true of positive attributes, but ite qually holds good of negative attributes also. 'The pen is not red,' though apparently a negative proposition, has a positive implication. The pen has some colour, which we know to be different from red. Even in what is held to be an absolutely negative proposition, *e.g.*, 'Air has no colour,' the negation of colour has a positive implication in that colour is existent in some other substance. If we now apply the law to the cases under consideration, we shall see that the propositions 'The jar exists' and 'the jar does not exist' are rather complementary to one another and not inconsistent. Existence, being a predicate and an adjective, must be concomitant with its opposite, non-existence, and similarly non-existence, being a predicate, will be concomitant with existence.[1] The Vedāntist complains of contradiction in the coincidence of existence and non-existence in one substratum. But the Jaina is emphatic in his repudiation of the charge. There is no incompatibility, as the existence of a thing *quâ* itself and non-existence *quâ* others are not unperceived. It is non-perception of co-existence, which is the determinant of contradiction, but this is conspicuous by its absence here. It is not a fact that existence is incongruent with non-existence, or that one supersedes the other as light does darkness. We have fully discussed the nature and scope of the Law of Contradiction in the first chapter and the arguments need not be reproduced here.

The justification of the first two propositions in the chain of sevenfold predication has drawn us into a discourse on the subject-predicate relation. But the position adopted by the Jaina involves him in open conflict with the Naiyāyika and we cannot avoid adverting to the controversy even though it may necessitate a digression.

The Naiyāyika believes in certain facts which are always existent and their opposites are inconceivable. For example, 'expressible,' 'cognisable' 'knowable' are attributes which are not inapplicable to anything and as such have no opposites. They are universally predicable. But as they have no opposites the Jaina's position that all predicates are concomitant with their opposites cannot hold good in these cases. Is there anything which is inexpressible or unknowable ? To assert that A exists and is inexpressible or unknowable involves self-contradiction, inasmuch as the very assertion of it as A presupposes its being known and the act of assertion constitutes its expression. This is certainly a plausible argument against the Jaina position. But

1. astitvaṁ pratiṣedhyenā 'vinābhāvy ekadharmiṇi. nāstītvaṁ pratiṣedhyenā 'vinābhāvy ekadharmiṇi.

AS, verses 17 & 18.

the plausibility will not bear scrutiny. 'Knowability' is a definite concept and it can have a meaning only if it negates its opposite. If a thing is called knowable by virtue of its being cognised by an accredited instrument of cognition, then of course fictions are not knowable. So the opposite of 'knowable' will not be wanting. If, however, 'knowable' be taken to stand for 'thinkable,' then also such expressions as "square circle" are available as the examples of 'unthinkable.' The question can be decided by a dilemma. Is the expression 'unknowable' unmeaning ? It cannot be entirely meaningless, as nobody would then care to assert it or feel called upon to rebut it. So the opposite of 'knowable' is not absent. Further if we descend from the realm of abstract speculation to the field of concrete reals, we shall have to acknowledge that the proposition, 'The jar is knowable' affirms the predicate in a determinate sense. The jar is knowable as a jar and not as a pen. Here the 'pen' will stand as its opposite. So all concepts, in so far as they have meaning, will have their opposites. The Naiyāyika's advocacy of purely positive attributes thus cannot create a difficulty for the Jaina standpoint. The fact can be made further clear from the consideration that the Naiyāyika would not have an occasion to make such assertions as that there are purely positive attributes, if there was no possibility of dispute. The Naiyāyika may succeed in exposing the inconsistency in the position of the opponent who would deny it. But the very necessity of logical defence shows that 'unknowable' may be logically untenable, but psychologically possible. As regards 'expressibility' the Jaina does not think it to be without its opposite. This has been made clear in our treatment of the concept of inexpressibility in Chapter V. We have seen that the law that the predicable attribute has its negative concomitant holds good also in the case of so-called purely positive attributes. We must consider the cases of fictions, *e.g.*, sky-flower, a barren woman's son, square-circle, phoenix, centaur and the like. Nobody would commit the absurdity of supposing that they are existent in any reference. These absolutely unreal fictions are logically predicable, but they have no positive concomitant, which they should have if the law of the mutual implication of opposites were universally true. But the Jaina would not take these fictions as purely negative ideas. If they are thinkable, they exist as thought constructions, though not as objective facts. Viewed from this point of view their objective non-existence is found to be commensurate with conceptual existence. It is not maintained that the negative concomitant should have coordinate status — an objective non-existence having subjective existence as its implicate or vice versa will equally meet the requirements of the law. And if we look deeper, coordinate status of the positive and negative concomitants can also be discovered in these cases. These fictions are complex constructions of incongruous elements. Both square and circle, sky and flower, a barren woman and a son, are objectively existent facts. But their combination is only non-existent. So the concomitance of existence and non-existence is found to hold good in these cases also.

The law of concomitance of opposites is only a deduction from the Jaina conception of determinateness of existence and as such holds good of all reals, irrespective of their rôle in logical thought. We have applied the law to predicates, but that is only by way of illustration. Predicate or subject, the law holds good of all facts. The conception of determinate existence is in direct opposition to the Vedāntist position of one universal existence which admits of no negation. It is again opposed to the Fluxist position that non-existence is only a fiction. A determinate existence is a complex of existence and non-existence, both being real elements of it. The first proposition is thus in need of being supplemented by the second — each being an incomplete description taken by itself. Let us now elucidate the import of the propositions in the light of the results of our speculations. 'The jar exists' would thus be correctly interpreted as 'X (the jar) is the substratum of existence as determined by the nature of jar.' The existence predicated of the jar is thus determinate and we mean this when we further amplify the original proposition, 'The jar exists,' by adding the restrictive clause 'as jar' to it. The second proposition is 'The jar does not exist' which is further amplified as 'The jar does not exist as pen and so on.' The non-existence of the jar is determined by the pen and the like which stand for the whole class of not-jar. The negative particle 'not' in connection with the verb means 'non-existence' and the latter is determined by the pen and the like. The non-existence predicated would thus be determinate. The full import of the second proposition thus amounts to the following — 'The jar is the substratum of non-existence as determined by the nature of pen-and-the-like.' As non-existence is identical with the reality in which it subsists, the non-existence of pen and the like would be identical with the jar. The propositions only affirm the truths which have been established by us in the second Chapter.

We have repeatedly asserted that existence and non-existence are always determinate. Existence is determined by the specific nature or individuality of the subject (*svarūpa*) and non-existence is in its tu n determined by the nature or individuality of things, which are different from the subject (*pararūpa*). There are also other determinants of existence and non-existence, *viz.*, substance (*dravya*), location (*kṣetra*), and time (*kāla*). What are we to understand by these determinants ? To return to the example given, 'The jar exists,' the predicate 'existence' is said to be determined by the nature of the jar. But what is the exact significance of the expression 'nature' of the jar ? The Jaina answers the question in his characteristic way. It is not necessary according to him to enter into a metaphysical discourse to determine the nature of the jar. It all depends upon the universe of discourse. By 'the nature of the jar' one can understand the connotation of the term, which, in terms of ontology, is the uniform attribute or attributes that characterize all jars, and by 'the nature of others' one can understand the connotation of the terms expressing pen and the like. The existence of the jar would thus be determined by the attributes which invariably present themselves to our mind when we think of the jar. The result is the same. A jar exists so far as it possesses the attributes which we associate with it in our thought. If a jar were to exist as partaking of the attributes of a pen, the jar would not be distinguishable from the pen. And if, again, it did not exist as possessed of the attributes which characterise it just as it does not exist as possessed of the attributes of pen and the like, it would be a non-entity like a sky-flower. The nature of a real is, however, composed of an infinite number of attributes, which cannot be fully comprehended by the limited intellect that mankind normally possesses. But that does not make our knowledge unreal or false, though undoubtedly it must be incomplete as we are at present constituted. Any attribute that we comprehend in a real will be a real part of its nature. What is necessary in a philosophical discourse is that we must stick to it throughout. Thus, one is at liberty to think of the jar as a name, as a substance, or as a mode. And in affirming its existence we must remember that the predicate belongs to the subject in respect of the nature in which we understand it. The predication of non-existence likewise will have reference to a nature other than this. It is quite legitimate again to take the jar in a very restricted sense, for example, as possessed of a distinctive magnitude. The affirmation of existence of the jar would then be determined by this magnitude and the negation of existence would then be determined by other magnitude, which it does not possess. The logical consequences will be the same in spite of the variation of our conception, as the affirmation and negation of existence will have reference to the particular conception. Thus, if the jar as possessed of the name, or the mode or magnitude were not to exist *quâ* these determinations like the pen, it would be a non-entity, and if it were again to exist in respect of opposite determinations, it would not be distinguishable from things which possess the latter determinations. We do not think it necessary to multiply instances. What is necessary is to recognize the metaphysical truth that things are possessed of an infinite plurality of attributes and the predication of one among these attributes is not false, though it is admittedly incomplete as a description of the nature of the subject. Every one of these attributes is true, but it would be a mistake, which is however traditional, to suppose that these alone constitute the nature of things.

We are now to consider the nature of other determinants, *viz.*, substance, time and location, which we have referred to. The word 'substance' (*dravya*) here stands for the material or stuff of which it is made. The substance of the jar is thus clay. It exists as made of this material and is non-existent in respect of another material, *e.g.*, gold. The proposition 'the jar exists' is thus to be completed by the insertion of the qualifying phrase 'of clay.' The jar of clay exists and not the jar of gold. That the material stuff is a necessary determinant of the predicate is obvious from the consideration that it has the same logical cosequences as the first determinant notified above. Thus if the jar were to exist in respect of another material, it would not be possible to assert that the jar is of clay and not of gold. A rich man may have a jar made of gold. But the gold jar would not be the same thing as the clay-jar. The difference is due to the difference of the material, though shape, size and function may be similar. The difference of material is only an instance of the difference of substance. The jar exists in clay and has no reality outside it. The same truth holds in the case of qualities also. The qualities must inhere in their respective substances and outside these substances, they have no being. Even in the case of those qualities which are known to inhere in more than one substance, the determination of the existence of these qualities by means of substance is also not wanting. Conjunction and disjunction, for instance, are qualities which relate to two things. It requires two things to be conjoined together and two again for one to be disjoined from the other. Though one substance cannot determine the existence of these qualities, the two together as their substrates will have the determining influence. Conjunction and disjunction can have existence only in their own substrates and not in others. Thus, the third substance will determine their non-existence. If these attributes were to have indeterminate substance, that is to say, if they could be supposed to exist in other substances than those in which they actually exist, the predicate of determinate conjunction or disjunction would be impossible. And if again they were not to exist even in their own substrates as they do not, in fact, in different substrates, they would be non-existent fictions.

Similarly, location is to be taken into account as determinant of the existence of things. The jar exists on the ground and not on the wall. The ground will be the specific location of the jar and the wall will be the location of other than jar. If a jar were to exist both in its own location and in the location of other things, the jar would not be a determinate existent. And if it were not to exist even in its own location, it would not exist anywhere, as it admittedly does not exist outside its own location. Location is thus a determinant of the existence of things, which are what they are by virtue of their possession of specific locations, which cannot be interchanged.

Time again is a determinant of existence. The jar exists in its own time and not in other time. The jar's own time is the present time and other time is the past or the future. If time were not a determinant of its existence, the jar could exist in the past and the future and thus would be an eternal substance. By the 'present time' we must understand the duration of time during which a jar endures. It has an upper and a lower limit constituted by its origin and its end. The upper limit separates the past from the present and the lower limit furnished by the end of the jar constitutes the future. Certainly it is absurd to suppose that the jar can exist in all these three divisions of time, or to suppose that it does not exist in its own time as it does not in the past and the future. The Vedāntist denies the reality of these determinations, but the denial of determinations is itself a case of determination. But unless a person is prepared to acquiesce in the Vedāntist's conclusion, or the Śūnyavādin's conclusion that nothing exists, he will have to accept the findings of the Jaina on the reality of these determinations. The full import of the proposition 'the jar exists' is thus to be elucidated as follows : 'The jar is the substratum of existence as determined by the nature of the jar, its substance (of clay), its present time and its own location.' The non-existence of the jar would likewise be determined by reference to time, place and substance.

The affirmation of the universal proposition, that the nature of reals is determined by the fourfold internal determinant as what it is and by the fourfold external determinant as what it is not, raises a problem about these determinants themselves. Are the determinants determinate ? If so, they must have internal and external determinants. And the same question will be raised regarding the second set, which again will require a third set of internal and external determinants, and the third set will require a fourth set and so on to infinity. The universal necessity insisted upon will lead to *a regressus ad infinitum* and the denial of this necessity at any stage will amount to surrender of a fundamental doctrine. It may be maintained on the analogy of the final self-determined stage that reals may be self-determined. The Jaina meets the problem by taking his stand upon concrete realism. He refuses to accept the solution that experience determines the nature of things as it is without reference to any determinant, external or internal. In the determination of the nature of reals the Jaina banks upon the testimony of experience, but he refuses to be a party to deliberate or undeliberate twisting of it. It is experience which envisages a real determined as existent and non-existent by its internal and external determinants respectively. If *a priori* considerations were depended upon in the determination of reality, there would be no check and no uniform standard. A real is to be accepted to be what it is found to be in experience. The dictum 'Things are determined by their proofs'[1] cannot be denied. If the knowledge of the determinant required another determinant, we would admit its necessity. If it did not require such determinants, we would not insist upon it. If the determination of the nature of the determinant actually depends upon another determinant, that need not cause a difficulty. A thing has a nature of its own and if the determination of the nature actually requires another nature of its own and that is found in experience, the first nature will be determined. And the second nature may or may not have a third nature. What is determined by another or is determined by itself has to be discovered by experience. The matter can be explained by reference to concrete facts. The specific nature (*svarūpa*) of a self (*jīva*) is to change into mental states and this mental change assumes one form as cognitive activity. Thus cognitive activity will be its internal determinant and the absence of cognitive activity will be its external determinant. This determinant again has its specific determinants. Thus cognition is of two kinds — mediate or non-perceptual and immediate or perceptual. The nature of immediate cognition is its lucidity (*vaiśadya*) and that of the mediate is the lack of lucidity. Immediate or perceptual cognition has again two varieties — perfect and imperfect. Perfect perception is cognisant of the complete nature of all things and imperfect perception takes note of parts of things. It is thus a matter of experience whether a determinant has another determinant. If a determinant is found ultimately to be self-explanatory and self-determinant, there is no reason whatsoever to question its validity.

1. vastuno hi yathaivā 'bādhitapratītis tathaiva svarūpavyavasthā, mānādhīnā meyasiddhir iti vacanāt. SBT, p. 34.

The contention that everything should be regarded as self-determined on the analogy of such determinants is a piece of hollow sophistry. Now, consciousness is found to reveal itself and its objects. Will it be a sound argument to maintain that brute material facts should be self-revelatory like consciousness ? The nature of reals should be determined to be exactly what they are found to be and not otherwise. Fire is hot and water is cold, though both are substances. Is it sound logic to argue that fire should be cold like water, as both are substances ? The difficulty raised by the opponent regarding the nature of determinants is thus found to be imaginary. As regards external determinants, there is absolutely no problem, since the number of reals being infinite and their nature being distinct and different in each, the nature of one can be easily distinguished from that of others. It cannot be maintained that things may be numerically different, yet they may have the same nature. 'A' is different from 'B' because 'A' has a nature different from that of 'B'. Either it has to be said that there is no plurality of things, or their different nature is to be conceded. Even if more than one entity is admitted, the second will determine the first and the first will determine the second externally. The difficulty about external determination is thus non-existent. And as regards internal determination we have shown that the difficulty is a figment of pure logic.

Another problem and we shall finish with the first two propositions. Let us examine the relation of subject and predicate in the first proposition. Let the proposition be 'The self exists.' Is 'existence,' the predicate in the proposition, different and distinct from the subject, 'self' ? Or, are they identical ? If the subject and predicate meant the self-identical thing, the relation of subject and predicate, substantive and adjective, and the relation of coincidence of the predicate with the connotation of the subject in the subject (*sāmānādhikaraṇya*) would not be possible. The subject and the predicate denoting the same thing would be two synonymous terms and the proposition would be tautologous. The statement of either the subject or the predicate would be sufficient. Of course it is possible to regard all propositions as analytical in character. But we do not solve the problem by such terminological devices. An analytical proposition is a proposition nonetheless. If the predicate did not mean anything different from the subject and vice versa, it is patent on the face of it that there would be no proposition. The problem is, 'Is a proposition possible' ? We see that it is not possible if the subject and the predicate are of self-identical import. The self-same difficulty is confronted even in what are called synthetic propositions. Let the proposition be 'The pen is red.' It is a synthetic proposition inasmuch as the predicate, 'red,' stands for a quality which does not follow from the connotation of the subject. But the question may be raised, does red mean the same thing as the subject ? Are they identical in meaning ? If the answer be in the affirmative, the objection of tautology stands unrefuted. Apart from this difficulty which is common to all propositions, the propositions 'the pen exists' or 'the self exists' are instances, in which the problem is further aggravated by grave difficulties. The predicate 'existence' is to be asserted of all entities and if the relation of the predicate to the subject were 'identity' all entities would become identical, being identical with a self-same predicate, 'existence.' This will be manifest from analysis of the proposition we have taken for consideration, *viz.*, 'The self exists.' The self is identical with existence, which is identical with all that exists. The result is, the self would be everything. This is the conclusion of the Vedāntist, but a realist would not take it to be true.

Identity cannot then be the relation between the subject and the predicate in a proposition, because of its untoward consequences, one logical and another ontological. The logical consequence of this view is the fallacy of tautology and the ontological consequence is the abolition of diversity and pluralism. Vedānta deduces these very consequences as evidence of the unreality of diversity, but a realist cannot be a party to it. Let us then consider the other alternative. Let the relation between the subject and the predicate be one of difference. 'The pen is red' is a proposition. If the pen were different from 'red,' it would not be red, and if 'red' were different from the pen, it would not be affirmed of it. But the difficulty is accentuated in a pronounced form in the proposition, 'The self exists.' If the self were different from existence, it would have no existence and it would be a fiction. And as has been observed before, existence being a universal predicate, each and every thing would be a fiction, being the subject of 'existence' and being different from it like the self. The consequence will be nothingness of the universe — the conclusion of *śūnyavāda*. The consequences are equally fatal to logic and realism. But it is equally difficult to maintain that the relation of the subject and the predicate is neither numerical identity nor numerical difference, since the two are contradictorily opposed and the denial of one involves the affirmation of the other according to the Law of Excluded Middle.

The Naiyāyika solves the problem by means of 'inherence' (*samavāya*). He would have it that though existence be different from the self, the former can be in the latter by relation of *samavāya* or inherence. Existence inheres in the self, though numerically different from it. But *samavāya* or inherence is a logical fiction apart from identity-cum-difference, which is the Jaina position. We shall examine this *Nyāya-Vaiśeṣika* concept in a separate chapter and shall see that it is only a device of philosophical escapism. The Jaina meets the difficulty by practically denying its reality. The difficulty is a creation of abstract logic, which the Jaina has condemned. The relation of the subject and the predicate is neither identity alone nor difference alone, but both together. If 'existence', as the predicate, were identical with the subject, the subject would be absolutely existent, and if it were different, the subject would be absolutely non-existent. But concrete reals are neither absolutely existent, nor absolutely non-existent. They are existent and non-existent both. If the predicate 'existence' be taken to stand for the whole substance, being concurrent with it, the relation can be taken to be identity. Existence as an attribute has no objectivity apart from the subject and is inseparable from it. Inseparability is concomitant with identity. The identity of a real is inseparable from it. And only that is inseparable from a real which constitutes its identity. Existence is inseparable from the self or the pen, because it constitutes its identity. But though inseparable and so identical, it does not constitute the whole of the identity. The pen and the self are both identical with existence, but still they are different and diverse, because existence is only a part of their being. We have to admit that the subject and the predicate are identical and different both, because we cannot get rid of the two, unless we are prepared to escape into the strangle-hold of Vedānta or to court intellectual death which the nihilism of *śūnyavāda* holds out as a temptation.

Section III

We have completed the survey of the first two propositions and discussed all the relevant problems in connection therewith. We now propose to survey the remaining propositions. 'The jar exists and does not exist (in their relevant contexts)' is the third proposition. Herein the two attributes, existence and non-existence, are successively predicated of the subject, 'jar.' It has already been established that the two attributes together form a different attribute from each of them and the resulting attribute is not a mere mechanical juxtaposition of two separate attributes, predicated respectively in the first and the second proposition. We shall further discuss and evaluate the objections that have been advanced by the absolutist philosophers against the entire system of predication at the end of the chapter. The import of the predicate nd of the subject has been fully discussed and that makes further discussion of the import of the proposition unnecessary. As regards the fourth proposition, the crux of the problem centres upon the predicate 'inexpressible' and we have discussed threadbare all the problems involved in the concept in the preceding chapter. It will be sufficient to observe here that the fourth proposition may be defined as one in which the attribute of inexpressibility is predicated of the subject. But inexpressibility is not the sole and sufficient characteristic. It is only one among many. That it is a different attribute from the predicates of the first, second and third propositions has been fully made out and we do not see anything to add to what has been said already.

The Jaina prefaces all the propositions by the word '*syāt*,' which indicates that it is only a partial characterization. Our previous investigations have made the task of explaining the remaining propositions rather an easy affair. The fifth proposition asserts the compresence of two attributes, existence and inexpressibility. Both are real and necessary attributes. Existence relates to the subject *quâ* a substance in respect of its internal determinations. The 'inexpressibility' is an attribute which relates to the substance standing in the relation of identity and distinction to its changing modes. The subject, so far as it is identical with and immanent in the changing modes, which are continually passing from being into non-being, is certainly not expressible by a word. It is also beyond the reach of logical thought, but is to be apprehended in intuitive experience alone. Logic can show only the possibility of such a concept. The sixth proposition stresses the negative aspect together with the attribute of inexpressibility. Each one of these attributes has been proved to be true of the subject and the compresence of the two is also a matter of fact. The seventh proposition asserts existence-cum-non-existence-cum-inexpressibility.' It gives a fuller and more comprehensive picture than the preceding ones, but does not supplant them. The predicated attribute is a synthesis of these attributes, which are separately asserted in three propositions. It has been shown that synthesis is not a mere summation, but entails the emergence of a new attribute different from the three elements. The seventh predicate is thus not a reduplication. It is one and three attributes at the same time. If it were three, it would be superfluous. But the unity is not secured by superseding the elements. The elements are preserved intact with all their individuality and it is through their co-operation that the seventh attribute is evolved into being.

Each of the seven propositions has been examined and none has been found to be unnecessary in virtue of the predicates being in each case new and real. The predicates from the third onward are synthetic in character, but their separate individuality has been proved. Each proposition constitutes an estimation of reality, which has been either advocated by a school of philosophers as a matter of historcial fact or is capable of being entertained as a possible evaluation. The Sāṅkhya believes in one *Prakṛti*, the prius of the material world. It is a substance which is undergoing constant change into modes and attributes. But still the plurality constituted by the modes is ignored and the unity is thought to be the sole characteristic. The assertion of the first proposition would explain the *Sāṅkhya* position. But this is only a partial and incomplete representation of reality.

The Jaina supplements it by the second proposition, and the remaining modes, being consequential, would *ipso facto* be true. The Buddhist fluxist concentrates his attention on the aspect of change and declares it alone to be the character of reality. The second proposition would represent his position. This is corrected by the introduction of the first. The *Sāṅkhya* represents one extreme by upholding the unitive character of substance, whereas the Buddhist advocates the other extreme by asserting the plurality constituted by the changing modes to be the sole reality and dismissing the unitive substance behind them. The Jaina asserts the reality of both in one, as each is attested in uncontradicted experience. The *Śūnyavādin* finds it impossible to reconcile the unchanging substance with its changing modes and he thinks being and non-being to be mutually contradictory. But he does not fail to recognize the factuality of both, though he characterizes it as inexpressible, and inexpressibility or logical indefinability is according to him the proof of the unreality of things. We have found that things are not absolutely inexpressible and how the advocacy of inexpressibility, as the sole and whole character of reality, leads to self-contradiction. Inexpressibility is a real characteristic which is not susceptible of being dismissed as a false appearance, since it is not sublated by a subsequent corrective experience like an error of perception. Nor does the cognition of inexpressibility involve a logical error, as we have shown.

The Vedāntist rightly shows that inexpressibility is invariably associated with the being of a real, but he is convicted of extremism by the Jaina for asserting the element of being as the sole and exclusive character of reality and for construing the element of inexpressibility as proof of the unreality of empirical facts following the lead of the *Śūnyavādin*. Jaina logic does not endorse this interpre ation, since it finds no contradiction in the coincidence of being and non-being. The coincidence of being and non-being in a real is certainly not capable of being grasped by a single concept or a linguistic symbol; but that is not proof of its unreality, but of the limitation of human language and conceptual thought. The Jaina accepts each one of the conclusions of these philosophers, as representative of a different aspect of reality. He does not repudiate their findings as false, but he insists that the fallacy of these philosophical positions lies in their exclusiveness and extremism. These philosophers taught true doctrines, but they erred by insisting on their discoveries being the exclusive nature of reality. The Jaina profits by their speculations and in his comprehensive philosophy finds room for them all. Each taken by itself is a true evaluation, but inadequate. He charges the philosophers with inadequacy and extremistic outlook, which, he thinks, is due to their preoccupation with their findings and impatience to look at the other side of the shield. The Jaina makes the extremes meet in his system of thought and calls his own philosophy by the name of non-extremism and non-absolutism (*anekāntavāda*). The non-absolutism of the Jaina is not the result of negation of absolutes and extremes, but of comprehension of them in a system. The empirical reality of the Vedāntist called *vyāvahārikasattā* is the absolute truth of the Jaina, and the latter refuses to accompany the Vedāntist in his philosophical excursion into the transcendental plane, which the Jaina thinks to be an airy abstraction hypostatized, as it lacks the sanction of experience, which is the only proof of existence.

The theory of sevenfold predication may be regarded as a logical elaboration of the position of the Jaina that each position is concomitant with its negation, or which is the same thing, that position is inconceivable without negation. This logical theory is in its turn derived from Jaina ontology that reality is determinate. We have shown that determinate reality is the focal point in which being and non-being coincide. Absolutism consists in maintaining either being or non-being as absolute truth and in holding that one is in absolute opposition to the other. The Vedāntist and the *Śūnyavādin* are paragons of absolutism. The former holds being, absolute and undetermined by non-being, as the whole truth, whereas the Buddhist nihilist accepts non-being as the only truth. The Jaina is non-absolutist in that he accepts both as the true determinations of the real, which is unique and common, particular and universal, positive and negative, rolled into one. But is this non-absolutism absolute and universal ? The proof of non-absolutism is the sevenfold predication. Does the sevenfold predication apply to non-absolutism itself ? If it does apply, non-absolutism will be concomitant with its opposite, which is the subject-matter of the second predicate. The first proposition will be 'non-absolutism exists' and the second proposition will be 'non-absolutism does not exist.' The negation of non-absolutism is equivalent to the affirmation of absolutism. Thus the universal advocacy of non-absolutism is vitiated by self-contradiction in that it ends in affirming absolutism. Non-absolutism is either absolute or non-absolute. If it is absolute, non-absolutism is not universal, which is the position of the Jaina, since at any rate there is one real which is *absolute.* If non-absolutism is itself non-absolute, it is not absolute and as such it is not the universal truth. Tossed between the two horns of the dilemma non-absolutism thus simply evaporates. The same result is attained from a further consideration of the implication of the second predication, which has been shown to amount to affirmation of absolutism. This absolutism, being in its turn, non-absolute, would require another absolute as its opposite, and the latter again another and so on to infinity. If sevenfold predication be not applicable to the truth of non-absolutism, the former would not be universal, which is again a contradiction of the Jaina position.

The Jaina holds non-absolutism to be the universal truth and as such it is not exempt from application of the sevenfold predication, which is the sole criterion of non-absolutism. The application of the test does not, how ever, lead to self-contradiction as alleged above. It has been observed, at the outset of the present chapter, that opposition is a logical relation and it is not necessary that the opposites must be of the same ontological status. It is enough if the other opposite is conceivable. Such being the case, the opposite of the non-absolute is not inaccessible. In point of fact, the absolute is of two types, *viz.*, the true absolute and the false absolute and similarly also, the non-absolute is true and false. The true absolute is one of the infinite attributes that are actually present in a real and is envisaged by cognition as it is without implying the negation of the remaining attributes. Such cognition, which takes stock of one attribute without implying the negation of other attributes that are actually present in it, is called 'partial knowledge' or *naya*. *Naya* is not false though it is partial knowledge, provided it takes stock of a real attribute without asserting or implying the negation of other attributes. Such an attribute or such partial cognition is regarded as the 'true absolute' (*samyagekānta*). But when one attribute is apprehended as constituting the whole nature of the real and thus implies the negation of other attributes which are really present, such attribute and such cognition are examples of 'the false absolute' (*mithaikānta*). Thus there are two types of partial knowledge — one true and the other false. The true nature of a real as consisting of an infinite plurality of attributes is, however, apprehended by a valid knowledge which is called *pramāṇa*. Such valid knowledge, which takes stock of the several attributes, existence and non-existence also, which are the real properties of the real, is the 'true non-absolute.' The false non-absolute is illustrated by that kind of knowledge, which takes stock of attributes, which are not really present in the object. It is non-absolute in the sense that it does not affirm one attribute only as constitutive of the whole nature of the real, implying the negation of the other attributes. It is the opposite of absolutism, which consists in the affirmation of one attribute to the exclusion of others. But it is false in that the attributes in question are unreal. So the non-absolute also admits of two varieties — one false and the other true.

Let us apply the results attained to the problem raised, *viz.*, whether sevenfold predication applies to the truth of non-absolutism. The 'true non-absolute' has been found to have its opposite in the 'true absolute' and the sevenfold predication can start on with these two opposites. 'It is absolute'; 'it is non-absolute'; 'it is both'; 'it is inexpressible' (as the two opposites together cannot be thought by a single concept or expressed by a single word); 'it is absolute and inexpressible'; 'it is non-absolute and inexpressible'; 'it is absolute, non-absolute and inexpressible.' It does not require any further proof to assert that the application of sevenfold predication to the universal truth of non-absolutism does not involve the consequences of self-surrender or infinite regression, which were believed by the opponent to be unavoidable. The non-absolute is constituted of absolutes as its elements, and as such would not be possible if there were no absolutes. If it be permitted to employ an imagery, the non-absolute may be compared with a tree and its absolute elements with the branches and members of the same. As the tree disappears if the branches and members are taken out, the non-absolute would similarly vanish if the absolute elements were not there.

We have established the sevenfold predication with the two attributes, existence and non-existence. Though we have repeatedly asserted that the attributes in question are only illustrative in character and our selection of these two was inspired by the recognition of the fact that the two attributes were the elemental characteristics of things, we now propose to add two more typical illustrations for the sake of easy understanding of the comprehensive scope of the doctrine. Let us take two pairs of attributes, permanent and impermanent, one and many, and illustrate the sevenfold predication with them.

The jar is permanent and 'the jar is impermanent' are the two elemental propositions and the predication is true of reality. The jar *quâ* the unitive substance is continuous through all the modes and as such is permanent. The substance of the jar is again earthy material, which is ever present. From the point of view of the material substance, the jar is again a mode of it. So the affirmation of permanence in respect of the jar *quâ* its material substance is true. The jar, again, as immanent in its modes and attributes, is identical with the latter and from the point of view of such identity the jar is as impermanent as the modes are. The construction of the derivative modes being quite consequential, it need not be discussed in detail. The import of the first proposition may be stated as follows : The jar is possessed of the attribute, permanence, so far as it is determined by its substantive character. The second proposition may present a problem according as the interpretation of the predicate may differ. 'Impermanent' may mean the attribute, 'absence of permanence,' or it may be interpreted as 'different from permanent.' The first interpretation does not present any specific problem as it is quite on a par with the attribute of non-existence. There is no difficulty that permanence and impermanence may co-exist in one substratum in respect of different determinations, *viz.*, as substance and as changing modes. There is absolutely no contradiction between the attributes as they relate to different facts, *e.g.*, permanence relates to the substance and impermanence to the modes. The contradiction would arise if both the predicates were to relate to the self-same thing, that is to say, if permanence and impermanence were affirmed in respect of the substance or of the modes in the same reference. But that is not the case and so the propositions are not incompatible. But a real difficulty occurs if the second interpretation is followed. The jar is a unit and cannot be both permanent and impermanent in the contemplated sense. 'The jar is permanent' means 'the jar is identical with 'the permanent' and 'the jar is impermanent' means 'the jar is different from 'the permanent.' The jar, which is permanent, cannot have 'difference' from 'permanent', since difference is an attribute which subsists in the whole of a real. It is not a part-characteristic like 'conjunction' (*saṃyoga*) or attributes derived from conjunction, red or blue. A jar may be red and not-red, red in one part and non-red in another part. These attributes are called part-characteristics, since the locus of one is not the locus of the other (*avyāpyavṛtti*). But difference is not a part-characteristic, as it belongs to the subject as a whole. Difference or identity, on the other hand, are whole-characteristics (*vyāpyavṛtti*). If 'A' is different from 'B,' it can be so if 'A' as a whole would be different, in other words, if it has an identity unshared by 'B' in any aspect.

The Jaina however does not believe in whole-characteristics at all and the denial of whole-characteristics is only a corollary of the dictum that the positive is the correlate of the negative.[1] 'Difference' would not be a determinate attribute, if it did not negate its opposite. An indeterminate attribute is only a contradiction in terms. The Jaina asserts that difference being a determinate characteristic must be concomitant with its opposite, otherwise it would cease to be an attribute at all. Such being the case, difference and identity, so far as they are determinate characteristics, must be co-existent in the same substratum, and this knocks out the Naiyāyika's differentiation between whole-characteristic and part-characteristic and the difficulty based upon it. The hollowness of the Naiyāyika's contention can be demonstrated further by the examination of a concrete instance.

1. astitvaṁ pratiṣedhyenā 'vinābhāvy ekadharmiṇi AMI, Chap. I, verse 17.

Conjunction is a part-characteristic even according to the Naiyāyika. Suppose a monkey is perched on a branch of a tree. It is to be said then that the tree is conjoined to the monkey in the top and not conjoined in the root. The 'conjoined' is a different attribute from the 'non-conjoined.' There is nothing repugnant about it, if one asserts on the strength of this difference that the conjoined tree is different from the non-conjoined tree. The soldier in uniform is different from the same soldier in civilian dress. The same person as a judge of the High Court is different from the man in a private capacity or in a different capacity, say, as Vice-chancellor of a University. It is sometimes found that the grant sanctioned by the same person as the official Head of a University is negatived by the same person as Governor of a Province. We regard such a procedure as an oddity or even as a case of contradiction. But logically speaking there is no contradiction, as functional identity and personal identity are two things. We shall clarify this point further in a subsequent chapter, when we shall deal with the problem of inherence (*samavāya*) as a relation.

Let us consider the pair of 'one' and 'many' (in the sense of 'other than one') and see how the sevenfold predication unfolds itself. 'The jar is one' and 'the jar is many' are the basic propositions. The 'oneness' is true of it, as the unitive substance, which owns up the modes and manyness, is the underlying entity of the modes themselves, which are identical with the substance. The substance and the modes are not different. And this identity of the substance with the modes constitutes its plurality. Both unity and plurality are true of each real. The Buddhist affirms the truth of the modes and on the basis of the identity of the substance with each mode, asserts the plurality as the only reality. The result is the doctrine of flux. The Vedāntist declares the modes to be unreal appearance in and over the unity. Both appeal to experience in support of their contentions, but as their logic stands in the way, the opposite aspect is repudiated as illusory. But the Jaina accepts the two together as constitutive of the true nature of reality and does not believe them to be incompatible, as they do not relate to the self-same thing, but to two different things, *viz.*, substance and modes. The identity of the two is felt in experience equally with the difference of the modes and the unification of the plurality is certified by perceptual intuition. But are these determinations, unity and plurality, capable of being predicated of *all* taken as one ? It is the position of the Jaina that a determination is concomitant with its opposite. But what about the universe — the totality of existents ? Is the totality an ideal unity and a real plurality? If the position be this, it follows that the unity being a subjective construction, plurality will be the true character of the totality of existence. So instead of a universe, we shall really have a pluri-verse. We postpone the discussion of the problem to a subsequent chapter, as we cannot do justice to the paramount importance which it possesses by dealing with it as a side issue. We may state in a dogmatic form that the Jaina takes the totality of existence as a unity with the plurality of existents preserved with all their individuality. The universe will be found on examination to be a unity of plurality exactly on a par with the individual, which is an epitome of the macrocosm, being a unity and a plurality in one and at the same time, though in a different reference.

The universality of sevenfold predication with regard to all that exists cannot be called in question. Even the totality of existents does not prove an exception, as it is also one and many. It is one *quâ* the universal being and many in reference to the plurality of things. So the sevenfold predication with the predicates, unity and plurality, is true of the totality as it is of the individuals themselves. As regards the individuals, all of which are undergoing change into modes, the plurality of the modes and the unity of the substance in each individual are attested truths and the sevenfold predication is the legitimate form of their evaluation.

We have discussed all the problems that were raised in connection with the specific instances of sevenfold predication and we have cosidered the objections advanced by the opponents regarding specific attributes. We now propose to consider the objections that have been advanced, not against specific predicates, but against the theory as a whole. In the first place, it is urged that the theory of sevenfold predication is only a quibble (*chala*). Whatever is existent is affirmed to be non-existent, whatever is permanent is asserted to be impermanent, in the sevenfold predication. It is only a jugglery in words and a despicable sophistry as it continually shifts the ground whenever confronted with a difficulty. But the charge is unfounded as the definition of a verbal quibble does not apply to it. A quibble consists in alleging a contradiction in the assertion of a person by putting a construction upon his words different from the intended sense.[1] It is resorted to when the assertion is susceptible of a double construction. In Sanskrit vocabulary which is exceptionally rich in sense, the occasions for quibble are numerous. The stock-in-trade example of quibble is the proposition 'The man has a new (*nava*) blanket.' The word for 'new' is *nava*, which also signifies the number 'nine.' The opponent charges the speaker with contradiction by taking the word '*nava*' in the sense of 'nine.' He says that the assertion is false. 'The man has not even two blankets, how can he have nine blankets ?' But there is no ambiguity in the Jaina propositions, nor is the assertion of existence and non-existence intended in different senses. The Jaina, on the contrary, scrupulously defines the meaning of his words and he insists on the uniformity of the sense of the same words occurring in the different propositions. The charge of 'quibbling' is the unkindest and the most frivolous accusation that can be conceived of against the Jaina position.

In the second place, it is alleged that the theory of sevenfold predication can only be the cause of doubt and not of certitude. The concurrence of opposite attributes in the same substance is impossible, yet the sevenfold predication asserts existence and non-existence, identity and non-identity, permanence and impermanence, of the same subject. This can only mean that the assertor is not sure of his position and is in doubt about the truth of either of the opposite attributes. What is doubt but this cognition of opposite attributes? Take, for instance, the notorious case of doubt. 'Is it a man or an inanimate tree' ? Doubt arises since the mind is confronted with two conflicting alternatives, man and tree, in respect of a self-identical entity. which cannot both be true. Similarly in the sevenfold predication, the assertion of existence and non-existence, which are

1. aviśeṣābhihite 'rthe vaktur abhiprāyād arthāntarakalpanā vākchalam NS 1.2.12.

mutually opposed, in respect of the same subject cannot but produce a doubt in the mind of the person to whom it is addressed. But the allegation is not well-founded upon truth. The conditions of doubt are not present in sevenfold predication. The conditions of doubt are three, *viz.*, the cognition of attributes common to the alternatives, the non-cognition of distinctive attributes, and the recollection of the distinctive attributes. An analysis of the instance under consideration will prove the truth of the assertion. A man sees at dusk a tall object ahead and owing to insufficiency of light cannot observe the specific attributes of the tree, *e.g.*, nests of birds upon it, the hollow in the trunk and the like, or of a human being, such as movement of hands and feet, the head-dress and so on. The object may be a man or a branchless tree, and whichever it is, it must have the attributes in question. But the attributes escape observation, though the man recalls them. He knows what is a man and what is a tree. But owing to the lack of perception of the specific determinations of either, he is in a fix and his mind oscillates between them.[1] In the case of sevenfold predication, on the contrary, existence and non-existence are each defined by their specific determinations, internal and external, and the cognition of these determinations makes doubt impossible. The cognition of common characteristics, when it is accompanied by the absence of the cognition of specific determinations, causes doubt, but not when such determinations are cognised. There can therefore be no room for doubt in sevenfold predication.

It has, however, been contended that though the conditions of doubt as enunciated above may not be present in full, there are certainly other conditions of doubt present in it. In the first place, there is divergence of opinion regarding the truth of the opposite attributes. Secondly, the Jaina must advance reasons in support of each of the opposite attributes and the consideration of such reasons must result in doubt, as one set of reasons will offset the other, and so neither existence nor non-existence can be asserted with certitude. But the second contention is also hollow like the first, since it is inspired by a misconception. It

1. The matter has been discussed in the beginning of this chapter.

is assumed that the predicates, existence and non-existence, are mutually opposed and so they would cancel each other. But the predicates are neither indeterminate nor have they the same reference, which would make opposition inevitable. Existence has reference to the identity of the substance, which never suffers lapse in spite of the evanescent modes which happen to it, and non-existence has reference to these modes, either defunct or unrealised. It may have reference to a distinct identity also. So there is no opposition, which would be irresistible, if the predication of opposite determinations were in the self-same reference. Fatherhood and sonship are opposed in the same reference. The same man cannot be the son and father of 'A.' But he can be the son of 'A' and father of 'B' and there is no contradiction, since the reference is different. A sound probans (*hetu*), *e.g.*, smoke, is existent in the kitchen and the hill and is non-existent in the lake. There is no opposition here and so also in sevenfold predication, as the opposites are asserted to be true not in the same reference, but in a different reference.

A charge-sheet of eight counts has been drawn up against the theory by another school of philosophers and this demands an examination and an answer. (1) The first charge is contradiction. It is asserted that affirmation and negation of the same attribute in respect of the same subject are not logically possible, since this would make self-contradiction inevitable. Existence is a positive attribute and non-existence is the negation of existence. The two are mutually repellent like heat and cold. (2) The second charge is consequential. The two opposites cannot exist in the same substratum and if existence and non-existence were predicated of the self-same subject, the identity of the subject would be split up into two — one as the substrate of existence and the other as the substrate of non-existence. (3) The third charge is that it makes infinite regress an unavoidable consequence. The Jaina position is that every real has a double character — one positive and another negative. Thus, jar, pen, table, chair and so on are all possessed of a double character, since they are both existent and non-existent according to the Jaina theory. Now 'existence' and 'non-existence' are real attributes and as such each of them must have a double character.

Existence will have existence and non-existence in its turn, and the second element of existence will have again existence and non-existence and so on to infinity. What is true of existence will be equally true of non-existence, as the postulation of an endless series of non-existences and existences will be necessary in the latter case also. (4) The fourth charge is the consequence of 'confusion' (*saṃkara*).[1] A thing will have existence and non-existence in the same manner. What is existent will be non-existent and what is non-existent will be existent. This is a case of confusion which consists in the overlapping of all things in one substratum. (5) The fifth charge is 'transfusion' (*vyatikara*),[2] the opposite of confusion. If existence were to occur in the very manner in which non-existence occurs, existence would be transfused into non-existence, and if non-existence were to have the same manner of incidence with existence, it would become existence. This is transfusion which is defined as the mutual transference of locus. (6) The sixth charge is the consequence, 'doubt.' If a real were existent and non-existent both, it could not be determined definitely as existent or as non-existent. The result is doubt as to which it is. (7) The seventh charge is 'indetermination,' which is the result of doubt. (8) The eighth charge is the inevitable consequence which is deduced by the nihilist that nothing is real, as every phenomenon is asserted to be possessed of both existence and non-existence — which is impossible.

This formidable catalogue of charges against the doctrine of non-absolutism, which is established by sevenfold predication, is really not so formidable as it appears at first sight. The fundamental charge is the allegation of self-contradiction and the remaining counts are only consequential. If the charge of self-contradiction can be shown to be unfounded and unreal, the disposal of the consequential charges will be a matter of methodical deduction. We have fully discussed the nature of opposition in the first chapter in connection with our critique of the Laws of Thought. The inflated list of objections recorded in the chargesheet is only an elaboration of the concept of

1. sarveṣāṁ yugapat prāptiḥ saṅkaraḥ. SBT., p. 42.
2. parasparaviṣayagamanaṁ vyatikaraḥ. ibid., pp., 42-43.

contradiction as endorsed by formal pure logic; but it has been established that *a priori* conception of opposition is untenable. It should, we think, suffice to say that the criterion of opposition is absence of proof of the co-existence of the opposites. In other words, it is from experience and not from pure thought that we should derive our notion of opposition. We have shown how the denial of this fundamental truth has divided idealists and realists and driven them to hostile camps. The only consistent logical conclusion of the *a priori* concept of opposition is the philosophy of Vedānta as taught by Śaṅkarācārya. Śaṅkara succeeds in denying the plurality with their relations by the application of the Law of contradiction, based upon the difference and opposition of being and non-being, which he thinks to be absolute.

But if we can persuade ourselves that *a priori* reasoning independent of experience is incompetent to yield insight into the nature of reals and their relations, we cannot accept the findings of idealists. The Jaina is a realist and if Vedānta is the paragon of idealistic thought, as James has observed, Jaina philosophy is with equal propriety and truth entitled to be called the paragon of realism. If experience be the ultimate source of knowledge of reality and its behaviour, we cannot repudiate the plurality of things. The admission of plurality necessitates the recognition of the dual nature of reals as constituted of being and non-being as fundamental elements. One real will be distinguished from another real and this distinction, unless it is dismissed as error of judgment, presupposes that each possesses a different identity, in other words that being of one is not the being of the other. This truth is propounded by the Jaina in that things are real, so far as they have a self-identity of their own unshared by others (*svarūpasattā*), and they are unreal in respect of a different self-identity (*pararūpasattā*). If being were the only character of reals to the exclusion of non-being, all reals would have the self-same being — in other words, there would be only one real, which is the conclusion of Vedānta. If non-being were the only character of reals, they would not be real even in their own self-identity, as the presupposition of self-identity is being, which is denied in the proposition. This is exactly the conclusion of *śūnyavāda*. Jaina thought steers clear of the Scylla of monism and the Charybdis of nihilism by accepting the deliveries of experience as the final truth. Of course experience must not be contradicted by subsequent experience if it is to be an authentic source of knowledge. But the crux of the problem lies in the very conception of contradiction and the Jaina refuses to capitulate to the Vedāntist or the Nihilist, who are adherents of pure logic.

The logic of Jaina is empirical logic, which stands in irreconcilable opposition to pure logic, and the advocates of the latter have to part company with the advocates of the former. If one were to pose the difficult question, 'Which of the two, realism and idealism, possesses the final truth' ? We can only advise him usefully by testing his logical convictions. "If you are a believer in absolute being or absolute non-being and in the absolute opposition of the two, you will find satisfaction either in Vedānta or Śūnyavāda. If, however, you have no such preformed faith, study the different systems of thought and understand the logic upon which they are founded, and you will arrive at your own conclusion in accordance with your logical sympathies that you will come to develop. If you come to believe in the truth of pure logic, you will become an idealist by faith. If, on the other hand, you are convinced by the contentions of realistic logic, you will be a realist. The form and nature of your philosophy will be determined by the strength of your convictions either way."

The Jaina position in logic, it can be expected, cannot be rejected by realistic philosophers. But as a matter of historical truth, realists also are not agreed in their views upon the nature of reality, although they are at one in rejecting the idealist's interpretation of logical truth. As regards the quarrel with the idealists, we do not want to act as umpire — an ambitious task which we leave to future prophets to adjudge. The realist can only show contradiction in the position of the idealist, which the latter does not believe to be a contradiction, and the idealist can show similar contradiction in the realist's position, which is believed by the latter to be the true description of the nature of reals as they are. I may be permitted to quote in this connection what I have said elsewhere about the differences of philosophers. "There is no reason to be optimistic that one day all philosophers will sink their differences and profess one philosophy. Philosophy is not so much a question of conviction or carrying conviction as it is a question of mental attitude and outlook of thought and habit of thinking. It will be therefore better and more consonant with truth to say that the task of philosophers is rather conversion than logical conviction. The phenomenon of rival schools of thought holding contradictory views and constantly fighting with one another, however unphilosophical it may appear, will not be a thing of past history, because the fundamental attitudes of mind, the bias of our thought movement, cannot be changed or destroyed."[1]

We have already alluded to the truth that the differences among realists are no less fundamental with regard to the interpretation of experience and thought. The Jaina deduces the conclusion that a real is constituted of being and non-being from the determinate nature that it possesses. The Naiyāyika also believes that existents are determinate, but declines to accept non-being as a factor of reality. The Naiyāyika believes in the opposition of being and non-being like the idealist and hence does not agree with the Jaina in respect of his assertion that reals are existent-cum-non-existent. It is contended by him, "The proposition 'A' is not 'B' or 'A' has not being as 'B' does not admit of the construction that 'A' has non-being of 'B' as an element of its being, which is the Jaina conclusion. The negation of 'B' relates to 'B' and not to 'A'. The proposition 'A' is not 'B' or 'A' has not the being of 'B' cannot be regarded as the equivalent of the proposition 'A' is not. What we seek to establish is that the identity of 'B' is absent in 'A' just as we assert non-existence of jar on the ground. The 'negation' is a determination of the jar and not of the ground and the legitimate form of assertion is 'the jar does not exist on the ground' and not 'The ground does not exist.' Similarly we should assert 'B' does not exist (in 'A') and not 'A' does not exist.' But the second proposition of the sevenfold predication just takes this illegitimate form."

The contention of the Naiyāyika seems to have much plausibility, but it will not stand scrutiny. The non-existence of the

1. *The Buddhist Philosophy of Universal Flux*, pp., 93-94.

jar is interpreted by the Naiyāyika as the attribute (*dharma*) of the jar. The non-existence of pen in the jar is similarly held to be an attribute of pen and not of the jar. The Jaina holds the opposite view. The dispute can be terminated by the determination of the substratum of negation. Negation will be the attribute of the substratum in which it subsists, just as 'redness' is the attribute of its substratum. In the proposition "The jar does not exist (*quâ* pen)" the non-existence of pen is predicated of the jar and the Naiyāyika takes exception to it. The question can be put as follows: 'Is the non-existence of pen a property of the pen or of the jar' ? The first alternative is not entertainable. If the non-existence of pen were a property of pen, the pen would cease to be pen. It cannot be maintained that what is a property of a thing does not exist in that thing. If negation as the property of the pen would subsist in the jar, why should not the other properties of the pen exist in the jar ? The first alternative must then be rejected and it must be admitted on pain of contradiction that the negation of pen is an attribute of the jar and not of the pen. And it is this truth which is asserted in the second proposition. What the Jaina seeks to establish is the truth that the assertion of existence yields only the knowledge of a part-characteristic, which is completed by the assertion of non-existence. Non-existence of the pen does not belong to the pen, as that would make it a non-entity. The truth can be elicited by the question, 'Does not the pen exist as pen ?' To say that the pen does not exist even as pen is a contradiction in terms. The non-existence of the pen is then to be asserted as its non-existence *quâ* not-pen. This is the Jaina position and no purpose can be served by twisting its plain meaning. The predication of existence and non-existence being thus necessary, the conclusion is undeniable that a real is existent and non-existent both.

But the Naiyāyika is not prepared to accept the Jaina interpretation so easily. It is contended by him that non-existence should be regarded as the attribute of the negatum. The meaning of the second proposition 'the jar does not exist as pen' is that the pen does not exist in the jar and it is plain that the non-existence belongs to the pen, which is non-existent. The non-existence is asserted of the pen and not of the jar. But here the Naiyāyika only lays emphasis upon one aspect of a complex situation. The Jaina does not deny that the pen is negated. The point at issue is the relation of attribute and substantive. The Naiyāyika admits that in the proposition 'The jar does not exist on the ground,' the non-existence of the jar is an attribute of the ground, which is the substratum of the non-existence in question. The non-existence of pen in the jar is exactly on a par with the case. And if the non-existence of the jar can be accepted as an attribute of its locus, why should an objection be raised regarding the non-existence of pen being an attribute of the jar, which is the import of the second proposition. We shall show in a subsequent chapter that all relations, irrespective of their apparent distinctions, are reducible to the relation of identity-cum-difference and the predicate is always a term which stands in this relation of identity to the subject. Non existence of the pen is affirmed in the jar and thus stands in a relation to the latter, and is thus a predicate of it.

It is seen that from whatever angle of vision one may approach the problem of negation, one cannot avoid the conclusion that non-existence is a real attribute of the existent. The Naiyāyika sets out to demonstrate the impossibility of the co-existence of non-existence and existence in an entity, but ends in asserting non-existence as the attribute of another existent, *viz.*, of the negatum. While he denies that non-existence of the pen is an attribute of the jar, he asserts that it is an attribute of the pen. But the pen cannot be non-existent as pen and existent as pen both — as that makes contradiction inevitable. It must then be admitted that non-existence can relate to the pen as determined by not-pen. The positive-cum-negative character of reals is the unavoidable conclusion even for the Naiyāyika. As we had an occasion to observe that it is only the Jaina who is the only consistent realist, and his *confréres*, the Naiyāyika and the Mīmāṁsist, have at times succumbed to the temptation of pure logic. The present case is only an illustration of the truth of our assertion.

But an objection of a formal nature has been raised. Granted that reals are positive-cum-negative in nature, still the form of the propositions as adopted by the Jaina is not correct. The propositions should be of the form, 'The jar exists' and 'The pen does not exist' and not 'the jar does not exist.' The negation of pen has always this form with the negatum as the subject, though as a matter of ontological fact, the non-existence of pen may be regarded as an attribute of the jar. The Jaina does not attach undue importance to formal disputes. He will be satisfied if the Naiyāyika accepts the Jaina position that reals are possessed of a double nature, positive-cum-negative, and abandons his wavering allegiance to the absolutist interpretation of the Law of Contradiction. As regards the form of verbal representation, the Jaina would only appeal to convention, that is followed. The form of propositions is not necessarily determined by philosophical truth. Take for instance the proposition 'John is cooking.' What is the meaning of the subject, John? Do we mean that John is only a physical organism, or a spirit, or an embodied spirit? According to the difference of import the subject should be stated differently in conformity with the objective truth. But no sane man, unless there is a special necessity for definition of the subject, raises any difficulty on the score of ontological truth regarding the form of proposition. It will suffice if the proposition is understood in the intended sense. As regards formal propriety the Jaina will only point to the large volume of usage and the time-honoured custom as his apology.

It may be claimed that the Jaina has succeeded in establishing his position that reals are existent and non-existent both. But if there still be left a lingering doubt or hesitation and further demonstration needed, it can be supplied by the following consideration. The Naiyāyika agrees that the pen does not exist in the jar.[1] The non-existence of pen is asserted to subsist in the jar. But such assertions must remain vague and obscure unless the nature of subsistence is determined in precise terms. Is the 'non-existence' in question numerically different from the jar in which it is asserted to subsist ? If it is different, it must be supposed that the non-existence is non-existent in its substratum. In other words, the identity of the jar and the identity of the non-existence being different, the latter must be non-existent in the former and vice versa. But the same problem

1. We have used 'pen' in the sense of penness or pen-character for the sake of brevity and for avoiding a clumsy expression.

will arise in the case of every subsequent non-existence and there will be no end of the process. The vicious infinite is not the only absurdity of the supposition. The second non-existence of the first non-existence will be equivalent to affirmation, according to the dictum 'Negation of negation is the original position.'[1] And, thus, this will be a case of self-contradiction, since the assertion of non-existence of the pen terminates in the affirmation of its existence. If, on the other hand, the non-existence of the pen be not different from the jar, the jar will have to be regarded as identical with non-existence, just as it is admitted to be identical with existence — the position advocated by the Jaina.

The aforesaid duality is repudiated by Prabhākara, the great Mīmāṁsist, who denies the reality of non-being. It is maintained by him that being is an indivisible simple characteristic of a real and non-being is only the self-same *being* as understood in reference to another real. It is 'being' all the same and all the while and non-being is only another name of it. The difference of nomenclature, however, does not presuppose a factual difference in the make-up of a real. The Jaina affirmation of being and non-being as elements in the real is thus an assumption based on the assumption of numerical difference of non-being from being, which is not a fact. But the Jaina thinks this contention to be based upon an unsound principle, which, if admitted, will lead to the abolition of many an accredited characteristic of reality. It is true that a *real* generates a positive cognition of 'being' *quâ* its self-identity as determined by its own context and the same *real* gives rise to the idea of 'non-being' in reference to another real in another context. If the difference of conditions and relations be a reason for denying the objectivity or numerical difference of the contents of cognition, we do not see how 'being' can be asserted as an objective characteristic in preference to non-being, both being equally conditioned. Moreover, such attributes as fatherhood and sonship of the same person understood in relation to different persons would also be unreal, or be the same. Again, number will be an ideal creation, or there will be no difference

1. abhāvavirahātmatvaṁ vastunaḥ pratiyogitā. NKU, Ch. III. 2.

of number as one, two, three and so on. A thing is one in its own self and thus has oneness as its determination; and the same thing together with another thing becomes two and thus comes to have the number 'two' as its determination. It cannot be thought for the reasons assigned that the attribute of number is an ideal creation or the different numbers are not really different. Being and non-being have no doubt the same substratum, but the sameness of substratum does not argue the sameness of the attributes. Nor again can it be maintained that being and non-being are identical with their substratum and hence identical with each other. In that case, the different numbers would be the same number having the same substratum and having the same relation of identity to the same substratum. Nor can the difference of 'number' or other relative attributes, as fatherhood etc., be preserved by virtue of the relation of inherence (*samavāya*), as inherence will be found to be only a name for identity-cum-difference (*tādātmya*).

There is, then, no logical justification for supposing that being and non-being are numerically identical. It ought to be accepted on the contrary that difference of relations and conditions is the cause of real difference of ontological status. The criterion of difference is the opposition of character and the proof of such difference is the difference of conditions[1] and this twofold criterion is fully applicable to the case of being and non-being. That being has a character which is the opposite of that of non-being and that the two are entailed by different conditions does not require proof, as the opponent also cannot deny them. The Jaina position that being and non-being are essential elements of the nature of a real should be taken as established. We have considered the various objections advanced by thinkers of opposite schools and it cannot be denied that the Jaina has met them with considerable force of logic. As regards the charge of contradiction involved in the compresence of being and non-being, which constitutes the main plank in the platform of the rival philosophers, the Jaina simply declines to accept the charge as authentic. We

1. sa eva hi bhedo bhedahetur vā yad viruddhadharmādhyāsaḥ kāraṇabhedaś ca—Quoted in the KP, Ch. V.

have considered the problem of contradiction in the first chapter and therein we have dealt with the four types of oppositional relation. The Jaina has made out that none of these types is applicable to the case of being and non-being, as both are perceived elements in a real. The Jaina has further made out that experience is the ultimate determinant of contradiction and the compresence of being and non-being is endorsed by experience. The Jaina has further resolved the opposition of reason and empirical knowledge. We do not think it necessary to enter into arguments that we have produced in the first chapter. We had to deal with the concept of opposition repeatedly as occasion required and we are perfectly sure that the careful reader of the present book does not stand in need of being pumped with the arguments that the Jaina advances in support of his position and in answer to the animadversions of his opponents. Suffice it to say that being and non-being are true elements of reality, which is determinate in all cases. The Jaina does not believe in indeterminate being and indeterminate non-being, which are according to him abstractions of formal logic. The opposition of indeterminate being with indeterminate non-being, on which the idealistic logician banks, has thus no force against the Jaina realist. The Jaina is an empiricist in the matter of determination of the nature of reality and it seems absolutely certain that in so far as the plain delivery of experience is taken into consideration the Jaina stands on unassailable grounds. It cannot be denied that the idealist also appeals to experience, but he subjects experience to critical analysis and examination. Uncriticised experience is suspect in idealistic philosophy. But the realist also has his own canons of criticism and he applies them to experiential data like the idealist. But there arises a fundamental difference in the results of the interpretation of experience by both the schools. It is no use making a complaint against the discrepancy of interpretation, which we must face as a necessary evil. The differences, on the contrary, should impel us to probe deeper and deeper into the problem. Differences of philosophy are not, to my mind, an unmixed evil. Criticism seems to be the very life of philosophy and it is necessary that we must stand by our convictions until we are made to see the drawbacks in our position by the criticism of the opponent.

To return to our problem, the Jaina is emphatic that the charge of contradiction against the co-presence of being and non-being in a real is a figment of *a priori* logic; and his dismissal of this fundamental accusation entails the collapse of all other charges, which are consequential upon the truth of contradiction. As regards the charge of *regressus ad infinitum,* it has been disposed of before. It will suffice to say that a real is a manifold of infinite plurality of attributes, and the infinity of attributes, which is the consequence of the charge, is true and authenticated by logic. So the charge does not invalidate the Jaina position.

We have finished our survey of the sevenfold predic ation and we have given serious thought to its implications and the criticism thereof. The dialectic of sevenfold predication is not easy to understand. It is not surprising that the doctrine has been misunderstood even in India. The critics of Jaina non-absolutism have not shown a critical grasp of this abstruse theory and their criticism has been rather shallow and superficial. It cannot be expected that the idealist logician will accept the logical theory of the Jaina realist. But the pity is that its implications were not sought to be understood even by those schools of thinkers who had much in common with the Jaina. The affinities of Jaina thought with other schools of thought are pronounced and momentous. Barring the Monists of Śaṅkara's school and the Buddhist Nihilist (*Śūnyavādin*), almost all schools of Indian philosophy, particularly those who have realistic leanings, have consciously or unconsciously followed the logic that is advocated by the Jaina. We do not propose to enter into the tangled problem of chronological priority and the consequent problem of influence of one school upon the other. It must be admitted that the systematization of Jaina philosophical thought and logic is rather a later phenomenon. We are concerned with the Masters of Jaina thought, who, as a matter of historical fact, flourished after Dignāga and Dharmakīrti. This has been a source of advantage to Jaina thought. It had the opportunity to study afresh the implications of the philosophy of non-absolutism called *anekāntavāda,* which seems to date back to a far remote past. But in spite of the chronological posteriority of the Jaina Masters, it must be admitted that the Jaina theory of sevenfold logical predication is the most original contribution of Jaina thought, which cannot be traced to the influence of other schools. In philosophy and other fields of abstract thought it is by no means the truth that the first is always the best or the most original. What we seek to emphasize is not the question of obligation this or that way, but the points of agreement among the different philosophies and their implications. It is undeniable that the Jaina siezes hold of these points of agreement and makes them proof of the inevitability of the truth of *anekānta* and not of personal or communal triumph.

The Sāṅkhya believes in one *Prakṛti,* the prius of the world of plurality, material and mental, standing in opposition to *Puruṣa*, the eternal, unchanging spirit. This *Prakṛti* is the unity of three principles, called *sattva, rajas* and *tamas*, which are mutually opposed in respect of their nature and functions. The compresence of three opposite principles in the unity of *Prakṛti* can be upheld only by the canons of non-absolutist logic as systematized by the Jaina. It is not suggested that the Sāṅkhya is indebted to Jaina thought. But the position of the Sāṅkhya is only an illustration of the validity of Jaina logic, no matter whether the Sāṅkhya is conscious of it or not. Moreover, the Sāṅkhya doctrine of the identity of substance in the midst of its changing modes is another illustration of the doctrine of identity in difference, which is another synonym of *anekāntavāda.*

The Nyāya-Vaiśeṣika school, which swears by the infallibility of the Law of Contradiction as interpreted in absolutist logic, advocates a number of universals of the second grade in contradistinction to the highest universal, 'existence'. Now these secondary universals, *e.g.*, substance-universal, quality-universal and action-universal, exercise a double function, which is mutually opposed. Substance-universal synthesizes all substances and at the same time separates them from other universals. So also the universals of the same grade. As regards the universals of lower grades, *viz.*, man-universal, cow-universal, horse-universal and the like, they also eminently discharge the opposite functions of unification and differentiation. These universals are therefore called universal-cum-particulars.

This constitutes evidence of the truth of the synthesis of opposites, which the Jaina propounds to be the universal truth.

As regards the Buddhists of Dignāga's school, who are the loudest in their protestations of the inviolability of the Law of Contradiction, they, too, are constrained to admit the validity of non-absolutism in exceptional cases. In the perceptual cognition of variegated colours in a carpet, the unity of the content *quâ* a carpet and the plurality *quâ* colours are admitted to be present together. Besides, the plurality of contents of the cognition and the unity of the cognitive act are affirmed to belong to a self-identical situation. The confession of the unity of the plurality is only an unconscious tribute to Jaina standpoint and if it is construed as corroboration of non-absolutism by the Jaina, we cannot accuse the latter of dogmatic zeal. The Sautrāntika and the Yogācāra believe in the plurality of powers of a single entity and this is an admission of the synthesis of plurality in one — which is the characteristic Jain position.

The Cārvāka materialist holds consciousness to be thepro duct of four elements, earth, air, water and fire. The product is not numerically different from the elements, as that would make it a separate principle; nor is it identical severally with each, as in that case even jars and tables would possess spirit. It is thus one and the four at the same time. This is only a confirmation of *anekāntavāda*. The affinities of Mīmāṁsist logic and ontology with the Jaina theory are too pronounced to be ignored. The Mīmāṁsist believes in the dual nature of reals, constituted by being and non-being as elements, and is thus at one with the Jaina. The later Vaiṣṇava philosophers, who believe in unity and plurality both and in their ultimate synthesis, cannot but endorse the Jaina logical standpoint. As regards the Prabhākara school of Mīmāṁsā, it also has to fall back on non-absolutist logic on occasions. One instance will suffice. According to Prabhākara all cognitions are cognisant of three elements, the content, the act of cognition (that is to say, their own identity), and the self as the knower. Accordingly all cognitions are held to be judgments by him of the form 'I know this.' The synthesis of three in one constitutes an endorsement of the Jaina logical standpoint. The purpose of this long schedule of affinities with other schools of thought is to show that the doctrine of the manifoldness of truth called *anekāntavāda*, which is proved by the application of the logical form of sevenfold predication, is not the outcome of logical aberration or abnormality of thought-proclivities, as the critics profess it to be. The logic of non-absolutism, as illustrated by sevenfold predication, seems to be the only kind of logic, that should be followed by realists. The refutation of the commonplace charges of indetermination and doubt against the theory should entitle it to serious consideration. The Jaina has succeeded in establishing that sevenfold predication is not a frivolous estimation of truth. And if I have succeeded in driving home this truth, I shall consider that I have accomplished a difficult task and fulfilled a sacred duty, which we owe to the philosophers of old, who are our own kith and kin spiritually and ethnologically.

CHAPTER VII

RELATIONS

It has been observed more than once that a relation is possible, if the terms are both identical with and different from each other. Relation cannot hold between absolutely different, or between absolutely identical facts. Identity and difference both are the presupposition of relation. Absolute identity would annul the duality of the terms and make them one self-identical entity. A self-identical entity is a unit, which is self-sufficient so far as its independent being is concerned, and as such it does not require any internal or external relation for its being. An internal relation would have been necessary, had the real actually broken up into differents. But that is *ex hypothesi* denied in the assumption of *absolute* identity. A relation is also not possible, far less necessary, between two terms, which are absolutely distinct and different. Now two reals, which are absolutely independent of each other in respect of their genesis, being and cognition, cannot be supposed to bear a relation to each other. They are unrelated and separate facts. It would be a travesty of fact, if not of logic, to think unrelatedness or separation to be itself a relation, as the logical form of predication might suggest. The logical relation of unrelatedness involved in subject-predicate form is only a conceptual relation, which is necessitated by the exigency of our thinking them together. It is the subject who thinks of the two terms and in the act of thinking superposes a relation upon them. Such a relation is ideal, conceptual or subjective. The opponent's denial of relation has reference to objective relation, and if a logician were to find a contradiction in this denial, he would be guilty of sophistry or lack of objective knowledge or perhaps both. The question — whether the totality of existents is only an ideational aggregate without objective nexus among them, or a system of reals with a connective link running through them all — is a grand problem of philosophy, which will engage our thought in the next chapter. We are here concerned with a less ambitious problem, firstly, whether there is any relation at all between reals *quâ* objective, and secondly, whether inherence as internal relation has any special claim to privileged treatment.

Now, the reality of relation has been denied by the Fluxist, the Vedāntist and by Bradley. It is a remarkable proof of the community of human thought that the arguments of Bradley were all anticipated by the Buddhist and the Vedāntist several centuries before. It has been urged that there can be no relation between two terms, which are independent. Relation presupposes that the terms are brought together. But what would bring them together ? If it be a relation, how does it supervene upon them, unless it is supposed that the terms are predisposed to be brought into a whole ? 'A' and 'B' are different and distinct, and if they are brought together by means of a relation, the relation must be supposed to induce a change in their nature, or to follow upon this change induced by an external factor. But this supposition only introduces a complication. If the relation were a *tertium quid*, it would necessitate another relation to bring this third entity into relation with the terms. Thus, the third would require the services of a fourth, and the fourth of a fifth and so on without end. But unless there is a predisposition in the terms to come to one another, it is unintelligible why a relation does not hold between anything and everything. The assumption of predisposition would again necessitate a relation between the term which develops predisposition and the condition which induces it. Not only this, the predisposition being a property of the term would require a relation, by the good offices of which it can belong to the term in question. And the same difficulty would arise with regard to this new relation and the relata.

Nor can it be supposed that relation is nothing but the absence of gap (*nairantarya*) between two terms, that is to say, the terms in relation are just close to one another and not separated by a gap in between them. But if absence of gap may be a relation, why should not separation by a gap be also a relation? However close the terms may be brought together, they cannot be supposed to abandon their separateness, unless there be a unification of the terms. But if this unification be a total merger of one in the other, no relation would be necessary, as the terms cease to be two and as relation is possible between two terms. Nor can there be a partial unification, which presupposes that the terms have parts and one of such parts is identified with another such part. But this also is no explanation, as it raises another problem. Is the part distinct from the term or not ? If it is not distinct, it is not a part, but the term itself. So the hypothesis of partial unification is irrelevant. If, again, there be real parts distinct from the terms, the unification of such distinct parts would be of no consequence to the original terms, as they would not be related on the relation of entities which are distinct. The parts again may have parts or not. On the former alternative, the question of partial or total unification would again raise itself in reference to the first set of parts and so also in reference to the second set and so on without end.[1]

Let it be supposed that relation is neither a case of unification nor mutual dependence, but something different which simply relates the terms. But the interposition of an independent relation has been found to be of no help. If the terms are left independent of each other, the introduction of relation as a *tertium quid*, equally independent, would not relate the terms. The two terms, on the latter hypothesis, would remain as they were, unaffected by the relation, which would thus be a third term resting in itself and self-sufficient. A relation which does not relate is only a word without meaning. It is concluded by the Buddhist that relation is only our way of looking at things and is not an objective entity.[2]

The charge that unreality of relation would make causal relation unreal does not affect the Buddhist, who does not believe that causality is an objective relation. The relation of cause and effect, it is asserted, is unreal, as the two do not co-exist at one time. The antecedent is called the cause and the consequent is called the effect. But this is only a conceptual characterization. It does not imply an objective relation, which is possible between

1. rūpśaleṣo hi sambandho dvitve sa ca kathaṁ bhavet ? Dharmakīrti's *Sambandhaparikṣā*, quoted in PKM, p. 503.

2. tau ca bhāvau tadanyaś ca sarve te svātmani sthitāḥ. ity amiśrāḥ svayaṁ bhāvās tān miśrayati kalpanā. ibid.

two co-existent terms. The *cause* ceases to be when the *effect* comes into being. Thus, the two terms are never synchronous and hence no relation can be posited between them. In the absence of one of the terms, causality also cannot be a real relation, but only an idea.[1] It is asserted that causal relation is sequential and not synchronous, and so the objection urged on the basis of the lack of synchronism is irrelevant. But Dharmakīrti, who does not believe in the reality of relation, which is according to him only a subjective way of evaluation, refuses to take this defence as a logically sound proof of the objectivity of causal relation. He argues, if the character of causality be really subsistent in the cause and in the effect in succession, it must be recognized that it does not depend upon the effect when it occurs in the causal antecedent, simply because the effect has not yet come into being. Similarly, causality *quâ* a characteristic of the effect is not dependent upon the cause, simply because the latter becomes defunct when the former comes into being. Thus, the character of causality, as an independent and intrinsic determination, either of the cause or of the effect, is self-contained, so far as its reference to the other correlate is concerned. Consequently, the connection between the cause and effect cannot be anything more than a subjective construction. If the relation were factual and the dependence of the effect were real, it must be shown that the cause is of real service to the effect or vice versa. But there is no possibility of service, mutual or solitary, between a non-existent and an existent fact. How could the effect be of service to the cause, when it was not even in existence and likewise how could the cause be of service to the effect, when the former has passed out of existence ? Certainly, dependence is ontologically possible only between terms which are related as benefactor and beneficiary (*upakārakopakāryabhāva*); but with regard to the cause and the effect, one of the two is always absent when the other is in existence. The relation of dependence is thus only a subjective interpretation so far as causality is concerned. A person observes the antecedent, unassociated with the consequent, and

1. kāryakāraṇabhāvo 'pi tayor asahabhāvataḥ. prasidhyati kathaṁ dviṣṭho 'dviṣṭhe sambandhatā kathaṁ ? ibid., p. 509.

the consequent, unattahed to the antecedent. But the observation of the consequent as following upon the antecedent, and the absence of observation of the consequent in the absence of the antecedent are interpreted as a relation of causality. The *observation* of concomitance in agreement and in difference is thus the only thing that can be posited as an actual truth; and the imposition of a relation between the antecedent and consequent events is only a subjective necessity of thought. The two events are not in reality related; and the conceptual relation, though it may be inevitable for our thought, is unreal and false as an estimation of objective truth. Dharmakīrti is positive that this conceptual relation occurs spontaneously in the mind of the observing subject and is not the result of a schooling received from a teacher,[1] It is worthy of remark that the Buddhist philosopher here anticipates Kant who may be regarded rather as a commentator and elaborator of the Buddhist position in this regard. It follows as a legitimate conclusion that all our judgments are false, as the relation of terms is only a subjective construction according to Dharmakīrti and Kant alike.

Dharmakīrti pursues the examination further. If, again, the relation were different from the terms, standing alongside of and aloof from them, how could the terms, *e.g.*, cause and effect, be brought together ? The impossibility of exchange of beneficiary services between the terms makes the relation a chimera and the recognition of this fact knocks out the pretensions of all other relations posited by philosophers. If things could be supposed to be related in spite of the lack of reciprocal services, there would be no logical bar to the postulation of a relation between anything and everything.[2] The reciprocity of services is thus the *conditio sinc quâ non* of objective relation, and we have seen that the condition cannot be fulfilled in causation. What is found to be true of causality is true of

1. paśyan nekam adṛṣṭasya darśane tadadarśane. apaśyat kāryam anveti vinā vyākhātṛbhir, janaḥ. darśanādarśane muktvā kāryabuddher asambhavāt. kāryādiśrutir apy atra lāghavārthaṁ niveśitā . . . . . etāvanmātratattvārtha-kāryakāraṇagocarāḥ. vikalpā darśayanty arthān mithyārthā ghaṭitān iva. ibid., p. 510.

2. tayor anupakāre 'pi samavāye paratra vā. sambandho yadi, viśvaṁ syāt samavāyi parasparam. ibid.. p. 510.

all other relations. Exchange of service may be possible between two existent terms. But what can be the nature of such service and why should it be required at all ? The service is not required by either term for achieving existence, which they already possess; nor can it be possibly required for the realization of an additional efficacy in themselves. For the efficacy, being distinct from the terms, would require a further relation in order to belong to them. And this relation might be possible, if there were again exchange of services between the efficacy and the terms. But the postulation of a second exchange of services would necessitate that of a third and so on to infinity. The truth of the matter is that relation, whatever be its character, either presupposes or involves causality, and if causality cannot be an objective relation, the reality of other relations cannot be established by logic. Take, for instance, the relations of conjunction and inherence. Conjunction may be considered as an effect of the terms The terms may be said to become conjoined by virtue of generating conjunction between themselves. But this supposition is not maintainable. If the characteristic of 'being conjoined' be a property of the generator of conjunction, it would be the property of motion (*karma*) also, which is posited as the cause of conjunction by the Vaiśeṣika. But motion cannot have the quality of being conjoined according to the Vaiśeṣika, as quality can in his theory belong only to substance. Conjunction with a part again is supposed to generate a fresh conjunction with the whole. If causality be the determinant of conjunction and of the consequential attribute of 'being conjoined', conjunction itself in such a situation should come to have the attribute in question. But this is absurd and is repudiated by the Vaiśeṣika himself.[1] Nor can conjunction or the quality of being conjoined be supposed to be a characteristic of the terms placed in a particular situation, because the supposition begs the question. What places the terms in that situation? Certainly situation is not an uncaused event. And thus the difficulties inherent in causality would crop up. As regards inherence (*samavāya*) it is also consequential to causality. The whole inheres in the parts,

1. saṁyogajanane 'pī 'ṣṭau tataḥ saṁyoginau na tau. karmādiyogitāpatteḥ sthitiś ca prativarṇitā. ibid. Cf. the comments of PKM, p. 509.

the quality or action inheres in a substance and the universal inheres in an individual. But why should they be brought together ? What ontological necessity would break the privacy of their aloofness and isolation? If there be a positive requirement on the part of the terms for one another and this requirement be supposed to be satisfied by inherence, the old problem of exchange of service would crop up again. The whole is supposed to be the product of the parts and *quâ* a product it was not in existence. It could not be either a receiver or a giver of service when it was not even in existence. Nor can causality account for the incidence of inherence for the efficient cause does not stand in the relation of inherence to its effect.[1]

And even if we grant the objective possibility of causal relation, it will have to be admitted that it will ever remain unknown and unknowable by the limited resources of mankind. Certainly, perceptual cognition is not competent to envisage such a relation. We may perceive either the antecedent, or the consequent, or both together, but all these perceptions are concerned with the terms as they are by themselves. It cannot be urged that perception of fire and smoke together in the kitchen gets hold of the causal relation between them. Fire and smoke are perceived as they are, and their togetherness is irrelevant, so far as the knowledge of causality is concerned. The pen and paper may be perceived together, but that does not warrant a causal relation between them. Nor again can the successive perception of the terms envisage the causal relation between them. One may perceive pen before and paper after, but there is no causality between them. Nor can the two successive cognitions be supposed to be synthesised by one cognition which may envisage causality, for the variation of contents of the two cognitions cannot allow them to be identified. It has been supposed that our organs, reinforced by the memory of the two cognitions, can generate a perceptual judgment having the two events for its terms, and this judgment is cognisant of causality. But this is opposed to the Law of the Uniformity of Nature, which

1. saṁyogisamavāyyādi sarvaṃ etena cintitam. anyonyānupakārāc ca na sambandhī ca tādṛśaḥ. janane 'pi hi kāryasya kenacit samavāyinā. samavāyī tadā nā 'sau no tato 'tiprasaṅgataḥ. ibid. p. 510.

presupposes that like causes produce like effects. Our organs were incapable of envisagingcausality by themselves and they could not be supposed to transcend 'this incapacity even if they were supposed to be reinforced by memory. Nor can perception of concomitance in agreement and in difference give knowledge of causality. We have seen that perception gives knowledge of the terms and not of the relation. As regards perception of concomitance in difference, it is nothing but the fact that the terms are not perceived, but only the empty locus where the terms could be perceived if they were present. So perception and non-perception together do not possess any special advantage over perceptual cognition, which has been found to yield knowledge of the terms in isolation and not in relation.[1]

Moreover, the causal relation in question is not supposed to be confined to the observed data. It is believed to hold good universally between the two classes of entities without exception and without failure. It is unthinkable that perceptual cognition, no matter whether determinate or indeterminate, may be competent to take stock of such universal relation. The aforesaid incompetency of perceptual knowledge can be entirely realised if we analyse the concept of causality. What is a cause ? It is nothing but that which possesses the power to produce an effect. So causality is nothing but power. But power is not capable of being perceived. It can be inferred from the observation of its effect. But inference of the causal power is possible only if the necessary universal relation between the power and the entity is known before. We have seen that perceptual knowledge is incompetent regarding this universal relation, and inference presupposes such knowledge as its condition. Causality is thus not capable of being known either by perception or by inference. The knowledge of causality must then be set down as a subjective construction or a way of thought. The necessity and universality felt to attend this relation cannot therefore be anything more than the necessity of our way of thinking, which has nothing to do with objective reality. And even if its objectivity be granted, it must remain *eo ipso* unknown and unknowable.[2]

1. ibid., pp. 511-12.
2. ibid., pp. 511-12.

The Jaina thinks that these objections proceed from *a priori* consideration and not from observation of the behaviour of things. It is undeniable that things are perceived to be related. A linen is perceived as related to its yarns, and colour and shape are perceived as related to the linen. That these are distinct and different is not open to denial. The whole is different from the parts and the quality is different from the substance, still they are perceived together. The given togetherness cannot be explained by any hypothesis other than that of a relation. Why should the Buddhist go out of his way to deny relation which is *given* to our sensibility, and posit lack of relation which is not *given* at all ? The Buddhist supposes that our senses are incapable of intuiting the terms and the relation between them and he explains the conception of relation as the construction of the intellect. But the supposition is based upon an assumption. The senses are but the channels through which external things present themselves to our consciousness. Our consciousness certainly does not lack the capacity of intuiting relation, even if the senses be incapable of doing so. The terms are felt to be *given* and so also is the relation holding between them. If the felt givenness of the terms be not denied, why should the givenness of the relation be impeached ? If the givenness of relation be explained away as appearance, there is no special reason for preferential treatment of the terms, which are equally given. So far as the psychology of perception is concerned, it is obvious that we do not perceive a difference between terms and relation in respect of their givenness. If there were again no substantive whole, but only a conglomeration of atoms, it would be impossible to account for difference of causal efficiency. Take for example a pitcher. The pitcher is supposed by the Buddhist to be nothing more than a collection of atoms existing side by side. The Buddhist admits that an atom does not possess the capacity for drawing water. But the pitcher has this capacity and as such cannot be supposed to be identical with the isolated atoms. If atoms alone were real, and if there were no relation amidst them and consequently no actual wholes, why should there be such a wide difference in the causal efficiency of things ? The theory of atomic constitution of material bodies is devised to account for the emergence of such bodies and not to repudiate the reality of the latter.

Let us now examine the grounds adduced by the Buddhist for the repudiation of relation one by one. The Buddhist asserts that relation is not possible between two independent entities. Relation presupposes dependence of one term upon another, but this is impossible between terms which are possessed of existence in their own right. And as regards a term or terms which are not in existence, they too cannot be supposed to depend upon one another, for dependence is a factual relation which cannot be thought to obtain between non-entities.[1] So relation is not logically justifiable and as such must be regarded as appearance. The Buddhist position has been summed up by Bradley, who independently reaches the same conclusion, in the following forceful words : 'The conclusion to which I am brought is that a relational way of thought — any one that moves by the machinery of terms and relations — must give appearance, and not truth. It is a makeshift, a device, a mere practical compromise, most necessary, but in the end most indefensible.'[2] The Jaina refuses to be convinced by such flourish of abstract logic.

The factuality of relation is attested by experience. Things in spite of their difference may transform themselves into a unity. It is a fact that things are dynamic and they maintain their identity in spite of their change, in so far at least as their nature is thought to unfold itself to our consciousness. If our intellect is not to be condemned to confusion and bankruptcy and if reality be not declared to be an unfathomable mystery, we must find an explanation. But why should we be sceptic of our knowledge ? We have elucidated the Jaina standpoint in logic in the first chapter and we need not go over the ground again. Suffice it to say that the denial of validity of experience ends in scepticism, entire and unqualified. If, however, we are to believe the testimony of our experience and if we feel called upon to give

1. pāratantryaṁ hi sambandhaḥ, siddhe kā paratantratā ? parāpekṣā hi sambandhaḥ, so 'san katham apekṣate ? saṁś ca sarvanirāśaṁso bhāvaḥ katham apekṣate ? NKC, pp. 305-06.

2. *Appearance and Reality*, p. 28.

an explanation of it, there is no possibility of denying the validity of relation. The Jaina explains relation by reference to an internal change in the terms, which makes it inevitable for them to come to a focal unity. The terms are numerically different no doubt, but when they come into relation they become changed into an identity of differents. The transformation into identity, which we have called unification, is believed to be neither complete nor partial and so the consequences alleged would not apply to them. The unification is different from both. It is neither a total merger nor partial identification. The unity of the terms in relation is *sui generis* (*jātyantara*). It is on a par with the unity of the cognition of a variegated carpet. The unity of the cognition in spite of the numerical difference of contents is an attested fact. The reality of total or partial identification is to be admitted on the basis of experience, and if experience records a case of unification of differents in which their difference is not annulled, but transformed into a different kind of identity, we have no reason to call in question its authenticity. The question would be futile if one were to ask how could the terms, existing independently of each other, come to be united ? He could as well question the truth of self-consciousness. It is as absurd as to ask why consciousness should be consciousness and not different from it. It is unanswerable. We can only assert that it is exactly what we know it to be. So with regard to relation. 'Why should there be a relation at all ?' is a question, which is equally unanswerable by logic. 'There is, however, no justification for the assumption that a relation is impossible, if it cannot inhere in something as a quality does. To the question 'in what is a relation ?' we may fairly answer that it is not in anything, but that it is between two or more terms, or between a term and itself, and that the conception of 'between' is as ultimate as the conception of 'in' and has as much claim to be regarded as valid. Both are ultimate, neither contains any contradiction, and the justification of our use of both lies in the fact that it is impossible to state anything whatever without asserting or implying the reality both of qualities and of relations.'[1]

1. *The Nature of Existence*, Vol. I, p. 82.

Relation then cannot be denied an objective status without involving consequences which we cannot acquiesce in. The problem how does relation happen to the terms can be determined by appeal to experience alone. Take for instance the case of solution of a powder in water. Here the parts of powder and the parts of water interpenetrate and we get practically an indistinguishable whole. In the case of conjunction of two fingers it is partial. The Jaina does not as a matter of fact believe in the existence of simples, which have no aspects, qualitative or quantitative. A real is the identity of an infinite plurality of aspects and modes, and we have seen how the Jaina solves the problem of incompatibility. A real is a unity and diversity in one, and the relation involved is neither one of absolute identity nor one of absolute otherness, but something different from them both. It is *sui generis,* which does not permit of being determined by absolute criteria. The parts or modes or aspects are neither different nor identical with the unity to which they belong. The relation inside the unity is also *sui generis.* The validity of such a relation cannot be called in question on the ground that it refuses to be determined in terms of identity or of otherness, because it is as ultimate and simple as identity and otherness are. If identity satisfies a logical necessity, so also should this unique relation. Each is unique and ultimate and there is no reason to condemn it as appearance when it is equally a given fact with identity or otherness. If, on the other hand, we are to rely upon the evidence of experience as the ultimate source of knowledge of the nature of reality and we feel the necessity of checking the results of discursive thought by reference to the verdict of experience, we shall be compelled to come to the conclusion that neither absolute identity nor absolute otherness has any reality beyond abstractions of thought. So far as reals are perceived and thought, they do not afford warrant for supposing identity or otherness to be veridical relations. Absolute identity is only an abstraction as ideal as Euclid's point and line are. But whereas Euclid's points and lines are useful fictions, the concepts of absolute identity and absolute otherness have been a fruitful source of confusion and acrimonious controversies which prevented philosophers from coming to an agreement where it was possible.

The assertion of infinite diversity does not make the conception of atoms impossible. An atom is *ex hypothesi* an indivisible unit. But though spatially indivisible it may be divisible in other dimensions. An atom has a plurality of aspects and thus it can be divided into these aspects. The Jaina would thus have no objection to McTaggart's view of the infinite divisibility of substance, as both are agreed upon the point that the manifold of qualities, original and derivative, that are possessed by reals, is infinite. As regards the objection of Dharmakīrti that relation cannot belong to existent or to non-existent terms, the Jaina meets him half way. The terms in relation are neither wholly finished entities nor non-entities. Relation is identity of different terms. Such being the case, the terms are neither what they were out of relation nor do they change their identity entirely when they come to be terms of a relation. Let us consider the relation of yarn and linen which we cited above. The linen is the product and yarn is the material cause of it. The linen was not in existence *quâ* linen before it came into being. But it was not an absolute non-entity as it existed as yarn. It is the yarn which becomes linen and so the two are not different in an absolute sense. The linen again abstracted from the yarn is only an idea and a fiction. So the linen as the other term of the causal relation was in existence before *quâ* yarn, though not *quâ* linen. The yarn in question was existent *quâ* yarn, but not *quâ* linen. Yarn and linen are not *quâ* substance two absolutely different entities, but they are the same substance with difference of qualities. The relation of linen and yarn is an instance of internal relation — internal in the sense that the change occurs in the causal stuff and the changed cause becomes the effect. The effect is the product of a process, which goes within the cause and so the production of the other term and that of its relation are rather simultaneous events. But so far as relation is considered as a separate fact, it must be recognized that it is not external to the terms in the sense that it can exist independently of the latter. Relation, whether internal or external, is integral to the terms and is the result of an internal change in the nature of terms. So also such external relations as conjunction of two fingers are nothing external in the sense of being independent. The fingers conjoined are no longer absolutely the same entities as they were while out of relation. The fact of being conjoined is a new attribute which they did not possess when they remained side by side in isolation. The emergence of the new quality is the result of a process of change in both the terms, which eventuated in the conjunction of both. The conjunction in question is thus the product of an internal change in the constitution of the terms and thus is as much entitled to be regarded as internal *quâ* relation as the so-called relation of inherence (*samavāya*).

The denial of relation, however, involves a self-contradiction. The Buddhist denies relation on the ground that the terms are not dependant. He assumes that dependence is the condition of relation and so the negation of dependence would entail the negation of relation. He must admit that negation of dependence is the condition of negation of relation and as such he tacitly affirms a relation between these two negations. If there were no relation between these two negative facts, he could not assert that the negation of the condition implies the negation of the conditioned. He flatly cotrandicts himself as he affirms one relation in the very act of denying another. But the Buddhist may defend himself by asserting that his denial of relation has reference to objective relation and the implicit assertion of relation involved in the denial of objective relation is only a subjective necessity of thought. We have alluded to this view just at the outset of this chapter. The Buddhist's contention draws its plausibility from an assumption which has had momentous consequences in philosophical thought. It is assumed that our thoughts do not necessarily represent reality. But is reality unknown and unknowable absolutely and without reservation ? If relation be an unreal figment of logical thought, no judgment can be true and no assertion can be made, as they presuppose relation between terms. Thus philosophy as a quest of truth by the pursuit of logical thought has to be condemned as a wild goose chase. But such scepticism and cynicism have not succeeded in the past in stifling the spirit of enquiry in thoughtful men and women. And the sceptic, who denies the validity of all judgments, succeeds in his task by means of a judgment of his own. The plea that his judgment has an ideal validity as contradistinguished from objective validity only aggravates the evil. "Our intellect, then, has been condemned to confusion and bankruptcy, and the reality has been left outside uncomprehended. Or rather, what is worse, it has been stripped bare of all distinction and quality. It is left naked and without a character, and we are covered with confusion".[1] We have already given an answer to the Buddhist's objection. It will only suffice to remark that wholesale condemnation of thought contradicts itself. That men fall into error and make false judgments is a truism. But because some judgments are false, that is certainly no ground for assuming that all judgments are false. The falsity of a judgment is determined by reference to a true judgment. If there be no *truth and if knowledge of truth were* absolutely unattainable, all our judgments would have the same value, *viz.*, they would be all false. But then there would be no criterion of falsity. When the Buddhist convicts judgmental thought of falsity, he certainly has an idea of what truth is. The Buddhist's plea that truth is revealed to unbroken indeterminate intuition does not improve the situation. An intuition, uninterpreted as intuition of a fact, is neither true nor false and as such cannot be the source of knowledge of reality. The Buddhist logician thus contradicts himself and he is compelled to confess the bankruptcy of our intellect. The criterion of falsity must be found in contradiction. And if a judgment is not contradicted by another judgment, it must be accepted to be true. The contradiction conjured up by abstract logic is only a perversion of logical thought and cannot be accepted as authentic appraisement of truth. We have discussed the implications of the Buddhist denial of conceptual thought as the vehicle of truth and we trust that the reader, who has carefully followed our arguments there, will not stand in need of further elaboration of the absurdities inherent in the Buddhist's position.[2]

The Jaina conception of relation may be summed up as follows. Relations are objective verities which are as much given to intuition and to thought as the terms are. A relation has no objective status outside the terms. It is the result of an internal change in the nature of the terms. It is *sui generis* in that it cannot be placed under the head of identity or of difference,

1. *Appearance and Reality*, p. 29.
2. *Supra*, Chapter IV.

both of which are contained as traits in its being. We have shown in Chapter V that the nature of reality is not entirely comprehensible by logical thought or expressible by language, but can be realized in all its uniqueness by intuition. Relation also shares this unique character which cannot be exhausted by the categories of thought, though they give a correct representation of reality so far as they go. The denial of relation is self-contradictory since the denial is possible by virtue of relational thought. The Buddhist plea that conceptual thought has only a subjective validity and relation is only an ideal fiction has been examined and found to be untenable as it leads to unqualified scepticism.

We now address ourselves to the examination of causal relation and we shall find substantial reasons for rejecting the Buddhist protestations about the unreality of causality. The Buddhist bases his denial of causality on the absence of synchronism of cause and effect. But neither synchronism nor succession is believed by the Jaina to be the essential characteristic of causal relation. Causality is a relation of determination. The effect is that whose coming into being is necessarily determined by the being of another. The determinant is called the cause and the determinatum is called the effect. The determinant may be synchronous with the determined or may be separated by an interval. If we take the case of clay and jar, the clay is found to continue and to synchronise with the jar. But the effect is seen to follow the cause in other cases, *e.g.*, death follows beheading. The essential character of causality is found in the necessity of determination. When the being of a fact determines the being of another fact they are held to be causally related. If we look deeper into the matter it will be found that causality as a sequential relation holds between two qualities or modes (*paryāya*). We call the earthy matter the cause of the jar. But strictly speaking it is the occurrence of a change in the causal substance which determines the occurrence of a particular shape, which distinguishes the jar from the earthy matter which was bereft of it. The Jaina believes in the timeless continuity of substance which is according to him not an event in time. Whether it is atoms or bodies that are the original substance makes little difference. The continuity of the substance in all its modifications is a fact which is emphasised by the Jaina. But if the change of qualities, original and derivative, be felt to give rise to different substances out of the original substance, there need not be any difficulty in connecting these occurrences as cause and effect.

It is true that time plays an important part in the relation of cause and effect. Between two terms the prior term is called the cause and the cause cannot be subsequent to the effect. In cases in which the terms are timeless or simultaneous neither can be called the cause, unless they appeared to be in time. It is to be admitted, then, that causality is a relation of determination as distinguished from extrinsic determination which holds between each fact and every other fact. Secondly, it is a relation which holds between existent facts: Thirdly, the earlier term is called the cause and the later the effect. It is perhaps more than a question of nomenclature. The earlier is followed by the later and the necessity of sequence seems to be an index to an inner necessity. It is not admitted that the cause exercises an activity upon the effect and thus does a good office to the effect. Causality is nothing more than this necessity of sequence. The question of dependence is irrelevant, if it is supposed to mean an occult influence exercised by one upon the other. The necessity and universality of the sequence of the effect to the cause are undeniable features of the law of causation, and if they cannot be made more intelligible by other laws, the law of causation should be regarded as an ultimate truth. In causation the two terms are related by sequence; and if a further intrinsic determination of the relation is demanded the Jaina supplies it by pointing out that the terms stand to each other in the relation of identity-in-difference. The effect is a modification of the cause and thus is not absolutely different from the cause or identical with it. *Quâ* substance the two are the same identity, but *quâ* qualities or modes they are numerically different. The Jaina view of causation differs from the traditional theories. It differs from the Sāṅkhya theory which holds cause and effect to be identical. The statement of the Sāṅkhya cannot be taken literally, as that annuls the duality of the terms. The effect is the result of a change in the cause or rather it itself represents the change in question.

Causation is a species of relation and as such it participates in the essential characteristic of relation. Relation in the ultimate analysis is found to be a case of identity-cum-difference between the terms, and this holds of the cause and effect also. But though identity-cum-difference is the universal character of all relations the specific differences of relations are not obliterated and there is no incompatibility between the general and the specific character. If, however, we probe the problem more carefully and deeply, it will be found that causality is the ultimate source of all other relations. As we have observed before, a relation is integral to the terms and is ontologically nothing but the occurrence of a change in the terms, which are so related. It is the product of a process which takes place inside the terms. Thus relations as external independent facts are only falsely hypostatized concepts. Two important results come out of this enquiry into the nature of relations. Firstly, relations are all internal having no ontological status beyond the terms. Secondly, they are the products of a change which occurs in the terms. The second characteristic proves that causality is the ultimate foundation of other relations, since they are the products of change and change presupposes causality, which is again reducible to identity-in-difference; and the latter is the foundational nature of all reals and their relations. But what is the occasion of change ? Certainly something more is needed to occasion a change in a real. According to the Jaina change is integral to the real. The stimulus of change is seated in the nature of the real. As regards the particular direction and the shape of the activity it may be determined by an external fact. But an external act being related to the fact under consideration is not entirely external, as it becomes identical with it, though it preserves its individuality. Being and change are necessary concomitants of reality and one is as ultimate as the other. So the question 'why there should be change at all' ? is unanswerable, being ultimate and simple.

We have now to dispose of the difficulty about the cognition of relation and particularly of the relation of cause and effect, which the Buddhist alleged to be unrealizable. The Jaina does not think the difficulty to be real. The Buddhist here is led away by *a priori* considerations in disregard of the evidence of psychology. Causality is perceived and the act of perception is one. The Jaina believes in the identity of the self which is inclusive of its changes. The self may perceive the cause first and the effect next. But it is the same self who perceives the two events. The self that perceives the subsequent event has not let the first perception go adrift. The perceptions are events in the history of the self and as such they occur as real changes in the self. The perception of the prior term spells a change and so also does the perception of the posterior term. But the change represented by the first perception is not lost hold of by the self when he perceives the subsequent event. So there is no difficulty that the self can perceive the two in succession and also as together. Of course, the Buddhiṣt may assert that it is only a hypothesis of the Jaina. But the hypothesis explains a real fact. It is undeniable that we connect the two events — earlier and later — as cause and effect. The Buddhist does not deny that this act of connecting is a fact. What he denies is that the accredited instruments of knowledge, perception or inference, are competent to apprehend this relation. He concludes that the knowledge of causality is an ideal judgment having no bearing upon the objective reality. But the Jaina thinks this to be a hasty conclusion, which is not only unwarranted but has also been a source of far-reaching mischief. It condemns all thought and all philosophical speculations. The difficulty of the Buddhist as well as of idealists in general lies in the supposition of incompatibility of change with identity. But this is the fundamental datum of Jaina thought and we have taken considerable pains to elucidate the Jaina position in the preceding chapters.

What is the organ of the knowledge of causality ? The Jaina answers that it is perception of the concomitance in agreement and difference. The Jaina position is found to be endorsed by J. S. Mill who recognizes the Joint Method as a distinct and different organ, severally from the Method of Agreement and the Method of Difference. The Jaina takes the observation of concomitance in agreement and in difference to be one observation. And as regards the universality and the necessity of causal relation, the Jaina posits another instrument which he calls *tarka*, which we may tentatively render as 'reasoning' which assumes the form of a *reductio ad absurdum*. It is by the aid of reasoning that we persuade ourselves that the occurrence of an event is impossible without the previous occurrence of another event. Armed with this knowledge of the impossibility of the independent occurrence of the subsequent event the self intuits the causal relation to be universal and necessary. Of course the development of the power of reasoning presupposes growth and advance of knowledge. There is nothing strange about the fact that the savage, who does not know the use of fire, fails to take note of the causality between fire and smoke. The Jaina posits a twofold cause for the perception of universal relation — an internal and an external condition. The internal condition is found in the developed state of our mind and the external condition is the repeated observation of the sequence of the two events. That the savage fails to intuit the causal relation between fire and smoke is due to his lack of this internal condition.[1] The Jaina here anticipates Kant and also differs from him, as he differs from the Buddhist. He admits that for the knowledge of causality the mind co-operates with our senses, and the cotribution of each of them is necessary. Let me quote what I have said at the very outset of this book. "Such concepts, as causality, substance, attribute and the like, are no doubt the ways in which the mind works up the data of experience, but this does not mean with the Jaina that they are true of the mind only and not of the extra-mental reality which they purport to understand. The Jaina would take them to be the instruments of discovery of the nature of reality, internal and external, which render the same kind of service as the sense-organs do".[2]

The opponent would ask, 'Why are smoke and fire not perceived as effect and cause', though according to the Jaina the character of being effect and the character of being cause are as integral to them as the character of being smoke or of being fire ? Fire is perceived as fire, that is to say, as possessed of the characteristics which determine its being. But it is not perceived

1. nanu nālikeradvīpādivāsinām akasmād dhūmasyā 'gner vo 'palambhe pi kāryakāraṇabhāvasyā 'niścayān nā 'sau vāstavaḥ, tad apy apeśalam bāhyāntaḥkāraṇaprabhavatvāt tanniścayasya kṣayopaśamaviśeṣo hi tasyā 'ntaḥkaraṇam, tadbhāvabhāvitvābhyāsas tu bāhyam. PKM, p. 518.

2. Chapter I, p. 1.

as cause until the concomitance of fire with smoke is observed. The Buddhist would conclude from this fact that the character of causality is only an ideal construction which is attributed to fire by uncritical thought. But the Jaina does not agree that the conclusion really follows from the premise. The nature of a real is constituted by an infinite number of attributes, which it is not given to us to know all at once and in one sweep. The fluxist believes that reals are momentary. This knowledge is reached at the end of an elaborate course of ratiocination, but the Buddhist would not, for the matter of that, accept the proposition that the fluxional character of reals is not true. There are attributes which are apprehended in an easy and simple fashion. But this is not true of all the attributes and even of the most important attributes. That 'material bodies gravitate' is a proposition which is the result of an elaborate process of thought. The Jaina would not again agree with those psychologists who think that the association of such subtle attributes, which are discovered by speculative reason, with the objects of experience is only an act of transference. The attributes are either real or attributed falsely to things. But if there is no proof of their falsity we must take them to be real characteristics of real things. As our knowledge advances our faculties of perception go on acquiring special refinement and proficiency. So what is unpresented to an untrained and uncultured person does present itself to a man of culture and knowledge. A thirsty man sees water and at once drinks it. He knows that water possesses the power of quenching thirst and he perceives it along with his perception of water. After all, it is not the physical organs that are the instruments of perception. The organs are but the channels or media through which the soul works upon the data. The percipient is ultimately the self, whose store of knowledge is constantly growing and with the growth of knowledge his powers of perception are being constantly improved and enriched. There is no logical necessity for supposing that the knowledge of attributes, which is reached by a laborious course of speculation, must be mental and subjective. To the question whether the attribute of causality is different from or identical with the entity the Jaina would give the characteristic answer. It is different and at the same time identical. Indentity-in-difference is the way of all relations and there is no reason for departure from this universal principle in the case of causality being the attribute of an entity.

(II)

We have finished our enquiry into the reality of relations and it is time to address ourselves to the problem of inherence (*samavāya*) which we promised to discuss in the beginning of this chapter. Although there is no specific necessity for dwelling on inherence as our findings recorded above will apply to it in full, we yet feel called upon to give a special consideration to inherence, since it has been postulated by the Vaiśeṣika philosopher to reconcile the discrepancy and antagonism of opposite entities. Substance and quality and action, universal and particular, are believed to be mutually opposed and irreconcilable by their very nature. But still they are held together in a unity by inherence in spite of the fact that they do not transcend their oppositional character even in the act of being forced into a unity. The Vaiśeṣika believes in the difference of reals and their mutual opposition. He holds identity and difference to be absolutely opposed to each other and asserts that relation by inherence effects a combination of the two in one entity without introducing difference into its constitution as an essential trait. The Vaiśeṣika theory of inherence is thus the antithesis of the Jaina position that the nature of things is composed of opposite characteristics. The Vaiśeṣika believes identity to be exclusive of difference and existence to be incompatible with non-existence. In other words, he retains his faith in the absolute validity of the Laws of Thought as propounded by pure logic and still seeks to reconcile the antagonism of opposites by means of inherence — which in his judgment is the universal solvent of all problems. If inherence can achieve all this, the Jaina metaphysics must be given wide berth. The importance of the problem is thus paramount and the Jaina must meet the challenge of the Vaiśeṣika. With these prefatory remarks we now propose to examine the Vaiśeṣika position as developed by the exponents of the school and we shall consider the Jaina's reflections upon it at the end.

The Vaiśeṣika maintains that inherence, in the first place, is a *relation* which is one in all such cases and the difference of terms does not affect the unity of inherence. In the second place, the notion of 'A is in B' demands an objective relation. In the third place, the terms are related as content and container (*ādhāryādheyabhūta*). In the fourth place, the terms so related are found to be inseparable (*ayutasiddha*). When these conditions are found to be present, the postulation of a relation is nccessary, and as the relation in question differs in fundamental respects from other types of relation, it must be distinct and different from them. The functional and numerical difference of the relation requires a separate name and so it is called inherence (*samavāya*). It is obvious that it is not a case of nomenclature, pure and simple. The notion of A is in B (*ihedampratyayahetu*) does not give insight into the character of inherence in full. A man perceives a park and a village together from a distance, though the two are separated and there is a gap between them as a matter of fact. In such a situation the trees are perceived to be situated in the village. The notion of the trees as existing in the village does not justify the supposition of a relation as it is due to the failure of observation of the actual gap between them. But inherence cannot thus be accounted for, as it is a real relation, not due to non-observation of gap. It is, therefore, necessary that it should be clearly stated as being a relation. The first part of the first condition and the second condition are thus logically justified, and as regards the unity of the relation it will be justified later. The third condition is necessary to exclude such cases as 'The bird is in the sky'. There is a relation, *viz.*, conjunction, between the bird and the sky, but it is not inherence, as it is not a relation of container and content. The sky is nothing but space and the bird is not only upon space, but space is also upon the former. The relation is not thus one of container and content, as it is not a relation of up and down. The container is always below the content and the latter is always *up* on the former. The three conditions are satisfied by the case of a fruit in a basket, but it is a case of conjunction (*saṁyoga*) and not inherence (*samavāya*). To exclude such a case the fourth condition is laid down as an essential characteristic of inherence. The fruits and the basket are not inseparable. 'To be separable' means that the terms may exist in different loci and may remain out of relation. But this is never found to be the case so far as the relation of whole and parts (*avayavāvayavin*), quality and substance (*guṇa-dravya*), motion and moving (*kriyākriyāvat*), universal and particular (*jātijātimat*) is concerned. The whole exists only in the parts and never outside, and such is the case with quality, motion and universal.

The relation of container and content and inseparability are both to be understood in a determinate and necessitarian reference. Thus, the following instances are not included within the scope of inherence. The word 'ether' (*ākāśa*) denotes 'ether' as an objective fact and as words are the qualities of ether (according to Vaiśeṣika), the word 'ether' is also a content of ether. Though word and ether are thus related as content and container, the relation holds good only because word happens to be a quality of ether and not that it denotes ether. The denotative relation holds also between a word and a thing which are not related as content and container, *e.g.*, bewteen the word 'chair' and the thing denoted by it. So the relation of denotation (*vācyavācakabhāva*) is not a case of inherence, as these terms are not as a matter of necessity related as container and content, nor are they inseparable. This consideration also suffices to exclude the cognitive relation, which holds between a cognition and its object. Now cognition and the like are the qualities of the self (*ātman*) and as such inhere in the latter The cognition of the self has the latter for its object also. Thus cognition is related to the self both by inherence and cognitive relation. But though cognition and the self are related both ways, the relation of cognition is not inherence, as it is found to hold in the case of things which are not inseparable, *e.g.*, the cognition of a chair. It then turns out that the terms in inherence must be universally and necessarily related as container and content and as inseparable. As the two conditions are not satisfied by the relation of denotation and of cognition universally and necessarily, the latter are excluded from the scope of inherence. It should not be thought that either of these conditions will be adequate and the two together are not necessary. The relation of container and content holds between a house and furniture. The furniture is always the content of the house and never the container. The relation is one of conjunction and it holds between the two universally and necessarily, that is to say, the relation of container and content is never reversed between them. So the condition of inseparability is essential to inherence, and as this condition does not hold in the case cited above, the relation is not inherence. Nor again can it be supposed that inseparability alone will suffice to distinguish inherence from other relations. Of course the cases considered above will be excluded by this condition alone, but it fails in the case of the compresence of several qualities in a substance. For instance, sugar is hard, white and sweet. The qualities in question coinhere in sugar and are inseparable from sugar and from one another. The relation of these qualities to sugar is certainly inherence, as sugar contains them as its contents and also because the latter are inseparable from sugar. But the relation between the qualities is not regarded as inherence, though they happen to be inseparable. The relation of inseparability between the qualities is due to their inherence in sugar from which they are not separable and thus their mutual inseparability is derived from the former. It inseparability were the sufficient condition of inherence there would be nothing to prevent the relation between the qualities being regarded as inherence. The relation is not inherence, but co-inherence (*ekārthasamavāya*), because the relation of container and content is found to be absent between the qualities themselves. The concept of inherence is thus found to be a complex one. It is a relation between terms, which are inseparable and which stand as container and content. That it does not hold between entities unrelated as container and content, *e.g.*, time and space, follows as a corollary.

What is the proof of inherence ? What is the source of its knowledge? These are the questions which naturally arise and require an answer. According to the Naiyāyika inherence is an object of perception. 'A' directly perceives a piece of linen as related to the yarns constituting it. Here inherence is between a whole and its parts. With equal immediacy again we intuit a substance and its sensible qualities as related to one another and so also do we intuit a cow and the cow-universal in it as related. As the relation is not anything else than inherence, the intuition of the relation is to be equated with the intuition of inherence. The Vaiśeṣika does not agree with the Naiyāyika in this matter. Inherence is a matter of inference according to the former. The Vaiśeṣika contends with great force of logic that the perception of a relation depends upon the perception of the terms. If the terms are perceivable the relation is perceived. But inherence holds also between terms which are not perceivable. For instance, the mental states of another self inhere in the latter, but as they are not perceivable the relation cannot be perceived. It cannot be contended that inherence may be perceivable and not perceivable according to the nature of the terms just like conjunction. Conjunction of the table and the pen is admitted on all hands to be a perceivable fact, but that between two atoms is not. Does not the same rule hold in the case of inherence also ? The Vaiśeṣka maintains this to be impossible. The analogy of conjunction is irrelevant, as conjunction is not numerically one but as many as the terms are. But inherence is numerically identical in all its incidences, and the difference of terms does not introduce qualitative or numerical difference into its nature. Barring this difference there is perfect agreement between the two schools about the factuality and necessity of inherence. The Naiyāyika does not disown the possibility of inference being the organon of inherence. The inference of inherence may be syllogistically set forth as follows. "All valid judgments of one term being content of another term are conditioned by relation. The knowledge of linen being the content of yarns is such a judgment. ∴The judgment in question is conditioned by a relation".

It cannot be urged that the judgment in question is unconditioned, or that it is conditioned by the terms and not by a relation. If it could be conditioned by either or both of the terms, the judgment would be either 'Here are yarns' or "The yarns are linen' and not 'The linen is in yarns'. Nor can the relation be conjunction of the yarns and the linen, as the latter is possible only between two-independently existing substances — which is not the case here. Nor can the relation be one of identity, as identity is incompatible with the duality of the terms. There can be no *two* identical terms except by way of metaphor. So by the method of elimination the relation inferred is known to be inherence. Inference is competent only to prove the existence of a relation, which is different from the other recognized types of relation. And this is sufficient for the purpose in hand and the appellation of 'inherence' is a question of nomenclature.

We have alluded more than once to the oneness of inherence in all its incidences. But why should it be one and why should it not vary with the terms as does conjunction on your hypothesis ? The Vaiśeṣika answers as follows. Inherence is on a par with being. Being is one in all existents. Though the number of existents is infinite, nobody thinks their being to be different numerically or qualitatively. The reason for the belief in a self-identical being is that it is perceived to be the same and that no difference is felt in any regard. On the contrary, if being were to differ in each case, the plurality of things would not be referred to by the same concept and the same expression, *viz*., being. A plurality of beings, on the other hand, would make the postulation of a higher universal necessary. But as this higher universal would itself be a being, that would only add to the number of beings and would itself remain unsynthesized with the rest of beings. But the synthesis of the different types of being is necessary for logical thought, as they are all referred to by the concept 'being'. The result of the attempted synthesis would be a *regressus ad infinitum* as a higher and a higher being were to be postulated. The same considerations apply to the case of inherence. Inherence is felt to be the same in all its incidences and though the terms vary from case to case the notion of inherence is not felt to be different. The concept of 'in-ness' is everywhere the same, be it a case of inherence of the whole *in* the parts, or that of a quality *in* a substance, or of a universal *in* a particular. Nor can the character of its being a relation be regarded as the ground of its diversity, since there is no necessary connection between relation and diversity.[1] That it is a relation is the proof of its difference from other types of existents, *e.g.*, substance, quality and so on, and not of its difference from other types of inherence. The analogy of the plurality of conjunctions does not apply to inherence. The numerical difference of conjunctions is not proved by the fact of their being relations. Conjunction is perceived in succession in the terms and that constitutes its numerical difference. That in spite of their numerical difference they are referred to by the same

1. na cā 'sya saṁyogavan nānātvam, iheti—pratyayāviśeṣāt, viśeṣa-liṅgābhāvāc ca . . . na ca sambandhatvam eva viśeṣaliṅgam asyā 'nyathā-siddhatvāt. NKC, p. 296.

concept is due to the presence of a self-identical universal conjunctionhood, in all of them. But inherence stands in a different position altogether. If inherence were to be many, this would necessitate the postulation of inherence-universal (*samavāyatva*) in order to account for the identity of conception, as is found to be the case with the individuals belonging to a class. But this hypothesis of one inherence-universal is fraught with grave difficulties on the score of its relation to the individual inherences. The relation of the universal to the particulars is always inherence. And if the inherence-universal were to be related by inherence to its individual members that would make *a regressus ad infinitum* inevitable. The second inherence connecting the inherence-universal with the individual inherences would itself require a third inherence to connect itself with the universal inherence of which it would be an individual instance. But the same fate awaits the third. Thus an infinite regress makes the hypothesis of a plurality of inherences impossible. But the difficulty does not arise in the case of conjunction, which, being an adjective of the terms, is felt to be different with different terms. So the postulation of a conjunction-universal is called for. And there is no difficulty about the relation of conjunction-universal with the individual conjunctions, as inherence will answer the requirement in the case. Inherence is thus on the same footing with the universals. It is one and the same in all its incidence just as the universal is the same in all the members of a class. Nor can it be called a universal, as the condition of plurality of individuals in which a universal inheres is impossible of fulfilment in the case of inherence.[1]

A number of difficulties has been raised as side-issues regarding inherence by the opponents, which the Vaiśeṣika feels no difficulty in meeting with convincing arguments. In the first place, it is urged that inherence cannot be a relation either between existents or between non-existents. The latter alternative is impossible as there can be no relation between non-existent terms. In the former alternative the relation would transpire to be conjunction. The supposition that it holds between an existent and a hitherto non-existent term is equally

1. Vide PKM and NKC. pp. 204-208, 294-296.

doomed, as relation is possible and necessary between existents alone. In the second place, inherence being a *tertium quid* must be related to the terms, otherwise it cannot be asserted as a relation of those terms. If, on the other hand, it be supposed to be related to the terms, it must be related either by itself or by the good offices of a second relation. The first alternative is not tenable, as self-relatedness is tantamount to unrelatedness. Moreover, if inherence can be related by its own self independently of the aid of another relation, the terms can with equal propriety be supposed to be related to each other by themselves. In that case there would be no logical necessity of positing a relation at all. Besides, if a relation *quâ* relation were self-sufficient for relating the terms and also for relating itself to the terms, why does the Vaiśeṣika make conjunction (*saṃyoga*), which is admittedly a relation, dependent upon another relation, *viz.*, inherence, to make it related to the terms ? This shows that relation as such is not capable of relating itself to the terms without the good offices of another relation. And if a second relation were posited to force the terms and the relation concerned into the framework of a relation, the second relation being equally unrelated would require a third relation and the third again would require a fourth and so on to infinity. In the third place, there is absolutely no logical or ontological necessity for positing a relation at all so far as the terms of the supposed inherence are concerned. Qualities are supposed to subsist in the substance by inherence. But no relation is necessary as quality, action or universals are not gravitating bodies, which would fall apart if a relation were not there to arrest their centrifugal activity.

The Vaiśeṣika regards these objections as frivolous and unfair. The dilemma raised in the first objection is a figment. The relation of inherence does not presuppose pre-existent terms, as the terms come into existence only by means of inherence. That a term comes into existence means that it inheres in its material cause or that existence comes to inhere in the effect. So existence implies inherence as its necessary concomitant, even though inherence be not identical with existence. The existence and the inherence take place at one and the same time.[1] So the difficulty does not arise as none of the premises is believed to be true. The second objection is based upon abstract considerations. Inherence is self-related to the terms. It is not, however, admitted that inherence is self-related *quâ* relation, but *quâ* inherence. If it were to stand in need of another relation in order to be related to the terms, that relation, again, could be inherence and nothing else. But it is not found in experience that a relation is related by means of a second relation which is of the same kind. The analogy of conjunction is irrelevant, as it is both a relation and a quality, and it is only in the latter capacity that it requires a relation. But the relation required by conjunction is inherence, which is not of the same kind with conjunction. So the analogy between conjunction and inherence is flimsy and superficial. Analogical arguments are very seldom safe, because analogy, if not based upon a fundamental community of nature, is no index to the uniformity of behaviour of things. The unreliability of analogical arguments is further attested by the third objection. It is true that gravitating objects require a relation to be held together. But the converse of the proposition that relation requires gravitating objects is not true. The point at issue can be made clear by a question. Are qualities perceived to be different from the substances or not ? The difference of quality from substance cannot be denied without condemning experience. And as difference implies distinction, there must be a relation to hold, the differents together. This relation is called inherence. If the opponent proposes to give a different name to the relation, the Vaiśeṣika would not quarrel with him over the question of nomenclature. What he is interested to prove is the reality of inherence distinct and different from the terms, and if this is conceded the quarrel comes to an end.

The Jaina does not agree with the Vaiśeṣika that inherence is an independent entity which connects terms absolutely different and distinct from each other. The specific characteristic of inherence is supposed to be unfolded in the inseparability

1. svakāraṇasattāsambandhasy aiva niṣpattitvāt. na hi niṣpattir ar.,ā samavāyaś cā 'nayḥ, yena paurvāparyaṁ syāt. NKC, p. 297. Cf. the dictum of Uddyotakara, jātaś ca sambaddhaś ce ty ekaḥ kālaḥ.

(*ayutasiddhi*) of the terms so related. But the concept of inseparability is not capable of being justified. If the meaning of the concept be supposed to be co-existence in the same substratum, that is certainly not a fact, if we are to believe in the Vaiśeṣika technique. The whole exists in the parts and the parts exist in a different substratum. Qualities exist in a substance, which, in its turn, exists in a different locus. So co-existence in the same substratum cannot be the meaning of the term 'inseparability'. Again if we are to follow the plain testimony of experience, milk and water mixed together exist in the same vessel. But the Vaiśeṣika does not posit inherence as their relation. Moreover, the concept of inseparability, being the negative counterpart of separability (*yutasiddhi*), derives its significance from the latter by contrast. And if existence in different substrata be the criterion of separability, and if its negation be the meaning of the opposite concept (inseparability), then time, space, selves (*ātman*), being ubiquitous and eternal, would be related by way of inherence. These substances are according to the Vaiśeṣika, simple uncaused entities and as such they cannot exist in parts or in any locus. They are self-existent, and besides, being ubiquitous, they are not separable from one another. But they are not supposed to stand in the relation of inherence, the terms of which have been specified as part and whole, quality and substance, universal and particular and so on.

It may be contended that inseparability connotes the absence of separate status. But separation in status is an ambiguous expression. It may mean separate perception or separate origination or separate existence. But the universal has a distinctive nature from that of the individual and as such they are known separately and as separate entities. As for separate origination, this does not hold good of universals, which are *ex hypothesi* eternal and uncaused entities. Besides, substance is held to be the cause of its qualities and as such the former must have its existence prior to that of the latter. So absence of separate origination cannot be maintained as the criterion of inherence. The third possibility is equally untenable as space, time, and the like have no separate existence from one another but nobody posits the relation of inherence between them. Let it again be supposed that inseparability means co-existence in the same time, or in the same space or location. But neither is tenable. The parts and wholes being causally related cannot be necessarily co-existent in time; and as regards location, the whole is held to exist in the parts and the parts exist elsewhere. Let it again be supposed to mean co-subsistence in the same substance, or co-production from the same cause or non-difference of nature. But the first alternative is out of the question, as wholes subsist in parts and the latter subsist in a different substance, *viz.*, their respective parts. The second is equally untenable, as the parts are prior to the whole, the latter being the effect of the former. If the terms of inherence be non-different in nature, this is intelligible in either of the two ways. The terms may be supposed to be identical in being and individuality, or to be produced together as inseparable members of a whole. The former supposition would reduce the two to one identity and thus relation would become unnecessary. The second alternative represents the Jaina view. Substance and quality emerge together. Substance changes into qualities and as such the latter have no independent being outside the former. They are different and identical both. So if inherence meant difference-in-identity, the Jaina would have no objection to the same. Inherence being a case of relation, it cannot be anything absolutely different from the terms. If the terms were absolutely different and distinct, there could be no positive relation between them and if they were identical, there would be no necessity for a relation at all. It must be admitted that the terms of supposed inherence, *e.g.*, parts and whole, substance and quality etc., are both identical and different, as they are felt together as inseparable from each other.

Moreover, there is no proof of inherence being a relation. The Vaiśeṣika infers the existence of inherence from the notion of *in-ness* (*ādhārādheyabhāva*), of one thing being the content of another. But so far as whole and part, substance and quality, the universal and the particular are concerned, it cannot be maintained that they give rise to the notion of in-ness. If we are not to twist the plain meaning of our experience, we cannot be said to conceive of the whole being in the parts as a content, or of the quality being in the substance. They are felt together as one entity. And if commonsense interpretation be followed, it points rather in the opposite direction. People think that the branches are *of* the tree and *in* the tree, the yarns are *in* the cloth and so on. The Jaina does not believe in a separate relation between parts and whole. The whole is according to him nothing but the parts arranged in a particular manner. The arrangement implies a change in the original substances, but the change is from separateness to unification. The change, however, is qualitative and functional and does not connote numerical difference, which might necessitate a relation. If the conception of relation be necessary from the point of view of discursive thought it should be termed 'identity-in-difference'. In fact, relations are nothing outside the terms themselves, and as such, they are all internal and integral to the terms. As regards the notion of one containing the other, we have seen how it varies with the variation of our angle of vision. The Vaiśeṣika would make the whole a content of the parts, and others would think the parts to be the contents of the whole. Truly speaking, the notion of in-ness does not presuppose a relation at all. It is only a way of our thought or of linguistic expression, which has no objective implication. 'Sugar is white' is a proposition, which can be stated in a different form *e.g.*, 'whiteness is *in* sugar'. The notion of in-ness here does not indicate the relation of container and content. Pre-non-existence is held to be beginningless and so beginninglessness may be supposed to be *in* pre-non-existence. Even the Vaiśeṣika does not suppose that the notion of in-ness has here an independent reference to an objective content or a relation. It may be urged that the relation is one of substantive and adjective, or subject and predicate. But the latter is not an independent relation; rather it is only symptomatic of an objective relation, which is, however, incapable of being posited between the terms under consideration. The conclusion is irresistible that the notion of in-ness or linguistic usage based on such notion is only the conventional way of expressing the fact of identity of the two terms. As it is the universal truth, identity is always to be understood as identity of differents—in other words, as identity-in-difference.

We have sought to prove that relation has no status outside the terms. It is the terms themselves which play the part of relation. In fact, this conclusion has been endorsed by the later exponents of Nyāya, who reduce all relations ultimately to the specific nature of the terms designating them as terms *quâ* relations (*svarūpasambandha*).

As regards the contention that inherence is one and consequently eternal, it too cannot stand scrutiny. Being a relation it is not intelligible without reference to the terms. And as the terms vary, the relation cannot be uniformly identical. That it is so is proved by the case of conjunction, which is also a relation The conjunction of the pen and the table and the conjunction of the table and the floor are certainly not identical. By parity of reasoning the inherence of sweetness in sugar and that of whiteness in the latter cannot be the self-identical relation. The numerical difference of inherence will be manifest from the consideration that inherence is supposed by the Vaiśeṣika to be subsistent in the terms. Subsistence implies that it is a content, and such being the case it is unthinkable that the content will not vary with the terms containing it.[1] The unity of inherence is thus seen to be an unjustifiable assumption. And eternity being only a consequence of the unity, it should be equally regarded as an unfounded assumption. Inherence has been compared to existence in respect of its unity. But existence is not absolutely one, but also must vary with the terms. As existence is one and manifold both, such also should be the case with inherence. But this is opposed to the Vaiśeṣika position. It has been further maintained that inherence, being a relation, does not stand in need of another relation to make it related to the terms. But if inherence be a distinct unity from the terms, it is absolutely a miracle that it should not require a relation to belong to the terms. A relation is unnecessary only if it is supposed to be identical with the terms. But in that case the terms alone will remain and they will function as relation, which is the Jaina position. The Jaina does not believe in a relation apart from the terms as something connecting them from outside. In point of fact it is the terms themselves which come to have relation as an internal determination induced by a change of their nature. The relation of part and whole, substance and quality, universal and particular etc., which are not capable of being separated in thought and actuality, is nothing but identity-in-difference. In conclusion,

1 ṣaṇṇām āśritatvam anyatra nityadravyebhyaḥ. PDS, p. 16.

it should be stated that the Vaiśeṣika has failed to maintain the independent reality of inherence and consequently his attempt to explain the relation of part and whole etc. by means of such an independent real is bound to fail. There seems to be no third alternative to the possibilities — either relation should be set down as appearance or the Jaina position of identity-in-difference be accepted as an ontological truth.

CHAPTER VIII

THE NYĀYA CONCEPTION OF UNIVERSALS

We have seen that relations are real and all relations are ultimately reducible to identity in difference. That things are related with one another means that they are identical in respect of a common nature and different in respect of specific individuality, which distinguishes each from the rest. It is relation which introduces order and coherence into the world. If things were absolutely distinct and discrete with no underlying nexus among them, they would all fall apart, and we could not think of them together as comprised into a system. Of course, the Buddhist fluxist does not believe in objective relations, and according to him the order and connection, that are conceived to prevail in the world of our experience, are subjective impositions or ideal constructions. But this position has been repudiated by the Jaina, the Naiyāyika and other realists on the ground that conceptual thought is as veridical as our perceptual intuition. We have discussed the problem threadbare in the foregoing chapters and we do not think any useful purpose will be served by embarking upon the same discourse again. But a problem naturally arises in connection with our discussion of relations. Relations, we have seen, are possible between terms which share in common an identity of being in spite of their diversity and difference of nature in respect of other characteristics. But what is this identity ? The problem pertinently arises in connection with groups of individuals which are put under definite class-concepts. Take, for instance, the class of individuals known as men. Now, individual men are numerically different from one another, just as they are different from cows and horses. But in spite of their numerical difference all individuals fall under a class, *viz.*, man, and not only are they synthesized under a common category, but as a whole class the individuals are distinguished from other classes, *viz.*, horses and cows. What is the ground of this classification and differentiation of groups? Is it merely due to a conceptual necessity — the necessity of human thought, or is the latter necessity derived from an objective necessity also? In plain language, the problem can be stated as follows. Do all the members belonging to a class actually possess in common an ontological identical principle by virtue of which they are arranged into a definite group? This identical principle is called universal (*sāmānya* or *jāti*). The problem then can be propounded in philosophical terminology in the following terms. Are the universals ontological reals, or subjective constructions, or absolute fictions?

The Buddhist thinks universals to be fictions. That the meaning of terms in propositions and that of the logical probans and probandum are common attributes, which are called universals, does not admit of doubt. The dispute arises with regard to the ontological status of the meaning. Whatever it may be, it is however impossible to suppose that universals as meant by the aforementioned terms are fictions (*alīkas*). Certainly, experience does not endorse the position that fictions are comprehended. If the term 'cow', for instance, in the proposition 'Fetch the cow' were indicative of a fiction, there would be no activity towards it. Now, is it a fact that the meaning of the terms under consideration is understood as a fiction? The contention of the Buddhist, that the meaning of the terms is negation of the opposite (*anyāpoha*) and that negation is a fiction, is not supported by experience. The meanings of positive terms and propositions are always understood as positive facts and neither as fictions nor as negations of the opposites. The proposition, for instance, 'The hill is on fire' is not understood as asserting that negation of fire does not exist, but that fire, a positive fact, exists. The Buddhist would reduce all positive terms and propositions to negative fictions — a position which is psychologically false and logically unjustifiable. A section of the Buddhists, however, contends that though negation be not felt as negation either as a substantive or as an adjective of the meaning, it is an element in the felt meaning none the less. The meaning of the term 'cow', for instance, is a determinate concept, felt as distinct from its opposite 'not-cow'. But it can be felt as distinct, only if distinction is a formative element of its being. The assertion of distinction, which is only a type of negation, as an element of the meaning of a term, is thus the necessary result of logical analysis. The Naiyāyika affirms universals to be elements of the meaning of terms. But what is the source of his knowledge of this universal ? The meaning of the term 'cow' is not expressly felt as a universal, but as a generic image which fits in with all the individual objects falling under the class. The presence of the universal is derived from an analysis of the generic image. Similarly, the Buddhist makes out negation to be the meaning of a term from an analysis of the concept felt as distinct.

But the Naiyāyika does not agree with the Buddhist interpretation. He insists that the meaning of the term 'cow' is a positive concept, which fits in with all the particulars, and there is no reference, implicit or explicit, to negation, either as a substantive or as an adjectival element in it. That the concept 'cow' is a determinate concept and is distinguished from all that is not cow is a fact, which is admitted by all. But the 'negation of the opposite' is only a logical concomitant of the positive concept and is never psychologically felt. The position can be made clear from an analysis of the concept 'cow'. To be sure, no man moves forward to tether a cow with the idea that it is not not-cow. Our idea of a cow is always of a positive entity and negation has no part to play in it. If, on the contrary, the concept were entirely negative in character, there would be no activity possible with regard to such a negation. Suppose, for instance, that a man were called upon to fetch a pitcher. The idea, that would move him to activity, cannot be supposed to be of the form that a not-pitcher does not exist, but it must be of the form that there is a pitcher. It should, therefore, be admitted that the idea of the pitcher is that of a positive real, which, though not absolutely identical with one particular, as it is appropriately capable of being affiliated to many such particulars, and as such something other than particulars, still, it must be something which particular things partake of. "It is not fleeting or changeable like the things of sense; it is eternally itself, immutable and indestructible".[1]

It might be contended, that the concept of a pitcher need not be cognisant of a positive universal, the objective existence of which is riddled with insuperable logical difficulties. The concept is negative and is cognisant of the negation of 'not-pitchers' as a

1. *The Problems of Philosophy* by Russell. p. 144

collective whole. But the contention is not tenable. The concept of 'not-pitcher' should include not only such positive things as pen and the like, but also the absence of pitcher. Such being the case, the negation of the absence of pitcher is nothing but the assertion of a positive fact, *viz.*, of a thing possessed of a character which is common to all individual pitchers, *i.e.*, of the pitcher universal, for negation of a negation is nothing but affirmation.[1] The fact cannot be denied that negation cannot be conceived without relation to a positive fact, either felt as its object or as its substratum. The Buddhist theory of pure negation, being the character of concepts, attempts an impossible feat, both logically and psychologically. If a positive idea is introduced as an element in the concept, this would involve surrender of his position by the Buddhist. We shall advert to this modification of the Buddhist theory at a later stage.

But the Buddhist insists that negation of the opposite must be admitted as the meaning of terms. If the negation of the opposite be not felt as the meaning of a term, there would be no determinate activity. Now if a man is asked to tether a cow, he excludes the horse and the like and moves towards the cow only. What makes the exclusion of the 'not-cow' possible ? Certainly it is the idea of the negation of the opposite. So the negative character of concepts cannot be denied, as this would make selective activity impossible. But the Naiyāyika is not prepared to concede this point also. He maintains that the possibility of promiscuous activity has absolutely no *raison d'etre*. The man who is asked to tether a cow does not move towards a horse, simply because the term cow stands for and signifies a positive fact, *viz.*, cow, and not horse and the like. The avoidance of 'not-cow' is not due to the comprehension of the negation of not-cow as the meaning of the term. It follows from the simple fact that the idea of the horse and the like does not arise, as there is no occasion for it. The negation of not-cow is only an ontological concomitant of the positive cow-concept and is not felt at all. The cow is understood as the cow *quâ* a determinate real and

1. aghaṭasyaive nivṛttir iti pratītau nāyaṁ doṣa, iti cet, na. ghaṭanivṛttyapratikṣepe niyamasyaivā 'siddheḥ. tatpratikṣepe tu kas tato 'nyo vidhir niṣedhapratikṣepasyaiva vidhitvāt, ATV, p. 283.

the element of negation is entirely unfelt in it. If the comprehension of the negation of the opposite be made a condition of the comprehension of the meaning of a term, *i.e.*, of a determinate concept, the result would be an absurdity. Is the negation of the opposite, *e.g.*, not-not-cow, which the Buddhist contends to be the meaning or a term, a determinate concept or not ? If determinate, is it felt to be so by virtue of the comprehension of its opposite ? If it be so, the negation of the opposite, *viz.*, of not-not-cow, would be felt as a determinate fact only by the felt negation of its opposite, *viz.*, of not-not-not-cow. But the second negation would again require another negation of the opposite in order to be made determinate. In other words, there would be an infinite regression and this would make a dead-lock inevitabe. If, however, the distinction of the negation, negatum and of the substratum of negation be not felt, no selective activity would be possibe.[1] If it be maintained, that negation of the opposite is a determinate concept felt by itself, without involving reference to any other negation, the contingency of infinite regress would be avoided, no doubt. But then there would be no logical or psychological justification for making the comprehension of the negation of the opposite a condition of the comprehension of a determinate concept. The cow-concept, being equally determinate, should be admitted to be felt by itself without reference to the negation of its opposite. The positive concept should be felt as determinate by reason of its being possessed of a distinctive character (*svarūpabheda*), in which negation has no part to play.

The Buddhist may contend that the distinctive character (*svarūpabheda*) spoken of is nothing but the negation of the opposite, and the positive character of a thing consists in what is distinguished from the opposite. Whatever it may be alleged to be, it is undeniable that this character must be real and not fictitious, which negation is avowed to be. A fiction has no character of its own, which can distinguish it from other fictions. It must, therefore, be admitted that the universal is not a fiction as it has a distinctive character. The cow-concept has a content which is different from that of a horse-concept.

1. Op. cit., p. 283.

Certainly this difference of character cannot be a figment of intellect with no reality underlying it. For a fiction has no character. The Buddhist attempts to equate the content of conception with negation, which, again, is asserted to be an unreal construction. The Naiyāyika does not admit the possibility of a fiction being the content of thought. Moreover, there is no evidence of negation being an element of concepts. That a person moves towards a cow and avoids a horse, when called upon to tether a cow, is due to the fact that the cow-concept has reference to the real objective cow, and the horse, either as an element of negation or as a substantive fact, is not felt to be meant. And even when by accident the horse is perceived on the way, the man avoids it simply because he is persuaded that the horse is not the 'cow', which he is directed to tether.

Jñānaśrī, a later Buddhist exponent, has given a new orientation to the theory of *apoha*. He admits that a concept has a substantive positive content, but the element of negation is also felt as an adjective to the positive substantive in it. Thus, for instance, the cow concept, though positive in character and reference, has a negative element, which serves to distinguish the cows as a class from other classes of animals. The cow-character, or the cow-universal as it is called, subserves a double purpose, *viz*., it not only assimilates the different individual animals called cows under a class but also distinguishes the latter from all that is not-cow. The cow-universal is thus felt to determine the individual cows by differentiating them from the opposite classes. "The meaning of the word is therefore neither purely positive nor purely negative with contrary logical implication, but even psychologically a distinctive concept with the element of distinction or negation as a part of the felt content. The word 'cow' is conventionally affixed to the distinctive cow-concept felt as divorced from not-cows. Though the negative element is not distinctly articulated in words it is there as a felt content none the less. Just as the concept of 'blue-lotus' to which the word '*indīvara*' is affixed by convention is a complex of blue and lotus and the blue is felt as much as the lotus in one sweep, so in the case of such expression as 'cow' which gives rise to a complex concept of 'cow-as-distinct from non-cow'.

Here the non-cow is felt as much as the cow — the negative and the positive factor being present alike".[1] Udayana seems to assent to the position asserted by Jñānaśrī, but the positive character conceded by the Buddhist makes a material difference which Udayana will show to be incompatible with the Buddhist denial of objective universals. But Udayana has all along denied that negation is felt as an element in a concept and this endorsement of the Buddhist position seems to be a make-believe. Śaṅkara Miśra takes Udayana's words at their face value and thinks that negation of the opposite is felt as an element in a determinate concept. But the other commentators, particularly Bhagīratha Thakkura and Raghunātha Śiromaṇi are decidedly of opinion that negation of the opposite is only a deduction from the positive concept and is understood at a subsequent stage.

And even if it is allowed that negation of the opposite is a factor of the meaning of a word, this negation cannot be understood without reference to a positive universal. This will be obvious from an analysis of the concept 'not-not-cow'. 'Not-cow', unless it be nonsense, must mean all that is different from cow. But one individual cow is different from another individual cow and if this difference of individuality be made the connotation, the word not-cow would denote not only horses, buffaloes and so on, but also other individual cows. In order to avoid this contingency it must be admitted that not-cow denotes all things that are different from each and every cow. But the number of cows being unlimited it is not humanly possible to know that a horse or a buffalo differs from an unknown cow. So the negation of cow must be admitted to refer to the cow-universal and not to the infinite number of cows as individuals. Even an ordinary assertion of negation is possible only because the negated object is never felt as an individual, but as a fact possessed of the universal that constitutes its essence. When we say 'there is no cow here', we mean not the absence of this or that individual cow, but of cows as such. To be explicit, we mean that all cows are absent from this place. How is this knowledge of all individual cows, past, present, future, near or remote,

1. *The Buddhist Philosophy of Universal Flux*, p. 133.

made possible ? Certainly a man would have to live for countless ages if he were to acquire this knowledge from direct acquaintance with all the individuals. But such a miracle is neither possible nor necessary. It is a simple intuition and is possible because the knowledge of one cow gives insight into the fundamental essence that makes a cow what it is. We know that whatever is to be a cow can be such provided it possesses that fundamental essence. And this essence is called the universal of the cow, because it is present in an unvariant manner in all cows in spite of the difference of shape, colour, dimension and such other qualities. These varying qualities do not affect the identity of the universal in the least. So when the Buddhist seeks to identify this universal with negation of the opposite he essays an impossible task, as the 'opposite' can be understood only in terms of a universal, which is sought to be denied by the theory. Jñānaśrī and Ratnakīrti realized this truth and so conceded the positive nature of universals,[1] while reserving the right to repudiate its ontologically objective status.

Dharmottara holds that the universal is a fiction of thought though it be a positive idea; but this is a contradiction in terms. A fiction is a non-entity and to say that it is positive is to erect a fiction into a positive entity. The question is whether the universal is felt or not. If it is felt it cannot be nothing. It has been contended in defence that it is not the universal as a felt idea that is denied, but its ontological reality which is riddled with insuperable logical difficulties. It is urged that the so-called universal, *e.g.*, cow-universal or horse-universal, cannot be a positive real as it is understood by negation of its contradictory opposite. But the negation of the opposite cannot be regarded as proof of its unreality, as even the particular, which is regarded as real by the Buddhist, is also possessed of a negative character in that its reality is concomitant with the negation of its opposite. If it be held that the universal is devoid of a character and so cannot be regarded as a real, then again it becomes a non-entity and the old difficulty of non-entity being a content of thought crops up with all its consequences. Nor can the felt positivity of the universal as a

1. Op. cit., Chap. VII, and ATV, pp. 289 ff.

content of conception be regarded as a case of superimposition. Because superimposition consists in the false perception of a characteristic, which belongs to a real. Take, for instance, the case of the erroneous perception of the shell as silver. Here the character of silver is falsely transferred to the shell. But the silver character is a real attribute which belongs to real silver. If the intuititon of the positive character in the universal were a case of superimposition upon a fiction, this positive character must needs be shown to be a real characteristic of a real entity. The only real entity admitted by the Buddhist is only a self-characterised particular, which is discrete and distinct from all other particulars. But this particular is believd by him to be left untouched by conceptual thought, which alone can envisage a universal, which is *ex hypothesi* a non-entity. So the denial of positive character to a universal reduces it to a fiction. To say that it is a fiction and at the same time felt as a positive fact is to speak unintelligible nonsense.

It has been contended that the felt positivity of the universal is not a case of superimposition. The universal is felt as positive, because it is not felt as distinct from positive real. But this is a desperate argument. A thing cannot be felt in the character of another thing simply because its distinction from the latter is not perceived. A pen as a fact is distinct from the whole world of reals which are comprised under the category of not-pen. It is not necessary that the pen should be felt as distinct from all these things. But this failure of realization of its distinction from the horse and the like does not make it appear as a horse or the like. So the non-apprehension of distinction of a fiction from a positive real cannot account for the felt positivity of a concept. Moreover, a real is always a self-characterised particular and is felt as such. A fiction is always a non-entity which can never be felt as a positive entity. A fiction could be felt as positive if the positive character could be detached from the particular and tagged on to it. But a real particular is an indivisible whole and has no character which can be set loose from it and attached to another. Nor can it be a case of erroneous perception which is possible only on the perception of a common character between two things. So the felt positivity cannot be explained away either as a case of superimposition or as due to non-apprehension of its distinction from a positive real.

It is undeniable that conceptual thought is cognisant of a common character which is felt to be identical in the different individuals of a class. The Buddhist also admits this to be the case. But the conflict of views arises when the Buddhist seeks to repudiate its objective reality and the Naiyāyika realist insists upon it. The Naiyāyika maintains that the felt universal cannot be a non-entity since a non-entity cannot be connected with different individuals. It is a fact that all cows are felt to be possessed of an identical principle which draws the individual cows close together and distinguishes them each and all from not-cows. The principle is continuous and undifferentiated in its incidence in spite of the variations of the individuals. This unvariant principle is regarded either as a fiction or as a subjective idea. But we have seen that a fiction cannot have the capacity for real assimilation and differentiation, to account for which a universal is postulated. The Buddhist, however, regards the continuity of the universal as only a subjective way of thought. But a subjective idea is a momentary existent according to the Buddhist and so cannot function as a unitive principle. Nor can the continuity be a case of transferred characteristic according to the Buddhist, since he does not believe in the real continuity of any thing.

A later Buddhist has sought to account for the felt identity and continuity of the universal-idea in a different way. He admits that the universal is nothing but an idea and the idea, so far as it is real, cannot have a continued existence. The so-called universal, so far as it is felt to be present in the different individuals, is not an identical principle. The concept of one cow is numerically different from the concept of another cow and so also their contents equally vary with each concept. But these conceptual contents are felt to be one identical principle owing to the non-cognition of their differences. Here the Naiyāyika would ask whether the differences of the conceptual contents are real. If they are real, the contents cannot be unreal being possessed of real differences. Nor could the differences be unreal because unreal difference of the contents would make them a real identity. It is a fact that the difference of A from A is not felt because it is really non-existent in it. The non-existence of difference of A from A proves that A is an identical entity. So if the difference of contents were really non-existent, that would prove the real identity of the contents. In other words, the existence of an identical universal as a reality would be left unrepudiated. The Buddhist is thus placed between the horns of a dilemma. The differences of concepts are either real or unreal. If real, the concepts would be real universals and if unreal they would be one identical principle. It may be contended that differences are superimposed upon the concepts. But the hypothesis of superimposition would make the intuition of differences inevitable and thus leave no room for the superimposition of identity. So the old dilemma would again crop up. *viz.* either the differences of the concepts are real or unreal and both these alternatives are fatal to the Buddhist position. To say that the concepts are neither real nor unreal, nor both nor neither, as none of these characteristics is appropriate to a fiction which a concept is, is tantamount to a confession of defeat and failure to explain a difficulty. And if the possibility of non-perception of such a fictitious difference be allowed and made the condition of confusion of identity, there would be no entity in the universe, which would not be felt as identical with every other thing. But the Buddhist would rejoin that such a contingency does not arise where the real differences of things are actually cognised. Thus, for instance, a book is not felt as identical with a pen because the difference of the pen from the book is real and is also felt as such.

Udayana observes that the Buddhist here asserts a truth, but he does not go deep enough into the implication of this discovery. It is a natural deduction that when the cognition of real differences operates as an obstacle to the possibility of mistaking of identity, the mistaking of identity should be set down to the absence of the cognition of real difference. To take a concrete example, a shell is mistaken for silver because the real difference of identity of the shell and silver is uncognised. Likewise in the case of concepts, they could be mistaken to be identical only if they were possessed of real differences and these differences were not cognised. But the reality of differences of the concepts would knock out the plea of the Buddhist that the concepts are unreal fictions. The contention of Udayana can be summed up as follows. The felt unity of the universal cannot be explained away as an error as due to the non-perception of the differences of the conceptual contents, no matter whether the said differences are real or unreal. Secondly, even the erroneous perception of identity is possible only if the differences are objectively real. There is no possibility for the perception of identity, if the differences are perceived. This holds good even in the case of erroneous perception of difference. For instance, a real silver may be mistaken to be something different from silver and this erroneous perception of difference would prevent the perception of the real identity of silver. Here the difference of silver is falsely felt, but it is a real attribute of lead. So even error of identity or of difference is possible only if the difference or identity is real somewhere. That the hair of a tortoise is felt to be different from the horn of a horse is due to the fact that hair and horn are real entities which are really different from each other, and the perception of their real difference cannot be done away with even when they are imposed upon a tortoise and a horse to which they do not belong. The law formulated by Udayana that the perception of real difference is an obstacle to the perception of identity, true or false, and that the perception of identity is due to the non-perception of such difference is not found to be inoperative even in such exceptional cases. The upshot is that the conception of identity of the universal cannot be conjured away by any amount of logic as an unfounded fiction or as a subjective creation, because the felt unity and continuity cannot be accounted for on the supposition of its unreality.

The nature of conceptual knowledge, so far as it is revealed in experience, has been examined and the Naiyāyika has shown that the Buddhist has not succeeded in explaining away the positive character of it. The element of negation, so far as psychological evidence is concerned, is problematic. Let us now consider the logical grounds on which the Buddhist bases his conclusion that conceptual thought is *per se* negative in character and reference. It is alleged that a concept is referable both by a negative and by a positive determination. This will be evident from an analysis of the propositions, 'The cow is here' and 'the cow is not here.' The cow that is referred to by 'is' and 'is not' cannot be a positive real, which has invariably 'being' as an inalienable part of its nature. A real cannot own the character of being and non-being. But both these characters are predicated of the cow. So the cow, which is the subject of the propositions. cannot be supposed to stand for an objective reality. It must, therefore, be a concept consisting in the negation of the opposite. It is only negative concepts that are amenable to a positive and a negative determination. The concept 'amorphous' is an instance in point. It can be predicated of such a real as space, thought and the like, which are accounted as positive reals, and also of such fictions, as a square circle. Neither thought nor square circle has any dimension. Our concepts are invariably such of which negative and positive predication is permissible without offence to logic. It should be concluded, the Buddhist argues, that concepts are of the nature of negation of their opposites on a par with the negation of dimension. The positive-cum-negative can belong only to a subjective idea and not to an objective real. Secondly, it is only negation of the opposite that can make a synthesis of absolutely divergent facts. The example of the concept 'amorphous' which applies to real and unreal facts alike, as set forth above, should be a pointer to the truth of the proposition. Concepts as synthesising ideas should, thus, be equated with negation and a subjective creation at that.

Udayana observes that the Buddhist here attempts to determine the nature and meaning of a physical existent by means of pure logic, a procedure entirely *ultra vires*. The Buddhist has failed to carry conviction when he maintains that our concepts are negative fictions. The question is, is the concept felt or not ? If it is felt, it cannot be a fiction. Even such constructions as a rabbit's horn or a square circle cannot be fictions, if they have a meaning. The unreality of these constructions does not belong to the elements, rabbit or horn, square or circle, but to their combination, which also in its turn has its foundation in objective reality. If any conceptual construction is inconceivable, it should be dismissed as unmeaning nonsense as abracadabra. But if it has a meaning, it must have elements and a relation which are found to be objectively real in another context. Whatever may be the ontological value of concepts, there is no reason for supposing that they are to be treated like such unreal constructions as a rabbit's horn or a barren woman's son. For instance, such concepts as the cow, the horse, man and so on, are simple ideas felt as such. The question, whether our thought is derived from reality or independent of it, should not deter us from pursuing our enquiry into the nature of concepts. Suffice it to observe here that if even uncontradicted experience is subjected to distrust, there would be no reason for believing in the existence of anything beyond experience. Not only this, even the existence of experience *per se*, which cannot be ascertained by any amount of pure logic, will be liable to doubt. Doubt, unqualified and universal, stultifies not only the whole fabric of human knowledge, but also its very existence. So the Buddhist cannot push his scepticism too far. He must rely on an ultimate criterion and this must be uncontradicted experience. The question at issue is whether our concepts are fictions or real facts. If they were unfelt fictions the problem would be at an end. We have observed before that the theory of felt fiction is destroyed by a contradiction in terms. It has been admitted even by Dharmottara and Jñānaśrī that concepts as psychical existents are real entities. An observation of the relative jurisdiction of logic and experience will not be irrelevant here. Pure logic is frequently seen to be worsted when it comes in conflict with uncontradicted experience. Thus, the inference of coldness in fire on the ground of its materiality is dismissed, in spite of its apparent cogency, as it is found to be contradicted by direct experience which finds fire to be hot. The attempt, therefore, to construe a concept, *e.g.*, a cow-concept as negation of buffalo, horse and the like, that is to say, of the opposite of cow, on the ground that these negations serve to include a number of divergent individuals, is stultified by the direct experience of its entitative character. The argument of the Buddhist is based on a partial finding that a negation serves as a synthesising principle. But he fails to consider whether a positive principle can also function as a synthetic principle with equal efficiency.

The question of contradiction by experience apart, let us examine the Buddhist's plea of the common possibility of positive and negative predication. What is sought to be proved by the fact that the cow is capable of being said to exist and not to exist ? Does he mean to say that the cow should be regarded as both existent and non-existent in the same reference ? Certainly this would be a contradiction in terms. Nor can it be meant that the cow-universal, which is the meaning of the cow-concept, is an attribute of both existents and non-existents. Nobody thinks that the cow-universal belongs to non-existents as an attribute. Let, again, it be interpreted as evidence of the cow being the subject of both these determinations. But if this be the point the Buddhist would seek to establish, the argument would be a case of pure non sequitur. It is a fact that the cow-universal has the positive character of being a universal and also the negative character of not being a quality, or not having a quality which can belong only to a substance. But the possession of such positive and negative character does not involve any contradiction. Even the self-characterized particular, which is the only reality according to the Buddhist, is also found to be possessed of a positive and a negative character. The individual cow is existent *quâ* a cow and non-existent *quâ* a horse. But this dual predication does not spell a contradiction even according to the Buddhist. It passes one's understanding why should this dual characterization prove the unreality of the cow-universal.

Let it be held that the meaning of the dual characterization is not anything of the kind considered above. But let it be supposed to mean that the universal has a definite community of nature with existent and non-existent. But this also is not a tenable hypothesis, as a universal is a determination of existents and not of non-entities. So it cannot be such a common attribute. It may be contended that negation of the opposite is found to be a common characteristic of both existents and non-existents, and this constitutes the neutral community of the universal. Thus, for instance, the negation of not-cow may stand for the cow as well as a fiction, and the universal being such a negation must have this common character. But this would be a case of *petitio principii*, as it takes for granted that a universal is a negative concept which is the matter of dispute.

Let us, then, suppose that the meaning of the dual predication is that the subject is thought of as existent and non-existent both. But is existence predicated in the same reference with non-existence? This is certainly impossible owing to the contradiction involved. Neither the Buddhist nor the Naiyâyika can maintain that this is meant by dual predication. If it is meant that they have a different reference, the objective universal will also not be unamenable to such predication. The predication of non-existence of the cow would only mean that the cow-universal has lost its substratum owing to the destruction of the individual. The affirmation of existence would mean that the cow-universal has a living substratum.

It has however been contended by the Buddhist that if the universal be a positive entity as the Naiyāyika maintains, the affirmation of it would be an unmeaning tautology and the negation of existence of such a positive fact would be a case of self-contradiction. But the Naiyāyika would rejoin that the Buddhist conception of negative universals also involves the same consequences. If the universal be a negative fiction as the Buddhist maintains, affirmation of existence would be a case of contradiction in terms and negation of existence would be a superfluous tautology. The Buddhist may rejoin that his conception of universal is one of a neutral idea, which is susceptible of affirmation and negation both and thus the alleged consequences do not affect his position. But this argument smacks of equivocation and evasion of a real difficulty. Even granting that it is an idea, it cannot be said to be both existent and non-existent, or neither existent nor non-existent, because of the contradiction involved in such suppositions. So the Buddhist does not gain an advantage by denying the objective reality of the universal or affirming its subjective character. We have shown that the universal cannot be conjured away as a fiction. The solution of the problem must be found elsewhere and this will engage our attention in the rest of our enquiry.

The predication of existence and non-existence should be held to refer to a hitherto unknown determination or the specification of a known determination. The predicate in the proposition "The cow exists" signifies the existence of the cow as an individual in a particular place and time. Likewise, the predication of non-existence would refer to the non-existence of the individual *per se* or in a particular context. This explanation of the problem has been propounded by the Buddhist, and the Naiyāyika, who believes in objective universals, can also accept this solution with equal propriety. The Buddhist, on the contrary, would have no logical justification in offering this explanation inasmuch as the universal being a fiction in his view can have no determination, positive or negative. The meaning of the proposition — 'The cow exists' can thus be analysed as follows : The word 'cow' means an individual possessed of the cow-universal. But individuals being scattered over diverse places and times would not be of any service, unless they are determined by reference to specific attributes, time, place and so on. The predicate 'exists' connotes the connection of the cow with a particular spatio-temporal setting. Thus the meaning of the whole proposition is that an individual possessed of the cow-universal is connected with the present time and a particular area of space, which may be specified again, according to the needs of a person, as the cow-shed or the like. The cow-universal as a meaning of the word or concept 'cow' is a positive entity, no doubt. But the predication of the existence does not involve tautology inasmuch as existence is not a part of the connotation of a 'positive'. A 'positive' is by itself bereft of time-determination, though the latter is not repugnant to the former. Thus the positive is not only present, but may be past and future also. The predicate 'existence' connotes presentness which is not a necessary concomitant of a real. The predication of non-existence is also not repugnant to a real universal as it means only the destruction of a particular individual as its substratum. So the compatibility of the universal with existence and non-existence does not prove its unreality. The universal is an eternal real and so is not affected by the existence or non-existence of a particular substratum. The non-existence of substratum involves the non-existence of its content only when the latter is a factitious product.[1] So the dual predication in question means something else than the reality or unreality of the universal.

Jñānaśrī has sought to prove that concepts or words have no objective meaning by an ingenious argument. A cognition, whose content is unaffected by the presence and absence of an entity, cannot have that entity for its object. Thus, for instance, the conception of cow, being unaffected by the presence or absence

1. atha bhāvābhāva-sādhāraṇyam āśrayasya sattva iva vināśe 'py avināśitvam, tad anyathāsiddham, nityatvāt, kāryasy aivā 'śrayanāśanāśyatvāt. ATVD, p. 316.

of a horse, has not the horse for its object. The conception of cow, again, is indifferent to the presence or absence of a real cow. It should thus be admitted that this conception cannot have 'cow' for its object, just as it cannot have the horse for its object. But this interpretation of the dual predication seems to be nothing but an unconvincing sophistry. The reference to the horse has no bearing upon the conception of cow. It is not yet established that the conception of cow does not relate to an objective fact. The Naiyāyika does not admit that the word 'cow' does not stand for the objective 'cow', just as it does not admittedly stand for the objective horse. The issue can be clarified by the determination of the significance of the dual predication in question. Does this predication of existence and non-existence mean that the concept is not caused by an objective existence ? If so, it does not help the Buddhist contention that the concept has not the cow for its object. It is not necessary that the object of a cognition should be what brings it into being. In that case, no other cognition, save and except perception, would have an object of its own — a position, which is absurd on the face of it. Thus inference would not have a genuine objective reference. Nor can it be supposed that dual predication means that the concept 'cow' necessarily requires for its fulfilment 'existence' or 'non-existence' as its predicates. No doubt this is a fact, but it proves nothing in the way of reality or unreality. If this be the meaning, the citation of the horse for example, becomes irrelevant, for no body thinks that the concept 'cow' requires the existence or non-existence of the horse for its self-fulfilment. The Buddhist may contend that the dual predication does not mean anything of the kind that has been proposed above. The meaning of it is that the concept 'cow' as the subject of the proposition does not signify the existence or non-existence of the cow. Yes, but what does the Buddhist seek to infer from it ? If he means that the concept or the word 'cow' does not signify 'cow' as a reality, then certainly the Buddhist is guilty of making an unfounded assumption. It has not yet been proved to the satisfaction of the realist that the concept 'cow' signifies a fiction or does not signify a reality. If it is supposed that the dual predication is proof of the fact that the concept 'cow' does not signify anything beyond the bare reality, the Naiyāyika would accept this interpretation. But if the Buddhist would seek to prove, from the incapacity of the concept to signify an additional attribute over and above the bare fact, that it would not signify any positive fact, then that would be an unwarranted inference. There is no necessity that a word should not signify anything if it cannot signify an attribute which may belong to it. The word jar does not signify that it is blue or red, but that cannot be made the ground of inferring that it signifies nothing—not even the 'jar' as a fact.

The Naiyāyika realist is never tired of emphasising the fact that a word signifies a meaning and the meaning is a real fact. There is absolutely no warrant from the psychological evidence of conceptual knowledge that our conceptual thoughts are unreal. The felt reality of their reference cannot be repudiated on psychological grounds. The Buddhist also has been constrained to admit this truth. But he seeks to repudiate the objective validity of the reference of concepts on logical grounds. He has made capital out of the supposed incompatibility of the predication of existence and non-existence with reference to an objective reality. The Buddhist contends that the reality of a thing is inseparable from its existence and so the predication of existence would be a case of hopeless tautology and the denial of existence would involve self-contradiction. But the Naiyāyika finds in this contention a confusion of thought. If existence meant the being of the subject which is inseparable from its reality, the Buddhist contention would be unassailable. But the predication of existence in the proposition, — 'The cow exists', does not refer to being of the cow, but to its connection with a temporal determination *viz.*, presentness (*vartamānatva*). The being of a real is indifferent, though not repugnant, to temporal determinations. And so the latter are not understood as part of the connotation of the subject. The predication of such determinations is, therefore, neither unnecessary nor logically absurd. The Buddhist, however, has sought to prove his contention by pursuing a different line of attack. He insists that the contemplated differentiation of attributes as essential and unessential, as made by the Naiyāyika, is not justifiable. If the predicate does not stand for an attribute which belongs to the subject as a part of its nature, the former would not belong to the latter.

Moreover, the relation of substance and attribute cannot be one of absolute difference. The attribute must be identical with the being of the substance. So a word or a concept, which does not signify an attribute of a thing, cannot signify the identity of the same. To take an example, the word or concept 'cow' does not signify an attribute of the horse and consequently the substance horse. If the concept 'cow' did not signify an attribute of the cow, it could not signify the cow as a real either.

The Naiyāyika observes that the argument is based on the supposition of identity between substance and attribute which is an unwarranted assumption. The difference of attributes from substance is a felt fact and there is no logical necessity for repudiating it. So the knowledge of the substance does not carry the necessity of the knowledge of the attribute. The subject predicate relation in a proposition is based upon this truth. The nature of a thing is determined by the evidence of undisputed experience and no amount of *a priori* logic can override its deliverance. The Buddhist contention, that the knowledge of the subject necessarily involves the knowledge of the predicate could be accepted, if it were true that the subject or the cognition of the subject or the conditions of the cognition of the subject involve necessarily the cognition of all possible attributes that could be predicated of it. But the fact is quite otherwise. The conditions of the cognition of the subject differ from the conditions of the cognition of the predicate and they are neither coincident nor simultaneous. The cognition of the attribute is rather conditional upon that of the subject and the Buddhist puts the cart before the horse by making the former the condition of the latter.[1]

The Buddhist puts forward another contention that if a word or a necessary logical concomitant were incompetent to convey these attributes, the organ of perception should equally fail to do so. But the contention is inspired by superficial analogy.[2]

1. yat tu śakter abhedād ity ādi, tat tadā śobheta, yadi dharmimātrādhīnas tadbodhamātrādhīnas tāvanmātrabodhasāmagryadhīno vā yāvad-upādhibhedabodhaḥ syāt, na caivam. ibid., p. 326.

2. etena bhedād dharmiṇah pratītāv api śabdaliṅgadvārā dharmāṇāṁ ced apratītiḥ, indriyadvārā 'pi mā 'bhūd ity ādikaṁ tu karṇasparśe kaṭicālanam apāstam. Ibid. p. 327.

If the conditions of the perception of attributes were not coincident with those of the perception of the substance the former consequence would be a matter of undeniable logical necessity. It is an unjustifiable perversion of truth to contend that all the accredited cognitive instruments (*pramāṇa*) should have the same efficiency. Thus inference is competent to prove only the fact with which the necessary concomitance of the probans has been cognised. The cognition of smoke is competent to deliver the cognition of fire and those attributes of fire, the conditions of whose knowledge are necessarily coincident with those of fire. That is to say, only the fire-universal is cognized with the fire, since the latter cannot be known without the former. In other words the conditions of the cognition of fire are coincident with those of fire-universal, and not with the condition of cognition of such attributes as the colour, dimension, specific temperature of fire though they are necessarily connected with fire. Language is competent to convey only those attributes of a substance with which its conventional relation (*samaya*) has been known. But sense-organ has got an advantage over the two aforesaid cognitive instruments. It cognizes not only fire, for instance, together with fire-universal, but with other sensible attributes also which fall within the ken of the aforesaid organ. The Buddhist contention, that the cognition of a substance is conditioned by the cognition of all attributes that are connected with it, is based on an unwarranted generalization. It is true that the cognition of fire as a substance is necessarily concomitant with the cognition of such attributes as the 'being' (*sattva*) of fire and of fire-universal (*vahnitva*). But to contend on the basis of this truth that the cognition of fire should carry with it the cognition of all possible attributes that are connected with it as a matter of fact would only be an unwarranted generalization. The cognition of substance and of attribute is governed by a law which is imperfectly understood by the Buddhist. The law should be correctly propounded as follows. The cognition of a substance is necessarily conditioned by the cognition of an attribute or attributes, which is a necessary antecedent to that of the former. The truth of the law is verified by the fact that a substance is never known without some attribute or other. Secondly, it is invariably known together with those attributes without the knowledge of which the knowledge of a substance is impossible.[1]

The Buddhist has raised another difficulty. It is urged that if inference and language were cognisant of the same objective reality as sense perception is, then the difference of contents of the cognitions in question would be unaccountable. The criterion of the identity of objects is the identity of contents of the cognition in question. Thus, for instance, the thing perceived with the left eye is known to be identical with what is perceived with the right eye because the contents of the perceptual cognitions are not different. Hence only the sameness of content is proof of the sameness of the object. But this condition is found to be lacking in the case of verbal and inferential cognitions as compared with the perceptual cognition. In perceptual cognition, a real is cognised with all its distinctive individuality, as determined by the specific spatio-temporal setting together with its specific qualitative characteristics. But in inferential and verbal cognitions the supposedly identical object is felt as indistinct and with a character in which the individuality, constituted by diverse attributes, has faded out. It is a blurred picture, which cannot be specifically identified with this or that individual, that is cognised with its distinctive identity in perception. We know from the testimony of perception that one individual cow is different from another individual cow and also from a buffalo or a horse. But in non-perceptual cognition of the cow the content is felt as something different from a buffalo or a horse, no doubt, but the mutual difference of individual cows has faded out of it. Certainly this difference of the contents of the different kinds of cognition cannot be accounted for, if they are supposed to be cognisant of the self-same reality. Nor can the difference be accounted for by the difference of the modes of cognition, if the object were a self-identical fact. A reality cannot be

1. vicitraśaktitvāc ca pramāṇānāṁ liṅgasya prasiddhapratibandhapratisandhānaśaktitvāt, śabdasya samayasīmavikramatvāt, indriyasya tv arthaśakter apy apekṣaṇāt. na tu sambaddho 'rtha ity eva pramāṇaih pramāpyate, atiprasaṅgāt. yasya tū 'pādher upalambha eva yena pramāṇena dharmy upalabhyate tasyā 'nupalambhe sa tena no 'palabhyata iti paraṁ yujyate, sarvopādhyanupalambhe vā, tathā ca siddhasādhanam iti saṁkṣepaḥ. Ibid. p. 327.

supposed to be possessed of mutually incompatible characters. If the difference of contents were no index to the difference of objects, the cognition of a jar could not be distinguished from the cognition of linen in spite of the difference of contents. It must, therefore, be admitted that the difference of contents must be set down to the difference of objects. It follows irresistibly from this premise that non-perceptual cognition, which has a different content from that of perceptual cognition, cannot have reference to the self-same object.[1]

The Naiyāyika has refused to be convinced by the Buddhist's argument. That difference of contents is incompatible with the sameness of objects is not universally true. That there is a qualitative difference between a perceptual and a non-perceptual cognition is not denied even by the Naiyāyika. But he thinks that this qualitative difference is due to factors other than the identity of the object. There is nothing repugnant in the proposition that perceptual and non-perceptual cognitions alike should be cognisant of a self-identical real. The contingent character of the proposition, which is believed to be universal by the Buddhist, can be demonstrated even by the evidence of perceptual cognition. Take the case of a variegated carpet possessed of blue, red, violet and other colour-patches. A man may perceive a blue patch alone and not the other patches of colour, if his angle of vision be such as can command the view of that particular patch, or if the carpet be folded. Suppose that the same man sees the carpet from a different position or when it is unrolled. That man would certainly perceive the carpet as variegated and not blue as he did in the first instance. The contents of the second cognition are different from those of the first, no doubt. But this difference does not annul the identity of the blue patch as blue, though in the first case it is felt merely as blue and in the second case as variegated. The Buddhist may contend that there is no incompatibility between the perception of the blue as blue and the perception of the same as a factor of the variegated. The blue does not cease to be blue even when it is felt as a part of the variegated. The blue is the same whether perceived as blue or as a factor of the variegated. The identity of the object of the two perceptions is

1. Ibid., p. 330.

confined to this much. The blue is, however, opposed, to the variegated as the two do not mean the same attribute. The Buddhist would conclude that the case of the perception of the variegated does not invalidate the universal truth of the proposition that the variation of contents is incompatible with the identity of the object.

The Naiyāyika acknowledges the justice and partial truth of the argument adduced in defence by the Buddhist. But he invites the attention of the Buddhist to the fact that the same principle, by which he resolves the conflict, is applicable in the case of non-perceptual cognition also with equal propriety. The difference of contents between perceptual and non-perceptual cognitions is not, to be precise, qualitative, but quantitative. The contents of a perceptual cognition are only in excess of those of non-perceptual cognition. The excess is due to the different qualities that are cognised in perception alone. But in so far as the identity of the object, irrespective of the excess or diminution of qualities, is taken into account, there is absolutely no difference between perceptual and non-perceptual cognitions. Thus, for instance, the perception of a cow and the inference of a cow have a common content, which is due to the common substance, *viz.*, an individual possessed of the cow-universal. The difference of contents of the cognitions is due to the varying number of qualities cognised. The Naiyāyika does not maintain that non-perceptual cognition is competent to envisage the spatio-temporal determinations or other sensible attributes that fall within the competency of perception alone. So the Buddhist does not prove anything which is not admitted by the Naiyāyika. He, again, fails to establish his conclusion that perceptual and non-perceptual cognitions are not cognisant of the same substantive object since the logical ground, *viz.*, the difference of contents, on which he relies, has been shown to be inconclusive. The Naiyāyika maintains that difference of contents of the modes of cognition has no reference to the substantive identity of the object, but only to the excess or diminution of qualities that are noticed.

Why should there be a difference in the quality of cognitions, were they equally cognisant of the same substantive real ? A thing is perceived as distinct and clear, but the inference or verbal cognition gives only a pale picture. Certainly, he makes an extravagent demand on our credulity when the Naiyāyika asks us to believe that it is the same substance that is distinct and indistinct, pale and bright. Why should there be a difference of quality in the contents if they are due to the same real ? It is also to be explained away by the quantitative theory by the Naiyāyika ? But the Naiyāyika denies that the situation creates a problem at all. So far as the substantive real is concerned it is neither distinct nor indistinct. Consequently, there is no qualitative difference in the content of consciousness relating to the substance.[1] The distinctness and indistinctness are due to the varying cognition of qualities. A substance is cognised with a greater number of qualities in perception and so is felt to be more vivid and distinct. In non-perceptual cognition the number of qualities is much less, as sensible qualities are not cognised in it.[2] So the distinctness or indistinctness of contents is due to the numerical ratio of the qualities, that are perceived or unperceived along with the substance. The variation of the contents has, therefore, reference to the adjectival qualities and has nothing to do with the substantive core of reality. The so-called qualitative variation of the contents of consciousness with reference to the same thing observed from proximity and distance should be regarded as a pointer. It can be explained only if the theory of numerical variation of qualities as the cause of the difference be adopted. The situation cannot be made the ground for repudiating the objective reference of non-perceptual cognitions. Nor can it be construed as evidence of perceptual cognition being the only type which is cognisant of reality.[3]

But the Buddhist has contended that the variation of contents due to distance is also an instance of unfounded cognition. The position, which he maintains, is this. There could be no variation in the quality of cognitions if they were conversant with the same reality. So perception from distance is not believed to be

1. kevaladharmyapekṣayā sphuṭāsphuṭa-pratibhāsabheda eva nāsti. Nārāyaṇa's Com. p. 140.

2. bahutarālpataradharmavaddharmibhedaviṣayatvam eva sphuṭāsphuṭa-pratibhāsatvam, nādhikam. ATVD. p. 336.

3. ata eva dharmiviṣayake 'pi dūrāntikapratyakṣe sphuṭā-sphuṭatvaṁ dṛṣṭam. ATVS. p. 336.

conversant with the real which admits of no such qualitative difference. The felt immediacy of the cognition is only a case of illusion. The Naiyāyika does not find any substance in the latter contention also. The entire line of argument followed by the Buddhist is based upon the assumption of identity of substance and quality. It is argued that when a quality is not different from the substance, there can be no veridical perception of substance without perception of the quality. But if the numerical difference of substance and quality can be proved, or if it can be shown that there are weighty considerations against the supposed identity of quality and substance, the Buddhist position will not be established. The difference of quality and substance cannot be annulled without stultifying either or both of them. Nor can we acquiesce in the Buddhist contention that substance and qualities are only subjective concepts. The admission of subjectivity will not be confined to these categories alone, but will extend to the entire objective world. The Buddhist also, so far as he believes in the objectivity of particulars, does not adopt the philosophy of absolute subjectivism. The quarrel in the present instance is concerned with the Buddhist realist, who believes in particulars, but denies objective universals and relations. To return to the point at issue the argument of the Buddhist would be valid if the difference of substance and qualities were unreal and if consequently a real were made up of all the qualities that are felt or associated with it. In that case the omission of even one quality would destroy the indentity of a real, and a cognition which was not cognisant of all the qualities would not be cognisant of the real.

The Naiyāyika does not believe that a substance is nothing but the totality of qualities. The felt difference of substance and quality cannot be dismissed as an illusion by a philosopher, who is not prepared to deny the validity of all our cognitions. But the universal denial of validity to all cognitions is vitiated by self-contradiction.

If the object seen from adis tance were not the same with what is perceived from a close vicinity, the belief in the identity of the object would be erroneous. The question of distance or nearness has no absolute standard by which it can be determined. Now, what is distant from one point of view is believed to be near from another point of view. In the absence of an absolute criterion we cannot legitimately place confidence in any one of our cognitions that are seen to vary with the relative distance of the observer. The contents of perception from a distance of one foot are seen to vary in degrees of distinctness from those of a perception from a yard's distance. Are all these perceptions to be condemned as false? Or is one among them to be regarded as the true perception ? The former alternative is untenable as it makes all our theoretical and practical activity impossible. The second altenative, too, does not afford any advantage as it leaves no criterion by which one can pick out the privileged one from among the series of perceptions under consideration. If verification be the criterion, that also does not help one to pick and choose. All the members of the series of perceptions, that a man can have of an object as he app.oaches nearer and nearer to it, should have an equal claim to truth. There is no doubt that each succeeding intuition acquires an added content, but there is absolutely no reason to prefer one over the rest. The contents of all the intuitions in the series are equally verified. The succeeding intuition does not annul the contents of the preceding intuitions though there is an addition in each successive instance. A man may perceive a tree from a great distance as only an entity. But in his progressive approach towards the object, he may successively perceive it as a substance, and that of a particular kind and finally as a tree. The final intuition of the object as tree does not cancel the validity of the previous intuitions of it as an entity and as a substance, since the reality of the tree includes all these characters within it. So all the intuitions, irrespective of the difference of contents, are to be regarded as veridical.

The Buddhist has contended against this conclusion that verification is to be understood in terms of causal efficiency (*arthakriyā*). It is unthinkable that a self-identical real can have a successive plurality of causal efficiencies. The content in consciousness is the effect of the external object. The difference of contents, qualitative or quantitative, cannot be set down to one self-identical reality. So only one cognition in the series can be veridical. But the contention does not help us from our previous difficulty of the impossibility of decision and choice. If the privileged member concerned cannot be picked out, the mere knowledge that one at least is true does not make a difference, so far as our theoretical belief and practical activity are concerned. Moreover, the self-identical causal activity, on which the Buddhist places his reliance, cannot be thought to proceed from one single condition, but from a totality of conditions, which forms a complex. An individual alone cannot produce any effect, but only when it is a member of such a group of individuals. A seed, for instance, cannot produce a sprout by itself, unless it is associated with a number of auxiliary factors, such as water, soil and the like. So the theory of one activity of one individual cause cannot be accepted as the explanation of the problem of perception we are considering. The hypothesis of the reduplication of similar facts in a continuum does not also give any advantage in this regard, since the several continuum of each of the factors involved in causation is also equally entitled to consideration. If, however, the application of the Joint Method be thought to throw a light on the specific contribution of each factor, the seed may be regarded as the specific cause of sprout, no doubt. But the same rule also holds good in the case of the different perceptions of the tree. The tree is a reality, a substance, a tree, oak or elm, and all these facts have their specific causal efficiency. The causal efficiency of substance is in respect of its qualities and that of a tree is in respect of its characteristic features, branches, leaves and the like. The objects of the series of perceptions are thus each real, as they equally pass the test of causal efficiency. Nor are the different causal efficiencies incompatible with the identity of the tree, as the tree is all the things rolled into one.

The difference of contents does not prove the numerical difference of the object, but only when they are incompatible with one another and with the identity of the substance. The same substance, *viz.*, light, produces illumination, removes darkness and generates heat. But the difference of effects or of causal efficiency is not believed to entail a difference of identity in the substance of light. The same law should apply in the case of perception. The differences of contents of perception have been shown to be the effects of the different elements, which are present in a self-identical real. The difference of contents in the cognitions of different cows is likewise to be accounted for by the mutual difference of the individuals; and the identical reference of these cognitions can be explained only if the reality of the universal as an identical principle present in the different individuals is allowed.

But the Buddhist refuses to admit that his difficulty has been accounted for by the aforesaid explanation. It is contended by him that the difference of content spells intrinsic difference, which cannot be explained away by reference to the different qualities of a substance. The perceptual cognition is direct and immediate and non-perceptual cognition has just the opposite character. It is absurd that the same thing should produce direct and indirect cognitions. The difference is fundamental and cannot relate to the self-identical object. Nor can it be set down to the different qualities or constituent elements, as the latter also like the former produce direct and indirect cognitions. If the identity of substance cannot be compatible with the difference of mediate cognitions, the qualities cannot fare better, as the problem is the same. The Naiyāyika submits in reply that the Buddhist here makes a lamentable confusion of issues. Immediacy or mediacy is the character of cognitions *per se* and has no reference to their objects. The difference or identity of the objects has no bearing upon it. A cognition admits of a twofold determination, external and internal. The external determination is constituted by the objects to which they refer and which are responsible for the variation of its contents. The variation of contents is thus regarded as proof of the difference of objects. But as regards the internal determination, which consists in the intrinsic difference of the character of cognitions, such as immediacy or mediacy, perceptional, inferential, verbal and so on, it stands in an entirely different position. The intrinsic difference in question is due to the difference of the internal conditions and has no concern with the objects to which they refer. We have perceptual cognition of various objects. The intrinsic character of the cognition *quâ* perceptual does not vary in spite of the variation of objects or of the contents. Similarly, we have perceptual and non-perceptual cognitions of the same thing. The identity of the object here does not make the character of the cognitions identical. Thus, variation or identity of objects has no influence on the character of the cognitions. The difference of cognitional character then can be accounted for by the difference of internal causes only, and not by the difference or identity of objects, which are responsible only for the difference of contents. The Naiyāyika's position receives further corroboration from the consideration that difference of character of cognitions is not felt along with the objects, but only by introspection. Were it a character of the object, it should be felt when the object is cognised. The difference of character, perceptual or nonperceptual, cannot therefore be made the ground for denying objective validity to non-perceptual cognitions, since the objects have been shown to have absolutely no bearing upon it.

Let us make a retrospective survey of the Buddhist arguments which have been put forward to negative the objective reality of the universal. The psychological interpretation of conceptual thought as negative fictions has been shown to be contrary to the verdict of experience as well as to the canons of logic. The attempt to controvert the objective foundation of concepts on the basis of positive-cum-negative predication has also been shown by Udayana to be inconclusive and indecisive in its results. The contention based on the difference of contents and qualitative difference of cognitions is aimed at disproving the objective foundation of non-perceptual cognitions. But Udayana has shown that a psychologically more plausible and a logically more satisfactory explanation of the knowledge situations, on which the Buddhist banks, is possible on a realistic basis. The further argument of Jñānaśrī, that synthetic reference of concepts is explicable in terms of negation, has been shown to be inspired by partial observation and imperfect study of the nature of conceptual thought. Udayana insists that the synthetic reference cannot be unfounded and uncaused. Nor can the unitive ideation be due to a plurality of reals which have no common objective bond among them. We shall advert more fully to this theory at a later stage. The attempt to affiliate the unitive meaning of conceptual thought to an identical principle, unrelated to a number of individuals, is equally doomed to failure like the previous hypotheses, because of the disastrous logical consequences. There can be no escape from the postulation of a unitive principle relating to a number of individuals in the same manner and degree. If such a principle be believed to be negative in utter disregard of the claim of a positive objective principle, it can only prove dogmatism and uncritical attitude which is deliberately blind to a competing explanation. Philosophy becomes a dangerous game when it degenerates into special pleading and partisanship. Udayana, on the other hand, shows that the balance of reasons is rather on the side of positive universal. The logical difficulties, that have been shown by Dharmakīrti to vitiate the reality of objective universals, will be examined later on. Without forestalling the discourse which will come in its proper place, it may be stated in advance that the difficulties alleged are more subjective than objective, more imaginary than real. On the contrary, one cannot succeed in offering a satisfactory and honest explanation, if one accepts the Buddhist theory of negation of the opposite as the equivalent substitute for an objective universal.

The negative universal, which only refers to the negative of the opposite, cannot account for the pragmatic success of conceptual thought. It is maintained by the Buddhist that language and inference yield only conceptual knowledge. The Naiyāyika has no objection to this interpretation of non-perceptual cognition. But he joins issue only when the Buddhist repudiates the objective affiliation of all conceptual thoughts. Besides, if concepts were not conversant with objective reals, how is it that they lead to the attainment of objective facts ? In other words, why should they be susceptible of verification ? It is sheer nonsense to say that the knowledge of one thing leads to the attainment of another thing. A man infers the presence of fire in the hill and goes forward to light his cigarette with it. He is not disappointed as he finds the actual fire there. If the conceptual knowledge, yielded by inference, were entirely unrelated to the concrete fire, how can there be fulfilment of the expectation and actual verification as a matter of universal and necessary occurrence ? The Buddhist seeks to explain the pragmatic success of conceptual thought by the theory of determination (*adhyavasāya*). But what is the nature of this determination ? Does it mean that it makes a fiction masquerade as the characteristic of a real or as identical with a real ? Both these alternatives are to be rejected. Determinate knowledge, being conceptual in character, cannot be supposed by the Buddhist to be cognisant of a real attribute or a real fact, which are, according to his theory, competent to be cognised by perceptual intuition alone. If the determinate conception were cognisant of a common character, it could not be accepted by the Buddhist as veridical, since reals are believed as a matter of universal truth to be uncommon particulars. But if the common character were not cognised, then conceptual thought would fail to embody the synthetic reference, and consequently the problem of universals would not arise simply for the lack of an organ for their knowledge.

We have already shown that the Buddhist's attempt to explain the pragmatic consequences of conceptual thought on the ground that it is not felt as different from veridical intuition is only a sophistry. Even if it is allowed for the sake of argument that a concept possesses difference as an attribute, which may or may not be felt, the mere failure to recognize its difference from what it is not cannot inspire activity towards the latter. If concepts were supposed to be different by virtue of possessing a distinctive individuality of their own, there would be no possibility for their being felt otherwise. If difference be the very stuff and essence of such concepts, it would be felt whenever the concepts will be known. It may be argued that concepts are mere fictions, which, however, are felt as distinctive reals, and so activity is possible. But it is extremely hard to be reconciled to such a theory. To say, that the concept of cow is a fiction with no ontological nexus with a real cow, and at the same time, that it is felt as different from a horse or a buffalo, is only to betray confusion of thought. Even if the possibility of a fiction being felt as a real be allowed, the activity towards a real cannot be justified, unless the former be felt as identical with the latter. And even an ideal identification of a fiction with a real is possible only if the two terms are felt together. But conceptual thought is asserted to be absolutely incompetent to envisage a real, and so ideal identification also becomes impossible. If concepts were admitted to be cognisant of reality, there would be an end of the controversy, since it would amount to an admission of an objective universal.

An alternative explanation has been offered by Jñānaśrī of the objective reference of conceptual thought. It is asserted that though conceptual thought does not envisage the objective real, it can inspire volition and motor activity towards the real, being derived from a veridical intuition. The intuition of a real leaves a subtle effect when it becomes defunct. The effect may be called a psychical leaven (*vāsanā*), which, though momentary like the intuition that generated it, is uniformly renewed. The continuum of the renewed leavens is suspended, when it attains maturity and is exhausted by the generation of its effect. Conceptual thought is an effect of the leaven left by a previous intuition. There is thus a bond of causal relation between conception and intuition on the one hand, and between intuition and an objective real on the other. That intuition is caused by the real, which is its object, is admitted by the Naiyāyika also. The volitional impulse, arising from conceptual thought, is directed towards the real, which is a remote condition of the leaven from which conceptual thought derives its genesis. The existence of the causal relationship prevents promiscuous activity. The presence or absence of the external object to consciousness has no bearing upon volitional urge or motor activity, which moves towards the real to which it is causally related.[1]

The plausibility of Jñānaśrī's theory is undeniable. It seems to succeed in explaining the definite reference of conceptual thought and volitional activity towards an objective real in spite of the fact that the latter is not present to the mind at the time. But the theory is based upon an assumption. There must be a relation between cognition and its object. Now, the question arises whether the cognitive relation is derived from the relation of causality. In plain language, the problem can be stated as follows. Is cognitive relation ultimate or derived from causality? The Jaina denies that causality is determinant of cognitive relation. Even those philosophers, who believe perceptual

1. svavāsanāparipākavaśād upajāyamānai 'va sā buddhir apaśyanty api bāhyaṁ bāhye pravṛttim ātanoti'. Jñānaśrī quoted by Śaṅkara Miśra, ATVS., p. 356.

cognition to be caused by its object, do not also think that causality determines its cognitive relation. The two are kept apart and never confounded. It is an accident that the cognitive relation between perceptual cognition and its object coincides with causal relation between them. In non-perceptual cognition the cognitive relation is independent of causality. The Buddhist makes the coincidence of the two relations in perceptual cognition a universal rule and so makes no scruple to deny the reality of cognitive relation in non-perceptual cognition on the ground of the absence of causality. It is to be decided whether the Buddhist's theory is based upon an assumption or truth.

Udayana observes that causality has nothing to do with objective reference. Jñānaśrī seeks to establish that the objective reference of conceptual cognitions is vicarious, being derived from its cause. The position could be accepted, if it were shown that the effect had the same objective reference with its cause as a matter of universal necessity. But this cannot be made out. The cognition of 'yellow' is believed by the Buddhist to be the effect of the cognition of 'blue' which has preceded it. The effect has not however the same objective reference with the cause here. But the Buddhist may contend that the rule does not operate in the case of perceptual cognitions, which have different objects as their causes. It has reference only to conceptual thoughts, which are derived from perceptual intuitions and purport to have the same reference with the latter. But the amendment of the original position also does not improve the situation. It is assumed that conceptual thought has no independent reference and the first assumption is derived from a wider assumption that two kinds of cognitions cannot have reference to the same object. But both assumptions are unwarranted as no proof has been adduced in support except those arguments which have already been shown to be inconclusive. If causal relation were determinant of objective reference, there is no reason to ear-mark it to specific cases. It is a simple matter. Is causality determinant of objective reference at all ? If so, is it direct or indirect causality ? In the first alternative, verbal and inferential knowledge should not inspire volitional activity, since they are derived from knowledge of conventional relation (*saṅketa*) or necessary concomitance, which are conceptual in character. Their affiliation to reality and intuition of reality is only remote. But it is a fact that these modes of knowledge have each an objective reference, which is proved by verification to be veridical. If a remote intuition could determine the objective reference of such indirect modes of cognition, the difficulty would be avoided in the cases under consideration. But the solution would give rise to another problem. The intuition of 'yellow' being remotely caused by the intuition of 'blue' should have the same reference with its cause. Thus, causality is found to have no influence upon the objective reference of pragmatic activity that follows from it.

Jñānaśrī however, complains that the Buddhist position has been misunderstood. The law of determination of objective reference by causality only relates to those cases of conceptual thought, which expose the being of intuition. Thus, only the determinate conceptual cognitions, which only expound and clarify a previous indeterminate intuition, are illustrative of the rule propounded by the Buddhist. Udayana observes that the nature of exposition (*puraskār*) requires to be clarified. If it meant that conception shared a common object with intuition, that would be untrue according to the Buddhist, who holds that conception is never in touch with the objective real. Nor can the meaning be that conception is felt to be identical with intuition. Intuition is free from ideation and has reference to the self-characterized particular real which is not amenable to verbal representation. But conception has exactly the opposite of these characteristics. So there can be no identification of the two. It may, again, be supposed that the validity of intuition is transposed to the conception which expounds its nature. But this transposition of validity is possible only if conception has reference to the selfsame real with intuition, because validity of knowledge is always determined by the reality of its object. The Buddhist cannot subscribe to the objective foundation of conceptual thought. As for the contention that conceptual cognition is cognisant of a fiction masquerading as a real, we have already shown the inherent contradiction involved in it.

It has been attempted to explain the apparent identity of objective reference by the theory of non-discrimination. It is asserted that conceptual cognition is not felt to be distinct from intuition and so is not felt to have different objective reference. But we have seen that there is no reason why the two cognitions should be confounded. Each one of them has a distinctive character and distinctive reference. And there is no ground why they should fail to be cognised in their true character. Can it be supposed that the felt immediacy (*apārokṣya*) of the two modes of cognition is the ground of confusion of identity ? The Naiyāyika does not think it to be possible. So far as the being of cognitions is concerned they are all on the same level, being self-intuited according to the Buddhist and being objects of introspection according to the Naiyāyika. Immediacy (*apārokṣya*), being the common character of all cognitions, perceptual and non-perceptual alike, is perfectly of no avail. If the immediacy of the object be supposed to furnish the key to the secret, it would suffice to remark that the object of non-perceptual cognition is believed by the Buddhist to be an unreal fiction, which is neither mediate nor immediate. Thus all these attempts to explain the pragmatic validity of the objective reference of conceptual cognitions are not successful. But the problem finds an easy solution in the Nyāya theory, which posits that the same object can be referred to by perceptual and non-perceptual cognition.

The Buddhist thinks that the solution of the problem can be found elsewhere. It is not denied that non-perceptual cognition has a definite objective reference, though the reality of the object referred to is denied by the Buddhist. But the object of non-perceptual cognition bears a definite similarity to that of perceptual cognition and this similarity of the objects accounts for the consequent volitional activity and its pragmatic success. Udayana would ask the Buddhist to explain the meaning of similarity. If the object of non-perceptual cognition be a fiction, what is the nature of its similarity to a real object ? Similarity can exist between two facts which have the same substance but different attributes, or between two substances, possessed of attributes numerically same or of the same class. But such similarity cannot be supposed to obtain between a fact and a fiction, which is neither a substance nor an attribute. As for the negation of the opposite serving as the bond of similarity, it would only suffice to remind the Buddhist that the negation of the opposite, being irrespectively predicable of a fiction and a fact, has no common element in it. So a fiction also cannot function as the bond of similarity. The Buddhist may rejoin that the similarity in question is not believed to be objective. It is only a subjective idea. The object of non-perceptual cognition is only believed to be similar to the real object. But Udayana would submit that the problem is, why should there be such a belief at all ? The grounds of belief adduced by the Buddhist have been examined and found to afford no light on the solution of the problem.

The Naiyāyika has heckled the Buddhist from all sides. Jñānaśrī has been constrained to admit virtually the failure of the aforesaid explanations. But he maintains that though a real is not envisaged by conceptual cognition, yet it can inspire volitional impulse towards a real by virtue of a natural power. It is admitted even by the Naiyāyika that a cause produces an effect which was not in existence before. But how can there be a factual relation between a real cause and an unreal effect ? For the explanation of the situation we have to appeal to the ultimate nature of things, which we have to accept without question. There can be no answer to the question, 'why should fire produce smoke and not water" ? The case of conceptual knowledge is on the same footing with causality. The Naiyāyika, however, is not satisfied with this explanation. He maintains that if conceptual cognitions did not bear a definite relation to reals, why should they refer to them or inspire activity towards them ? The appeal to natural power is only an argument of despair. The Naiyāyika admits that conceptual knowledge has by its very nature a reference to an object. This objective reference is determined by its very nature no doubt. But that does not mean that the reference in question is possible without a real objective relation. The relation is nothing else than one obtaining between an object and its cognition (*viṣaya-viṣayībhāva-sambandha*). That this relation is ultimate and simple is not open to question since no other ultimate relation can explain it. As regards the analogy of the causal relation trotted out by Jñānaśrī, it would suffice to observe that there is a definite relation between cause and effect. The cause and effect are always determined by reference to their relevant universals. It is, therefore, possible to assert that fire as such is the cause of smoke as such.

In other words, not this or that fire, but fire as determined by its universal (*vahnitva*) is the cause of smoke as determined by its universal (*dhūmatva*). This determination by means of universals makes the relation between cause and effect universally valid. But the Buddhist cannot appeal to any such determinant as he seeks to repudiate objective universals.

The Buddhist may contend that if the determination by universals be necessary for the universal validity of the causal relation, such a determinant is not lacking in the case of conceptual thought and activity towards a real. The concept of fire will lead to the attainment of real fire and all such concepts have got a common content, *viz.*, the negation of the opposite. So there is no difficulty in the way of the causal relation. But the question is whether activity presupposes a knowledge of its object or not. If the knowledge of the object of activity were a condition of the said activity, then conceptual knowledge would not lead to activity towards a real, as no real could be the object of conceptual knowledge according to the Buddhist. If, on the other hand, the Buddhist would maintain that conceptual thought leads to the attainment of a real by virtue of the necessity of causal power and that the knowledge of the real object of the activity is irrelevant, then conception of fire should always lead to the attainment of fire. But it is common knowledge that when the light of a jewel is mistaken for fire, the activity is directed towards what is not fire. If the causality between conception and activity were to operate as a law of blind necessity, then the conception of fire would of a necessity lead to the attainment of a real fire just like the causality of fire and smoke which never fails. If it were conceded that the erroneous cognition of fire in default of the expected cognition of the jewel's light were determinant of causal activity, there is absolutely no reason why the cognition of the object of activity should not be made the universal condition of activity towards it. But this would mean that a cognition is invariably cognisant of an object. When the object is actually present in the relevant spatio-temporal context, the cognition in question, perceptual or otherwise, is veridical. If the object be not actually present, the cognition is regarded as erroneous.

Jñānaśrī has contended that the Buddhist does not rely upon

the blind force of causality to account for volitional activity. What he seeks to establish is that conceptual knowledge is out of touch with reality. But though independent of reality it possesses similarity of structure (*ākārasārūpya*) with a real. So a conception of fire inspires activity towards real fire and not anything else which lacks such similarity of structure. The Naiyāyika observes in reply that structural similarity of content and object cannot be the universal condition of selective activity. In erroneous cognition the object of activity has no structural similarity with the content of the cognition and yet the activity takes place. So the hypothesis of structural similarity is abortive. The Buddhist however rejoins that the objection of the Naiyāyika is only a cavil, since the causal relation between activity and structural similarity holds good in normal cases and erroneous cognition is only an exception. Even the Naiyāyika, who makes the cognition of the object the condition of activity, has to admit that the causal relation in question only holds between veridical cognition and successful activity. He must therefore admit that the law does not operate in cases of unsuccessful activity. If the Naiyāyika would appeal to the abnormal conditions that frustrate the operation of the causal law, the Buddhist would also offer the same explanation. So the problem is not peculiar to the Buddhist theory and has to be met by the Naiyāyika and the Buddhist alike. They will both have to make allowance for abnormal cases.

Udayana would submit that the hypothesis of structural similarity is preposterous. How can there be similarity, structural or otherwise, between consciousness and matter, which are possessed of diametrically opposed characteristics ? If there could be similarity, there would be no necessity for postulation of two different kinds of being, spirit and matter, as either of them would do. Similarity is possible only if there be a nucleus of identity in the midst of variations. The elemental identity in any two products is possible only if both of them were derived from an identical condition. But consciousness and its object cannot be supposed to be derived from a self-identical condition. Thus for instance smoke is the product of fire, but awareness of smoke may occur even in the absence of fire. The difference of causes proves the difference of the identity of the effects. So there can be no similarity between consciousness and its object. Moreover, if the 'blue' character were only a property of a cognition it could not be referred to the object. If, on the other hand, it were an attribute of the object, it could not appertain to cognition. The assumption of similarity between consciousness and matter is therefore preposterous, and consequently the attempt to explain volitional activity on the basis of structural similarity of cognition and object falls to the ground. It must then be admitted that a cognition generates volitional activity towards the object which is cognised by it.

Let it be supposed that what is felt as an object in cognition is not anything else but a subjective content. It is the content that is felt as object, and consequently inspires volitional impulse. The attainment of the external object is due to the similarity of the two. But this theory is not also free from the difficulty of the previous attempts. The volitional activity is due to the conviction that the object in question is capable of satisfying a practical requirement. For instance, a man moves towards fire, if he is in need of heat. So volitional activity is inspired by a belief in the practical efficiency of the object. If the content were felt to be possessed of the causal efficiency that actually belongs to a real fire, it could be supposed to inspire a volitional urge. But the case is just otherwise. The situation could be explained if the content were felt as identical with external object. This is also not possible. Even the illusory perception of identity would be possible if the content were superimposed upon the external object. But the external object is beyond the ken of conceptual thought according to the Buddhist and so there can be no superimposition of one upon the other. Nor is there any possibility of a subjective content being felt as external object as a subjective entity is felt by itself, being essentially identical with the cognition.

The belief in the existence of a subjective content, as standing between consciousness and external object, is not only a superfluous hypothesis, but is fraught with serious difficulties. If cognitions were conversant with subjective contents alone and external objects were shut out from their ken, their external objective reference would become an unintelligible mystery. There would be no logical necessity for believing in an external reality. We should, on the contrary, be imprisoned within the four walls of subjective experience. Nor can the inference of external reality be necessitated by a *reductio ad absurdum*. The external reality has been supposed to be the cause of the content of its cognition. But the supposition seems to be a gratuitous assumption. The content could be accepted as the effect of external reality, if it were observed to be concomitant with the external reality in agreement and in difference. But the external reality is *ex hypothesi* cut off from consciousness. So the observation of concomitance between the content and the external object is by the very nature of the case ruled out of court. It has, however, been urged that the contents of consciousness are variable and the succession of contents must be due to a succession of causes. As the blue content of the antecedent cognition cannot be thought to be responsible for the red content of the subsequent cognition, the cause of variation must, therefore, be sought outside. This is the reason for believing in external objects since variation of contents of consciousness cannot be accounted for by any other theory.

The contention of the Buddhist Realist is, however, vitiated by a fundamental defect. In abnormal cognitions, *viz.*, illusion and dreams, the contents are believed to be independent of external objects. The felt objective reference of these contents is asserted by the Buddhist to be false. The contents of these abnormal experiences are supposed to be due to the revival of past experiences as represented by latent traces left behind as their legacy. The contents of such cognitions are purely subjective in character and in origin. But why should not our supposedly normal experiences be not self-contained like abnormal experiences ? In other words, what is the line of demarcation between normal and abnormal experiences ? Verification and pragmatic success cannot be supposed to be a proof of their objective foundation and thus furnish the criterion of normality. Verification is nothing but a cognition conversant with its content and thus does not stand in a better position. The Buddhist theory of knowledge gives all our experiences a tinge of subjectivity, and this makes the determination of objective bearing impossible. And as regards the strengthening of conviction by verification, that also cannot be supposed to throw any light on the objective affiliation of the confirmed belief. The verification of one cognition by another in dream experience prejudices the truth claim of such experiences. Udayana would press the Buddhist to shed his belief in the reality of contents or to throw off the disguise of realism.

The results of our enquiry can be summed up as follows. The hypothesis of the universal being a fiction or a subjective content has been found to be disappointing as explanation of our theoretical and practical system of thought. We now propose to conduct an examination of the remaining Buddhist theory, which makes the particular responsible for the thought of the universal. It has been supposed that the individual may be the object of conceptual thought. Though by itself the individual cannot be referred to by a word, which is the external equivalent of a concept, yet the individual may assume a general character by virtue of its difference from its opposites. Thus the various individual cows share this common characteristic that each one of them is different from not-cow. We have already examined the meaning of not-cow and found that it cannot convey a meaning unless it presupposes an objective universal. In short, 'not-cow' may mean either what is different from an individual cow, or what does not possess the character of cow. The first alternative does not give any advantage. The cow A is different from the cow B just as it is different from a horse. So the term 'cow' or the concept 'cow' would not relate to cow B. It may be urged that in spite of the numerical difference of individuals the cow B is cow none the less and that constitutes its community with the other individual cows. But it is the nature of difference from what is not-cow, which is the matter of dispute. Difference of one individual cow from one individual not-cow, *e.g.* a horse, is easily apprehended. But the difference of all individual cows from all individual not-cows cannot be known unless they each and all are known. This is however, impossible unless there be knowledge of a simple characteristic determining them one and all. The admission of such a characteristic would put an end to the controversy between the realist and the nominalist.

Nor can it be supposed that the individuals as identified with one another may be referred to by a concept for they have no identity, real or ideal. The individuals are known as individuals, different from one another. So they cannot be even ideally thought to be identical. Nor can there be ideal identification of their attributes, since the Buddhist does not believe in an attribute different from its substrate. The admission of such an attribute, different from substrates, would, on the contrary, amount to the affirmation of the universal.

It has been supposed that the individuals, in spite of their mutual difference, could give rise to an identical concept. The capacity of one individual for producing such a concept is not open to question. It is not necessary that a concept should be grounded in one identical objective universal. It is found that the different universals, *e.g.*, a horse-universal or a cow-universal, are so many individuals without sharing a common universal. But nevertheless these individual universals are all referred to by a common concept and a name, *viz.*, universal. So the universal may be only a conceptual identity and not an ontological principle. The realist also cannot point to the existence of an objective universal as comprising the different individual universals. If the identical conception and linguistic expression in this case may be allowed as legitimate the Buddhist also may with equal propriety and cogency offer the same solution in the case of the individuals.[1]

But the Naiyāyika does not think the two cases to be analogous. If the unitive concepts were not determined and conditioned by objective unitive principles and the discrete particulars could account for the former, then how could it be denied that one single principle might give rise to the idea of a plurality of individuals which is the position of the Vedāntist. The appeal to natural capacity is equally available in both the cases. If particulars may be supposed to possess the capacity for generating concepts of unity, a unitary principle also may with equal logical propriety be thought to yield the knowledge of a plurality of particulars. If it be contended that the admission of such a possibility would make the knowledge of plurality unaccountable or unconditional, then the Buddhist hypothesis also would make the idea of unity unfounded and unintelligible. If the

1. ekapratyavamarśasya hetutvād dhīr abhedinī. ekadhī-hetubhāvena vyaktīnām apy abhinnatā. PV.

knowledge of plurality is to be accepted as the proof of the objective plurality of things, the knowledge of unity should also be considered to be the proof of objective unity. The Buddhist denies the existence of a unitive universal in the plurality of individuals and seeks to explain the knowledge of unity by postulating the existence of a self-identical capacity in the different individuals for such concepts. But the assumption of an unperceived and unknown capacity does not seem to have any ground for preference over a unitive universal which is admittedly a matter of perception. If, however, the said capacity be supposed to vary with each individual, the knowledge of unity would have not *raison d'etre*.[1]

If the cognition of a universal were independent of a corresponding objective principle and individuals were alone real, it would be a case of erroneous cognition just like the cognition of two moons in lieu of one. If it further be contended that the said cognition is erroneous in spite of the absence of contradiction, then the cognition of plurality should also be liable to be considered as erroneous. It has been contended that the different causal consequences are proof of the reality of the different individuals and so the cognition of plurality is veridical. The identity of an entity is proved by the identity of its causal efficiency and likewise the numerical difference of reals is established by the difference of their causal consequences. But the same kind of proof is also available in the case of unitive universals also. A real has an individualistic as well as a universal reference. It is on account of the sameness of universal reference that a number of individuals fall into a class distinct from other such classes each of which possesses a different universal reference. The sameness and difference of universal reference presuppose as their conditions the same or different universals. There is no reason to suppose that such universal reference is erroneous. Even the distinction that some cognitions are erroneous and some veridical is possible on the basis of a common character. If the classification of a number of cognitions under

1. sāmarthyaṁ yadi tādṛśanikhilavyaktiniṣṭham ekam, tarhi kim aparāddhaṁ pratyakṣasiddhena gotvādinā, atha prativyakti bhinnam, na tarhi tasyānugatavikalpotpādaniyāmakatvam, mitho vyabhicārād. ATVD, p. 389.

the head of error were not due to an objective common character possessed by each one of them, there would be no justification for regarding them all as erroneous. Thus the very attempt to dismiss the cognition of a universal as false ends in the affirmation of a real universal. In fact even the false cognition of universal is possible on the basis of a true cognition. Not only this, even error as such has been found to be impossible without the admission of a veridical universal.

As regards the analogy of several universals which are referred to by the same name and concept. *viz.*, universal, that also does not afford any advantage to the Buddhist. Though the universals do not admittedly possess a higher universal, the sameness of reference is not ungrounded in an objective character. In fact, the latter is the proof of an objective common character possessed by all the universals. The common character in question may be defined as the character of existing in all the individuals of a class without existing in the individuals of other classes.[1] This common character is not a universal but that does not argue that it is not objective. In fact, it is admitted by the Naiyāyika that there are two types of common character (*sāmānya*), *viz.* (1) universal (*jāti*) and (2) non-universal (*upādhi*). The Buddhists have sought to explain the unitive reference of individuals on the analogy of that of universals as unfounded in an objective universal. But the explanation could be accepted if the Buddhist could point to the existence of an objective common character in the individuals which the universals have been shown to possess.

Let us again take a retrospect of the results attained. The Buddhist's hypotheses that the universal is a fiction or a subjective construction have been shown to be unsatisfactory. The third hypothesis that it is the individual, which gives rise to the conception of a universal, has just been examined and found to be inadequate. Let us now examine the objections that have been advanced by the Buddhist against the possibility of an objective universal.

1. vastutaḥ sāmānyeṣv api taditarāvṛttitve sati sakalatadvṛttitvam-upādhisāmānyam ekam asti, ATVS, p. 390.

It is contended by the Buddhist that the postulation of an objective universal is contradicted by logical considerations. This contradiction is regarded as the ground for the proof of the universal being a negation of the opposite (*anyāpoha*). But the Naiyāyika does not believe in a real contradiction in the situations. The contradiction may be found in the character of the universal itself or in its cognition. As regards the first alternative the contradiction may consist in the absence of all proof or in the presence of mutually contradictory characteristics in it. It is not a fact that the common nature is uncognized. Were it so, the problem would not arise. The Buddhist also has not denied the existence of the concept, though he is sceptical of its ontological bearing. It has already been established that the Buddhist theory of unfounded concepts has absolutely no justification. But it may be asked that if the universal be eternally present everywhere, then why is it that it is not perceived in the interval between two individuals ? The answer is that the condition of its perception is not present therein. The universal is perceived only in its relevant individuals wherein it inheres and not in any other place. That the universal is a ubiquitous principle follows from the fact that it is perceived in different individuals at the same and different times. If it were limited in its being confined to the individual in which it occurs, it would not be perceived in another individual. It cannot be supposed that the universal moves forward from one individual to another, since in that case the universal would not be a universal but a substance which alone can possess locomotion. The enternity of the universal is further proved by the fact that the destruction of an individual does not affect its being so that it is equally perceived in a subsequently born individual. That it is not perceived except in individuals is rather evidence of the peculiar nature of its manifestation. As has been observed, the universal reveals itself only in an individual and this shows that the condition of its manifestation is the presence of an individual and its inherence in the latter.

But why should it not be perceived distinctly like a fruit in a basket if it were really existent in it ? The question is ambiguous. If by distinct perception it is intended that it should be perceived outside an individual, the answer is that the universal has no medium of manifestation outside the same. As has been remarked before it is only an individual which can reveal a universal. The ultimate nature of things is to be accepted on the evidence of experience exactly in the way in which it manifests itself. It will be over-stepping the limits of our jurisdiction to expect things to behave according to our preference. That the universal is perceived distinctly from the individual is not open to question. Its numerical difference from the individuals is attested by the fact that it is felt as different from the individuals in which it was previously perceived when it is perceived in a new individual. And even when it is perceived in a new individual, it is felt as distinct from the individual and as related to it. It is never felt as identical with the individual. The possibility of its identity with individuals would on the contrary make the universal a gratuitous assumption, for which we have not found the slightest warrant.

As regards the charge of mutually contradictory characteristics that the universal does not exist either in its entirety or in its partial extension in the particulars the Naiyāyika reads in it the fallacy of *petitio principii*. The universal does not admit of degrees of dimension. So the question of extension is irrelevant. It exists in its own nature, which is non-dimensional. In this respect it is rather on a par with spiritual entities to which the question of dimension is entirely repugnant.

The difficulty of relation to unborn individuals is also a figment of Dharmakīrti's imagination. The Naiyāyika does not hold that a universal moves forward from one individual to another nor that it is born with the individual. It is existent all the while and even before the birth of the individual and after its destruction. It cannot be contended that its existence in space or in time should make the latter understood as a cow or a horse just as the existence of a cow-universal in an individual makes the latter understood as a cow. The answer is that it is not merely the existence of the universal but rather its inherence that makes the individual understood as a cow. The universal does not inhere in space or in time and so the question of the latter behaving like a cow or a horse does not arise. This also disposes of the further objection of the Buddhist that the co-existence of all universals will result in confusion. It is a fact that the cow-universal co-exists with the horse-universal. But that does not make a cow to be understood as a horse or vice versa. It is inherence and not mere existence that determines the cognition of an individual in terms of class-character. The horse-universal inheres in the individual horse and not in the cow. If the different universals were admitted to co-inhere in the same individual, the difficulty alleged by the Buddhist would be irrefutable. But the Naiyāyika never admits this possibility of co-inherence of different universals.

The question where the universal should inhere can be decided by the evidence of experience alone. That the cow-universal inheres in the individual called 'cow' and not in the horse is proved by the very fact that it is felt there and not elsewhere. Nor can there be any inherent impossibility in the co-existence of different universals since they are not objects of limited dimension. It is only seen in the case of the latter entities that one excludes the other from its locus. The horse and the cow cannot co-exist in the same substratum. But the entities like space and time which are not subject to limitations of dimension are in a different position. In these cases the existence of one does not cancel the existence of the other since the opposition imposed by dimension is absent. Universals also share this character and so their co-existence does not involve any difficulty.

The distinction between its existence in and by itself and its inherence and consequential manifestation in an individual is essential to the understanding of a universal and its function. The difficulties raised by the Buddhist mainly spring from their deliberate refusal to subscribe to this distinction. In fact, the Naiyāyika considers universals to be self-existent principles. The Individual only serves to manifest its being and the existence or non-existence of the individual does not induce any modification in the manner of being of a universal. The proposition the cow-universal is in the cow' would be illegitimate if it were understood to connote the actual existence of the cow-universal in the individual.[1] The position would be legitimate if the copula

1. tathā ca piṇḍe gotvam iti vyavahāro na mukhyaḥ kintu lākṣaṇikaḥ. ATVB, p. 407.

'is' meant 'is manifested'. Our ordinary assertions such as there is no cow here or its explanatory form 'it does not possess cow-hood' are only loose modes of expression. The denial of cow-hood in such propositions is to be understood as nothing more than the denial of manifestation due to the absence of an individual. The absence of an individual, due to its non-existence or departure from a place, is expressed as the non-existence of the universal concerned. But these assertions are not based on a correct estimation of the nature and relation of universal and the individuals.

The universal is a self-existent principle and the predication of its non-existence in respect of space or time is logically false just as it is ontologically unreal. The non-existence of an individual before its birth can only mean that the universal is not related to it. It does not mean that the universal was not existent at the time that the individual was non-existent. The universal is self-contained so far as its existence is concerned. The individual is required only to make the universal related to it.[1] It may be urged that the relation of inherence, being eternal like the universal, cannot also be non-existent like the latter. So universal and inherence being present all the time the former should always appear as related. But this contention is based on forgetfulness of the fact that the apprehension of relation presupposes not only the actual existence of relation but also of the terms. The relation is not therefore apprehended so long as the individual, which is the other term, does not present itself.[2] *The raison d'etre* of our assertions, *viz.*, 'there is a cow' or 'there is not a cow' is to be found in the presence or absence of the individual called 'cow' and not in that of the universal which is ever-existent. The situation can be brought home by a concrete example. Suppose a man stands in a place and somebody puts in his hand a stick. The man may then be legitimately stated to be one who bears a stick. Suppose that somebody takes away the stick and this makes a difference in the

1. svarūpasattvāsattvayor dvitīyānapekṣatvāt sambaddhatvāsambadddhatve tu dvitīyāpekṣe. ATV. p. 408.

2. yady api tayoḥ sambandhaḥ samavāyaḥ sa cā 'styeva tathā 'py asatā piṇḍena tannirūpaṇaṁ nāsti. ATVB. p. 410.

quality of the man and this can be expressed in the form that the man does no longer possess a stick. The case is similar with the universal. The universal is all the while there, but when an individual appears on the scene, we say 'there is a cow here' and when the same individual departs from the place, we say 'there is no cow here'. The universal may be compared with the man of our example and the individual with the stick. The presence and absence, ingress and egress, of the individual do not mean the corresponding change of attributes so far as the universal is concerned.[1]

A difficulty has been raised by an advocate of non-absolutism. If the universal and the individual were absolutely different, the co-existence of the two would be logically indefensible. It should therefore be admitted that the two are neither absolutely different from nor absolutely identical with each other. But the Naiyāyika does not subscribe to the justice of this contention. He asserts on the contrary that if co-existence means relation with a common substratum, it is quite legitimate, nay logically necessary, that the terms so related should be numerically different. It is a fact that the universal and the individuality do co-exist in the individual and their co-existence is not incompatible with their numerical difference. It has been asked why should not then the cow-universal and the horse-universal co-inhere, if numerical difference be no bar ? But the question is nothing short of a cavil. It is maintained that things co-related to a common substratum are numerically different. It does not follow from this assertion that all numerically different things should be co-existent or co-related.

The fact that there may be things which though different are not co-existent or co-related does not invalidate such co-relation between all numerically different facts. But why should such a relation exist between some facts and not others ? The Naiyāyika replies that the co-existence or co-relation in question is not due to the partial identity of the terms, but rather to an inherent difference of nature of them, which is to be admitted as

1. deśe kāle ca sāmānyasvarūpam asti, piṇḍopagamāpagamādinā gaur asti gaur nāstī 'ti vyavahāraḥ, yathā 'vicalati Caitre daṇḍopagamāpagamābhyāṁ daṇḍī Caitro nā 'yaṁ daṇḍī 'ti vyavahāraḥ. ATVS. p. 410.

a matter of logical necessity. Thus it is asserted by the Naiyāyika that the relation of inherence is possible only between definite classes of entities and it does not lie in us to call in question its propriety or to demand its extension outside its observed scope. Things have a determinate nature of their own which can be discovered by experience and not by *a priori* consideration. The difference between the Naiyayika on the one hand and the Jaina or the Mīmāṁsist on the other is thus fundamental. The former does not believe in the possibility of identity in difference, far less its logical necessity as the presupposition of relation. The Naiyāyika would answer the question 'why should not the horse-universal be found in a cow ?' by saying that the nature of the terms does not permit of the combination, which would make the perception of the horse-universal possible.

It has been shown that the Naiyāyika has ultimately to appeal to the determinate nature of the terms for the explanation of the relation of the universal and the individuals in spite of their numerical difference. Numerical difference, it has been argued, does not connote incompatibility and so does not preclude a relation. It is assumed that identity of being, partial or total, of the terms is not the condition of relation and consequently numerical difference is not repugnant to it. The condition is to be found in the nature of the terms themselves. But the opponent observes that this appeal to nature is only a camouflage for disguising the failure of rational explanation. If the unquestionable nature of things can be accepted as an explanation of a philosophical problem, the Buddhists also can make this appeal. Dharmakīrti denies the existence of universals and asserts that it is the individuals themselves, which in spite of their lack of a common nature do possess a natural capacity for generating identical concepts. The hypothesis of Dharmakīrti satisfies the Law of Parsimony. And his attempt to take shelter under the ultimate nature of the individuals does not stand in a position of disadvantage as compared with the similar appeal made by the Naiyāyika.

The Naiyāyika is emphatically of the opinion that the two cases are not similar. The appeal to the ultimate nature of things is the last resource which is necessitated by the failure of other possible explanations. The postulation of a universal distinct from the individuals is dictated by a logical necessity and the consequential problem of its relation demands an explanation. And when an explanation is not available except one based upon the nature of things, we have to accept it as a matter of metaphysical necessity. The Buddhist hypothesis could be accepted if the universal were found to be an impossible fiction.

If one attribute could not by its very nature be related to a number of individuals or conversely a number of individuals could not share in common one identical attribute, then the hypothesis of one individual as doing duty for a universal were to be accepted as a matter of logical necessity. But the unity of a real is not incompatible with its connection with a plurality of individuals. The Buddhist also admits that one cognition can have reference to a number of reals. This shows that the unity of the cognition is not annulled by the plurality of the objects with which it is related, and conversely, the plurality of the objects is not jeopardized by the unity of the cognition which includes them within its field of reference. That being so, the unity of the universal cannot be supposed to preclude its connection with a number of individuals. The denial of a unitive universal on the contrary would make the unitive reference of concepts unintelligible. If the idea of plurality is not the proof of the objective existence of a plurality, then the Vedāntic position of one absolute serving as the prius of the plurality of phenomena has to be accepted as a satisfactory explanation of the world order. Thus all the objections regarding the ontological status of universals have been weighed in the balance and found wanting.

The last objection regarding the knowledge of universals is equally doomed to failure. That there is knowledge of a common nature cannot be denied without contradicting the plain verdict of experience. The fact that it is felt as such presupposes that it must have a reason for it. The validity of such cognitions cannot be impeached without impeaching the reality of their objects. But it has been shown that the reality of universals as objects of conceptual knowledge cannot be repudiated and consequently concepts cannot be condemned as false.

There are two problems of a consequential nature, which we cannot help adverting to with a view to making our representation of the Naiyāyika's criticism of the Buddhist theory of universals as thorough as the original account. The problems are, *viz.*, (1) Are our sense-organs competent to envisage universals ? (2) Is language directly cognisant of reality as it is ? The Buddhist denies both the possibilities. According to him particulars are alone real and universals are subjective constructions. Accordingly our sense-organs are in touch only with particulars and not universals. Consequently particulars are alone sensed and universals which are cognized in perceptual judgment are non-sensuous in character. The felt immediacy of determinate judgment is only a case of transference of character. The immediacy of the indeterminate cognition, which is alone perceptual, is wrongly transferred to the determinate judgment that directly follows in its wake. But the Naiyāyika does not agree with the Buddhist interpretation of perceptual knowledge. He not only believes in the reality of the universals, but also in their being perceivable like the individuals in which they are manifested. The Naiyāyika does not deny that there may be universals which are imperceptible. But he strongly refuses to believe that the universals attaching to perceptible individuals are imperceptible.

The Buddhist thinks that all judgments are non-perceptual in character. But why should the determinate judgment following an indeterminate sense-intuition be non-perceptual ? Whether a cognition is immediate and perceptual is to be determined by the bearing of the sense-organ involved. When a thing is judged to be seen or heard following the operation of a sense-organ, there is no reason to deny that the judgment is sensuous. The felt immediacy of the judgment proves that it is perceptual and sensuous. There is no psychological or logical consideration which should compel us to regard the felt immediacy as a case of vicarious cognition. It is no objection that the sense-organ does not at once generate a determinate perceptual judgment when it is capable of doing so. The Naiyāyika maintains that possession of capacity is only one of the conditions of the generation of an effect, and left to itself, it cannot produce the expected result. Capacity comes into play only when it is associated with the other necessary conditions. Now the full set of conditions for the production of perceptual judgment consists of a sense-organ and indeterminate perception, which facilitates the recognition of identity of the present datum with the previously felt data. The non-appearance of the perceptual judgment immediately after sense-object contact is thus not a real difficulty.

Let us now consider the second problem. The Buddhist holds that verbal knowledge is entirely out of touch with reality. Verbal knowledge deals with concepts which are unfounded since they refer to universals which are unreal. But concepts have been shown to be based upon reals. The denial of validity of all verbal knowledge on the contrary would make the use of language absolutely unjustifiable. The Buddhist cannot endorse this consequence as forced by a logical necessity. In fact, all his philosophical speculations are recorded in language and if language be incompetent to convey truth, all his efforts will go in vain. When the Buddhist asserts that 'reality' cannot be the subject of affirmation or negation, he claims that his assertion is true. But the truth of the assertion can be accepted only if the subject of the proposition, *viz.*, 'reality', be a fact. But this would mean that at any rate there is one proposition which directly refers to reality. If this assertion also be false, the Buddhist would fail to establish his position absolutely and irretrievably.

Chapter IX

THE JAINA CONCEPTION OF UNIVERSALS

In the foregoing chapter we have given an elaborate evaluation of the nominalistic and conceptualistic positions of the Buddhist critics of objective universals from the point of view of the Naiyāyika realist. We now address ourselves to the Jaina theory of universals. We must confess that the Jaina conception of universals, as represented by such eminent writers as Jinabhadra, Akalaṅka and Vidyānandi, down to Yaśovijaya Sūri, has been systematically given a turn which smacks of profound influence by the Buddhist philosophers. The first Jaina writer, who has given an elaborate consideration to the problem of universals, is undoubtedly Samantabhadra, the author of the *Āptamīmāṃsā*, which has been commented upon by Akalaṅka, Vidyānandi and Yaśovijaya. According to these commentators, whose views have created a uniform tradition in subsequent Jaina speculations, the universal is rather a qualitative aspect of the individuals numerically different in different individuals. The unity of universals is set forth as more or less a conceptual figment, which they seek to equate with the concept of similarity. Individuals belonging to a class are similar to one another and the similarity, though numerically different, is accorded the status of the universal. Thus the universal *quâ* similarity is numerically different and discrete in different individuals and so the universal as a unitive self-identical principle is asserted to be an ontological fiction. We postpone an elaborate discussion of this Jaina reorientation of the Buddhistic conception of universals for the present, which will be given in its proper place later on. We now propose to interpret the position of Samantabhadra without allowing ourselves to be influenced by the views of the commentators.

Samantabhadra seems to be quite explicit that all entities are unified by one common existence running through them all. That things are different numerically and qualitatively from one another is undeniable. But this numerical difference does not cancel their unity in respect of the universal characteristic, *viz.*, existence.

All things, spiritual and material alike, are united by their participation in one common existence, though they differ from one another as substance, quality and so forth.[1] There is no antagonism between unity and difference as they are equally attested by experience and necessitated by logical thought. Even the Buddhist cannot deny that unity is the presupposition of plurality and vice versa. A logical ground, which proves the existence of the probandum in a subject, must possess triple characteristics. It must exist in the subject (*pakṣa-sattā*); secondly, it must exist in all cases known to possess the probandum (*sapakṣasattva*); and thirdly, it must not exist in cases which are definitely known to be destitute of the probandum (*vipakṣa-vyāvṛttatva*). Now these three characteristics belong to the logical ground without abrogating its unity. Similarly the numerical and qualitative difference of entities does not involve an antagonism to their unity. Their unity of being cannot be denied, as no intrinsic distinction and separation are felt in their nature of existence. Now what is the proof of unity except this lack of self-diremption and separateness ? The unity of the particular is admitted by the Buddhist and the proof of this unity must be found only in the absence of self-diremption and self-alienation as felt in it. The same absence of self-diremption is present in the case of existence which makes all things one and identical.[2] The identity in respect of existence does not, however, involve the disappearance of their separate individuality just as unity of a cognition does not disappear in spite of the plurality of its contents or to put it the other way about, just as the plurality of the contents does not disappear notwithstanding the unity of the cognition apprehending them.

1. satsāmanyāt tu sarvaikyaṁ pṛthag dravyādibhedataḥ — AM, p. 34.
2. sarvam ekam sadaviśeṣāt, TSB, 1-35.

Also, jīvādibhedānām aikyam, yathā ekabhedasya svabhāvavicchedābhāvāt, na hi svabhāvāvicchedābhāvād ṛte nīlasvalakṣaṇasya saṁvedanasya vā kasya cid ekasya svayam iṣṭasyā 'py ekatvanibandhanaṁ kiṁ cid asti. nā 'pi kathaṁ cid bhinnānām api bhāvānāṁ satsāmānyasvabhāvena vicchedo 'sti, tathā vicchedābhāvasyā 'nubhavāt. anyathā ekam sad anyad asat syāt. tataḥ samañjasaṁ sarvam ekaṁ sadaviśeṣāt. AS, p. 273.

It must be remembered that the Jaina cannot be a party to the advocacy of a universal, existence not excluded, which is purely a unity. The Jaina does not believe in an unchanging principle. Existence as a characteristic of all entities is related to the latter by way of identity-cum-difference. And in so far as it is identical with the individuals, it is different in each case. But difference does not annul its unity as it is equally felt along with the former. The law of concomitance of opposites also involves that unity and plurality must coincide somehow. The charge of contradiction is simply dismissed by the Jaina as a creation of abstract logic. Thus the Jaina conception of universal is bound to differ from the Naiyāyika's conception. The universal is regarded by the Jaina as also dynamic. But the dynamic constitution does not make away with its unity in spite of variation of the media. The Jaina can only affirm that the universal is not an unchanging unity existing as uniform and unaffected by the plurality of its substrates. What is asserted of existence equally holds good of the minor universal, *e.g.*, substance-universal etc. They too are dynamic and related by way of identity-cum-difference with their substrates. Thus these universals are not impartite principles bereft of intrinsic plurality. So the common universal is also uncommon, singular as well as plural, identical as well as different.[1]

It will be a perversion of the fundamental Jaina position as well as of the plain deliverance of experience to declare that difference is incompatible with unity. Difference as a quality cannot at any rate be different from the substance to which it belongs, otherwise the relation of quality and substance will not hold between them.[2] As has been explained in Chapter VII, relation presupposes that there must be a point in which the terms are identical. So difference and identity, separation and unification, are bound to go on *pari passu*.

1. sattaikā yugapad anekatra vartata ity apy asidhham, tadanantaparyāyatvasādhanāt svaparyāyebhyo 'tyantabhedāsiddheś ca dravyatvādisāmānyam api naikam anaṁśam anekasvavyaktivṛtti..,tasyāpi svāśrayātmakatayā kathañcit sāṁśatvānekatvapratīteḥ. AS, p. 164.

2. pṛthaktvaikāntapakṣe 'pi pṛthaktvād apṛthag hi tau — op. cit., v. XXVIII.

But are different things different in respect of their existence ? In other words, is the existence of one absolutely different from the existence of another ? The Jaina answers that this is not possible. Thus, for instance, the existence of cognition cannot be different from that of the object. Both are existent, because both have a common existence. If cognition were different from its object, even in respect of its existence, it would mean that the cognition is not existent. The non-existence of cognition would involve the non-existence of the object, as there would be no proof of it. A thing is known to exist only when it becomes the object of a cognition. But the subject-object relation presupposes that the two in spite of their separate identity are held together by a common bond of unity. This bond of Unity is the common element of existence. It has been contended that the numerical difference of one existent from another existent does not prove that one or both are non-existent fictions. The difference can at most imply that one existent is not identical with another existent. So there is no logical necessity for positing one identical existence running through all. But the Jaina does not endorse this contention. The question is whether the different existents can have existence without a common existence. It is not denied that the existence of one is also different from the existence of the other. But the separate existences are only specific instances of one common existence. If this common existence were not an objective fact but only a subjective idea, the different entities would also be deprived of their title to existence. In other words, they would become subjective fictions as unreal as the universal is represented to be by the Buddhist.[1] It follows therefore that even cognition and its object are identical in respect of their existence although they differ in respect of their individualities.[2]

The different categories, *viz.*, the selves, matter, time, space and so on, are deductions from experiential data. They have been posited since general concepts presuppose their existence and

1. satsāmānyasyā 'bhāve sāṁvṛtatve vā tadviśeṣāṇām abhāvaprasaṅgāt saṁvṛtatvāpatteś ca. Ibid, p. 167.

2. sadātmanā ca bhinnaṁ ced jñānaṁ jñeyād dvidhā 'py asat. AM, p. 30.

since without these principles the data of experience cannot be organized into a system. These categories in spite of their general and comprehensive character are not only not incosistent with the existence of individual entities, but on the contrary they are entirely based upon the objective data. Without the individual existents these categories would be reduced to unmeaning class-concepts. The affirmation of categories as objective principles is thus proof of the existence of individual reals, which are included within the ambit of these categories. Without the individuals forming their contents the categories would be empty and barren, and the individuals without the categories would be reduced to a welter of chaos. The Jaina is a believer in plurality no doubt, but that plurality is not an unrelated chaos. The plurality is a system inasmuch as each individual is cemented with the rest by definite bonds of relationship.

The different categoies are but different articulations of *one existence*, which runs through them as the underlying common bond. It would be a perversity of outlook and an anomalous inconsistency on the part of the Jaina philosopher, who always insists upon the necessity of a total view of reality that should be on guard against the abstractionist habit of thought, if the aspect of plurality were only emphasised by him to the detriment of the reality of unity, which is equally attested with plurality in the being of a real. It is a matter of gratification and relief that the Jaina philosopher has not been caught napping. The aspect of unity is emphasized not only in the individual's constitution as an individualistic trait, but the unity of all reals in spite of their infinite variations is not ignored and slurred over.

The individuals are in the first instance brought under comprehensive universals called categories. Thus, the individual substances, in spite of their varying individualities and without the slightest prejudice to their status as autonomous individuals, have been placed under one category, *viz.*, substance. The grouping of individuals under a universal is not a matter of procedure or of convenience of methodological treatment, which is more or less of subjective value to the philosopher. The universal as a unitive principle is not regarded as the figment of speculative thought, but as an immanent principle having a co-ordinate status with the individualities inherent in things.

But the different categories, if taken by themselves, are nothing more and no better than so many individuals in their mutual relationships. Notwithstanding the fact that as unitive principles they reduce the discrete individuals to a system, the different categories will remain as unrelated individuals unless there be a still higher unitive principle to bind them together. So the order introduced by them will be incomplete and partial. There would be as many different orders as the categories Instead of one universe we would have a pluriverse — as many universes as the number of categories, if these categories were left unaffiliated to a higher all-inclusive category in the last resort. It is a matter of felicitation that the Jaina philosopher did not fail to notice the problem. The metaphysical system, they have given, is not a hopeless pluralism but a pluralism reduced to a system. The plurality is an ontological fact, but their mutual relations are no less ontological. The Jaina did not also fail to note that the plurality is woven together by an all-inclusive principle, which makes a unitary cosmos of them without annulment of the plurality. From the analytic point of view (*paryāyārthikanaya*) the world is an infinite plurality with their infinite variations and modes. But the analytic view does not give us the whole nature of reality as it is. It is a partial picture that we derive of the world by means of such approach. The whole gamut of reality, however, reveals its universal unitive nature *as one existence* when it is envisaged from the synthetic angle of vision (*dravyārthikanaya*). All things have the common element in their possessing this unitive existence. It is existence which makes a substance what it is. It is one identical existence that underlies them all.

It seems legitimate to conclude that the universe is one existence which manifests itself, as substance (*dravya*) as it unifies the modes and attributes. The selfsame existence again reveals itself as Space in so far as it provides accommodation for the infinite plurality of existence within itself (*kṣetra*). It is the same existence which manifests itself as Time in so far as it changes into aspects, as precedent and consequent, as earlier and latter, as present, past and future modes. It is the same existence that evolves as phases and modes, attributes and states. The substance, time, space, attribute and relation are thus evolved from the same existence. The different categories, thus viewed as functional variations of one principle, are no longer in a position of antagonism or indifferent isolation.[1]

The world of reals is thus not only a plurality but a unity also. It is one universe that the Jaina metaphysics gives us. But the oneness is not secured at the sacrifice of the many, nor are the many left in unsocial indifference. The Vedāntist immolates the plurality at the altar of unity and the Buddhist fluxist sacrifices the unity to preserve the plurality. The Jaina ethics of *ahiṃsā* (non-injury) has its counterpart in Jaina metaphysics also. In it neither the unity nor the plurality is slaughtered, but both are preserved and kept in harmony. The system adumbrated by the Jaina is thus an anticipation of Hegel's metaphysics in important respects. But unfortunately the Jaina metaphysic was not allowed to develop along this line and the result is an unrelieved pluralism, which in the hands of later exponents degenerates into the particularism of the Buddhist type. As Sir Sarvapalli Radhakrishnan observes, "One thing, however, is clear, that it is only by stopping short at a half-way house that Jainism is able to set forth a pluralistic realism."[2]

SECTION II.

The exposition that has been given in the foregoing section is found to be contradicted by later writers on Jaina philosophy beginning with Jinabhadra of the 7th century A.D., Akalaṅka Bhaṭṭa and Vidyānandi of the 9th century, and Prabhācandra, the author of the *Prameyakamalamārtaṇḍa*, who was a contemporary of Bhoja of Dhara, of the 11th century A.D. down to Yaśovijaya who flourished about the end of the 17th century. These writers are emphatic in their repudiation of Vaiśeṣika conception of the universal as one self-identical principle, existing in several individuals in the same fashion and manner. These Jaina writers were profoundly influenced by the arguments of Dharmakīrti, who set forth the universal to be identical with the individual. Consequently the universal in one individual is numerically different

1. sattā sakalapadārthā saviśeṣarūpā tv anantaparyāyā. sthitibhaṅgotpādārthā sapratipakṣā bhavaty ekā. AS., p. 113.

2. Indian Philosophy, Vol. 1, p. 340 (Indian Edition).

from the universal in another individual, even of the same class. In other words, the universal as a unitive principle is repudiated and the individuals are made out to do duty for the Vaiśeṣika conception of universal. Like Dharmakīrti these Jaina writers asserted that it is the different individuals that only exist and their synthetic unitive reference is due to their similarity. Though different, the individuals are referred to by a common concept and a name owing to this qualitative similarity of nature. Even existence, which is regarded as the summum genus, the highest universal, is believed by the Jainas just like the Buddhist to be as particularistic as the particulars are. The assertion then that things are particulars and universals rolled into one is to be understood to mean that there are particulars which are similar. It is the similarity of the individuals that is interpreted as their unity and identity. In point of fact there is no common self-identical element in the different individuals and it is their similarity which is equated with identity.[1] Jinabhadra, the author of the *Viśeṣavāśyaka-bhāṣya*, who seems to have preceded Akalaṅka, is also of the same opinion. Thus unity of being is only a metaphorical expression for similarity. Individuals are always changing and the similarity of change is regarded as the universal informing and enlivening the different individuals. The dissimilarity of change is said to constitute their difference. The sameness of reference of different individuals is again interpreted in terms of similarity, which, ontologically speaking, is numerically different in different individuals. That two individuals are called cows does not argue that the two individuals possess a self-identical character. It only means that they are similar. The difficulties raised by Dharmakīrti regarding one universal relating to different individuals separated by a gap of time and space are believed to be insurmountable. And so the same solution is offered by the Jainas as has been done by Dharma-kīrti, but whereas Dharmakīrti unhesitatingly declares the unitive universal to be an illusion, the Jainas rather adopt an apologetic tone. According to the latter, the sameness of thought and expression is only a customary characterization which sets

1. tasmād abheda ity atra samabhāvaṁ pracakṣate. NVi, 206.

forth similarity as identity. This identity is as metaphorical as the identity of man with an ass in the proposition "the man is an ass". The case in apposition is not an evidence of real unity but of a make-believe unity which is asserted for emphasizing closeness of analogy.

Vidyānandi definitely asserts that the objections, that have been urged against the mode of existence of a unitive universal by Dharmakīrti, do not affect the Jaina position in the least, since the Jainas do not believe in the existence of a selfsame universal in several individuals. The universal is nothing but the similar transformation of different things, numerically different in each case. The assertion of unity of class-character or of being is only a case of rhetorical device.[1]

We need not reproduce the arguments of the different writers as they are all couched in the same strain. So let us now consider whether the Jaina version of the Buddhist position really effects an improvement on the original Buddhist position. We do not see any material difference between the Buddhist position as expounded by us in the previous chapter and the Jaina representation of it. It will be too much to expect that the idea of unity can be successfully accounted for by a plurality without a unitary principle running through them. We have recorded the objection of the Naiyāyika against the Buddhist's position that if the unity of members of a class be only an unfounded idea, why should not the plurality be successfully affiliated to a unity ? This objection also applies to the Jaina position which is nothing but a re-statement of Dharmakīrti's conclusion. The criticism of the Buddhist's position by the Jaina, that the individuals are not exclusively dissimilar and the element of similarity in them should be regarded as a distinctive attribute, savours of prevarication and intellectual dishonesty. The Buddhist also does not deny similarity among the different individuals. The attempt to criticize the Buddhist position therefore on the ground that dissimilar entities cannot account for identity of conception is only a pretence or a deliberate misrepresentation.

1. na hi vayaṁ sadṛśapariṇāmam anekavyaktivyāpinaṁ yugapad upagacchāmo'nyatro'pacārāt — TSV, p. 320.

The Jaina seems to have been completely unnerved by Dharmakīrti's criticism. It is a pity that he failed to gauge the force and cogency of the Naiyāyika's reply to the Buddhist's criticism. The Jaina here seems to have unconsciously surrendered his doctrine of non-absolutism. It has been repeatedly asserted by the Jaina that difference is not inconsistenct with identity. The Jaina could at most assert in conformity with his allegiance to the doctrine of non-absolutism that the universal is different in so far as it is identical with individuals and identical in all cases of its occurrence in so far as it is different from the individuals. The universal would thus both be different and identical, permanent and impermanent, — permanent and identical in so far as it is the selfsame principle, and impermanent and different in so far as it is identical with the individuals. But by impeaching the clear deliverance of experience certifying the unity of the universal in different individuals the Jaina has unwillingly walked into the spider's parlour. If similarity can account for unity, how can the Jaina establish the identity of substance ? The substance is identical with the modes that occur in it. The Buddhist asserts that there is no unitive substance running through the modes. It is the aspect of similarity of the modes that is mistaken for identity of the substance. In fact, the Jaina cannot give a satisfactory answer against this contention of the Buddhist when he admits similarity to be the equivalent of identity. The Jaina repeats the empirical argument that our experience takes note of the identity of the substance together with its changing modes which are transitory as they endure only for a moment and pass out of existence the very next moment. But if the experience of the unity of substance be deemed valid in spite of the logical difficulties alleged by the Buddhist, we do not see any reason how can the Jaina deny validity to the experience of unity in different individuals. The logical difficulties in the way of unitive universals have been met by Udayana and his predecessors; and the Jaina could easily solve the logical problem by means of his non-absolutist logic, which finds no contradiction in the identity of differences.

The unity of the universal and the particular has been sought to be explained by Yaśovijaya as the lack of the difference of substratum. In other words, unity is made out to be a case of simple co-incidence. It is argued that the universal is different from the individual and the identity of the universal is only a case of its coincidence with the specific character of the individual in the same substratum. The criterion of difference is the distinction of the locus of the incidence of attributes. The very fact that the universal has no locus independent of the individuals shows that the universal is not distinct from the individual. This explanation of unity as the absence of separation does not seem to be materially different from the concept of inherence as propounded by the Nyāya-Vaiśeṣika school. If the sameness of substratum does not connote the sameness of being in some respect, the unity will be only a question of juxtaposition. The Naiyāyika asserts that though numerically different, the universal and the particularity can co-exist without losing their specific character. The coincidence does not argue that they are identified with one another in some indefinable manner. The Jaina position also, so far as it is represented by Yaśovijaya, does not appear to be different from the Vaiśeṣika standpoint. Yaśovijaya explicitly states that though difference is to be understood as numerical difference, absence of difference is nothing but the absence of separate substratum.[1] Inherence, as conceived by the Vaiśeṣika, has been sought to be replaced by identity in difference. But the substitution would mean only a verbal change and a difference of nomenclature, if identity were to be understood as the sameness of substratum. The difference of the Jaina position, so far as the relation of inherence is concerned, would thus turn out to be only a show and a pretence. If however the sameness of substratum and the necessity of coincidence were regarded as symptomatic of real identity, the Jaina conception of identity in difference as the necessary character of relation would make a material difference. But unfortunately this point has been slurred over by the later Jaina writers without realizing the consequences which are fatal to the fundamental position of non-absolutism.

1. so 'py abhedaḥ, pravibhaktapradeśatvarūpa-bhedābhāvarūpatvāttathā ca jātau vyakter anyatvarūpo bhedo 'nanyadeśatvarūpo 'bhedaś ce 'ty ubhayam apy aviruddham — NKK. p. 272.

If the universal be numerically different in different individuals and the conception of unity be explained away as a case of pseudo-unity due to similarity, the Jaina metaphysical position would be reduced to an unmitigated pluralism. In that case there would not exist a universe but a pluriverse. Different individuals could only be described as similar or dissimilar without any common bond binding them together. The assertion that the totality of existents is bound by identity of being and the difference of entities is not absolute would thus transpire to be a mean verbal quibble. The Jaina position thus would not be a bit different from the position of the Buddhist fluxist which asserts that the plurality of entities is undisturbed by any unitive bond. Thus difference will be the absolute characteristic of reals, each individual being put in a place of its own and existing side by side without commingling their being in any wise and manner. But this would only amount to the repudiation of non-absolutism.

It is refreshing to note that the fallacies involved in the conception of numerically different universals were fully realized by a late Jaina philosopher. It is Vimaladāsa, the author of the *Saptabhaṅgītaraṅgiṇī*, an adherent of the Digambara school, who realized the dangerous implications of the Jaina position as expounded by the later writers. It is unfortunate that Yaśovijaya, who was well-trained in the dialectics of the Neo-logical school of Mithilā and Navadvīpa, failed to detect the fallacy involved in the position. Instead of effecting an improvement Yaśovijaya has rather complicated the issue and made the confusion worse confounded. Unfortunately he shows more ingenuity than insight. In fact, in the interest of truth and philosophic candour we are bound to admit, if we are to follow the representation of these writers, that the Jaina doctrine of non-absolutism is only a make-believe and a hollow pretence. Fortunately for us there has been at least one solitary writer, we mean Vimaladāsa, whom we have just referred to, who has voiced his protest against this traditional interpretation.

Vimaladāsa raises the problem in connection with the universality of sevenfold predication. In Chapter VI we raised the problem whether the totality of existents is an ideal unity and a real plurality.[1] We postponed the discussion of the problem there and rather dogmatically affirmed that the totality of existence is a real universe of which the determinations, one and many, are equally predicable. We asserted that the totality is one whole — one in respect of the universal, being, and many in respect of the plurality of the individuals. We anticipated the conclusion, "The universe will be found on examination to be a unity of plurality exactly on a par with the individual, which is an epitome of the macrocosm, being a unity and a plurality in one, and at the same time, though in a different reference."

Vimaladāsa observes that if the existence of one particular were absolutely different from that of another particular, then the totality of particulars would have no common element to bind them together. If the particulars were possessed of a common existence as the fundamental element of their individuality the totality of existence could be determined as one and many, which the universality of the law of Sevenfold Predication demands. But the assertions of the traditional exponents of Jaina thought seem to contradict this possibility. Vimaladāsa maintains that the statements of these masters should be understood not to imply the absolute difference and discretion of individuals. The implication of these statements consists in their repudiation of absolute identity. Though existence is variant and manifold in so far as it is identical with each individual, it does not for that reason forfeit its unity and self-identity *quâ* universal. Thus things are identical with and different from one another — identical in respect of a common existence and different in respect of their distinctive individuality. The denial of a common universal on the contrary would make the difference of individuals absolute. The absolutism of particularity has been emphatically repudiated by Samantabhadra and his commentators. In order to bring this denial of absolute particularism into harmony with the denial of absolute common existence underlying the diverse existents it is necessary to conclude that things are neither absolutely diverse nor absolutely identical, which are the respective positions of the Buddhist Fluxist and the Vedāntic monist. The Jaina philosopher cannot

1. Vide *supra* p. 159.

be a party to either of these positions without neutralizing the fundamental principle of non-absolutism. So the apparent repudiation of universals is to be interpreted as the repudiation of absolute unity of existents involved in the conception of unchanging self-identical universal running through them. In other words, the universal *quâ* existence is a unity in difference, which does not entirely merge its being in the particulars in spite of its participation in them.

Vimaladāsa further contends that similarity cannot account for the identity of reference of individuals, if the former be ontologically different in each case of its incidence. Similarity cannot be an ultimate category. Similarity is nothing but the possession of a common identical attribute or attributes by numerically different entities. The face of a lovely woman is compared by the poet to the moon. But where lies the similarity of the two ? It must be supposed that the face shares a common attribute with the moon, the selfsame attribute of beauty, which causes delight to the connoisseur. Similarly, the similarity of one pen with another pen, of one man with another man, is to be traced to an identical attribute, namely, the pen-universal or the man-universal, which is shared in common by the individuals concerned. The denial of a self-identical quality in several individuals would on the other hand make the distinction of common and uncommon attributes indefensible. A common attribute is but the selfsame attribute which exists in more than one individual and an uncommon attribute is but what is peculiar to a particular individual, unshared by any other. If the possibility of the occurrence of a selfsame attribute in more than one substratum is denied, then no quality would be common. There is no valid ground for dismissing this distinction as an unfounded illusion, since it is not contradicted by experience as other illusions are.

The idea of similarity is there and it cannot be explained without reference to an identical element. The reality of similarity again cannot be repudiated unless the knowledge of the same be declared false, for which there is no warrant, and similarity again ultimately presupposes a universal. But it may be contended that similarity is an unanalysable characteristic — as ultimate as identity or difference is. In point of fact, the school of Prabhākara and following them the school of Madhva maintain that similarity is an ultimate category which cannot be reduced to a simpler and more self-evident category. These philosophers have further endeavoured to prove the identity of reference of concepts in terms of similarity. Similarity is not deemed to be susceptible of being reduced to identity, which is done by the Naiyāyika.

But the attempt to equate identity with similar ty seems to be an extremism of pluralistic bias. Let us take it for granted that similarity can account for identical reference of concepts and the postulation of unitive universals is not logically necessary. But the question must be answered whether similarity is an identical principle subsisting in the particulars thought to be similar or numerically different in each instance. The first alternative, if granted, would only make the difference of views a question of nomenclature. An identical entity existing in different individuals may be designated as a universal or similarity, but the designation does not make any difference to the ontological problem. And the second alternative, which makes out the varying similarities to be numerically different, raises further problems. Is the similarity *quâ* characteristic different from the individual or identical with it ? If it is different, how can it belong to the individual and introduce a change into its constitution, that is to say, make it similar ? The Jaina philosopher at any rate cannot maintain that the relation of a characteristic to its substratum is either one of absolute otherness or of absolute identity. Even the Mādhvas, who believe in the absolute difference of things, are compelled to admit that the relation of a characteristic to the thing characterized is not one of absolute difference or of absolute identity, but as identity-cum-difference. At any rate the element of identity involved in the very constitution of relation makes the situation far from intelligible if identity of being is denied.

'A is similar' is a proposition and it follows that similarity is identical with A in some respect, which the relation of subject and predicate between the two logically entails. But similarity is not only a characteristic but also a relation. The similarity of A is not confined to A, but has necessary reference to B. To say that similarity is a characteristic entirely self-contained is to speak unintelligible jargon. Similarity holds between A and B and as such must belong to them. Now the question arises whether similarity is a relation or a characteristic or both ? It is no doubt a relation so far as it obtains between two terms. It is no doubt again a characteristic so far as it is conceived to be the attribute of the term in which it subsists and we have seen that the concept of similarity as an attribute presupposes a relation which is admitted to be identity-in-difference. But irrespective of whether it is a characteristic or not, it is not self-contained in its reference and requires a second term to which it relates. If the similarity be supposed to function as a relation between A and B, it may fall outside the terms and thus fail to relate them. Or it may function also as a characteristic of both the terms and thus require a second relation in order to belong to them. But relation has been admitted to consist in or presuppose identity-in-difference. So the similarity of A and the similarity of B, whether characteristics or relation, must be identical in some respect with A and B both. And this means that there is an element in both A and B which is identical.

Let us again suppose that similarity is a self-contained attribute of each of the terms, numerically different from one another. The similarity of A will then be numerically different from the similarity of B. There will be thus two similarities and not one. But this does not make the problem of identity of reference any more intelligible than before. The question irresistibly arises, whenever one states a proposition *e.g.* A is similar to B, where does the similarity consist in and what is it due to ? The question presupposes that there must be something in both the terms on which similarity is founded. But it may be maintained that the question is wrong and illegitimate since it derives from an unwarranted presupposition. Similarity is an ultimate simple fact and does not presuppose any further characteristic as its basis and ground. But this reiteration of the ultimacy of similarity does not help us to understand its nature a whit more clearly. We do not mean to say that the opponent seeks to escape under a prevarication but our grievance against the solution offered is that it does not care to appreciate the difficulty, which we confront in trying to grasp the nature of similarity as a self-contained attribute of each of the terms.

Suppose that the similarity of A is numerically different from the similarity of B. But what makes A and B to be similar ? Let us take a concrete example. A cow is similar to another cow and a buffalo is similar to another buffalo. But if the similarity *quâ* characteristic of one cow be numerically different from the similarity *quâ* characteristic of another cow and again the two similarities be numerically different from the similarity which characterizes buffaloes, we can account for the difference of function of the two types of similarities by assuming a qualitative difference in each. We must admit that the similarity that obtains between cows is different qualitatively and numerically from the similarity that holds between buffaloes. So there are similarities which are functionally identical and different. The similarity that governs one class is functionally different from the similarity that governs another class. The difference of function naturally presupposes an intrinsic difference in the similarities and thus similarities must fall into definitive groups. The similarity of cows stands apart from that of the buffaloes. But this grouping of types does not make an appreciable difference, procedural and ontological, from the classification of universals as propounded by the Nyāya-Vaiśeṣika school. The Jaina and Madhva classification on the contrary makes the postulation of an enormous number of ultimate types of similarity inevitable by making them numerically different in each individual.

The Nyāya-Vaiśeṣika scheme of universals has the merit of making a system of the plurality of individuals on an intelligible basis. The number of cows is classed together by reason of a definitive characteristic called the cow-universal and this accounts for the similarity of cows to one another. The cow-universal again has the advantage of differentiating the class of cows from the class of buffaloes on the basis of distinctive characteristics — the universal of the latter being numerically and functionally different from the former. But the theory of numerically different similarities will fail to account for the classification unless similarities fall into groups, and this grouping becomes arbitrary unless the types of similarities have each a distinctive common character. The assumption of types of similarities, however, is tentamount to a reinstatement of the Nyāya scheme of universals in different language.

The inherent difficulties of the theory of similarity as the substitute of universals pronouncedly manifest themselves when it is realized that similarity is both made an attributive characteristic and a relation. The similarity of the cow A is an attribute of it and is numerically different from the similarity that is the attribute of the cow B. But what makes A and B mutually similar ? The two similarities are each self-contained and unless they can function as a transitive relation they cannot make A and B similar to each other. But if similarity be a relation between A and B, we do not see what advantage is gained by positing two self-contained similarities as the properties of A and B. Unless there be a relation of similarity holding the two together, A and B will not be similar; and if the relation be there what do the two similarities *quâ* characteristics avail ? Do the latter serve as the ground and basis of the relation ? If so, the similarity *quâ* relation must be numerically and functionally different from the similarities *quâ* characteristics. But in that case the postulation of similarity as a characteristic does not seem to have a *raison d'etre*.

Perhaps the difficulties may be avoided by supposing similarity to be both an attribute and a relation of the terms. Granted that there is no logical difficulty in the selfsame attribute functioning also as relation, we do not see the logical necessity of postulating more than one similarity. The similarity *quâ* relation will make the terms similar and there is no necessity for positing another or more similarity for the same purpose. Similarity *quâ* relation will subsist in both the terms and thus may function as their attribute also. But similarity is a transitive symmetrical relation. If A is similar to B, B is similar to C, and C is similar to D and so on, then A is similar to C and D, and B, C, D etc. are similar to A. If one similarity functioning as a relation and also as an attribute can account for the similarity of the terms concerned, the similarity in question will serve the purpose of a common universal. So we do not see any difference, so far as the ontological status of universals is concerned, between the theory of similarity and the theory of objective universals.

But can one similarity meet all the situations and thus enable us to dispense with the plurality of universals ? If it could do this, that would be a positive advantage no doubt. But this is quite impossible. We have already seen that there must be different types of similarity. The similarity of cows as a class is different from the similarity of buffaloes as another class. Thus there will be as many types of similarity as there are classes, each different from the other. But this is nothing but a reinstatement of the different universals in a different guise.

The admission of similarity as a relation again makes the admission of a core of identity in the terms inevitable as we have seen that relation is possible only if the terms are identical and different. The admission of an identical element in the terms will be tantamount to the admission of a universal. Moreover the assertion that similarity is an ultitude concept does not carry conviction. The question of ultimacy can be decided if it is found to preclude the demand of a further explanation or to show such a demand to be unintelligible and absurd. Thus existence is an ultimate concept and no further explanation of its character is possible which does not presuppose the idea of existence in it. But is similarity self-explanatory like existence ? So far as the psychology of our experience and thought is found to testify, we do not see it to be the case. If a person asserts that A is similar to B, the question naturally arises, "What is the ground of their similarity ?" And the question is set at rest when one can point to a common element existing in both. The Naiyāyika is certainly in the right when he asserts that similarity is a characteristic derived from the possession of a definite common attribute.[1] Vimaladāsa evinces greater insight and love of truth when he agrees with the Naiyāyika in regarding similarity as a deriva'ive characteristic.

The incongruence of the same thing serving as the attribute and as the relation unfortunately did not occur to the Jaina realists of the Post-Dharmakīrti period. Relation is at any rate logically posterior to quality. It requires at least two terms to make a relation possible. Similarity, if it be an attribute, must be prior to and hence different from relation. This will be apparent from the consideration that one cannot satisfy the

1. tadbhinnatve sati tadgatabhūyodharmavattvam.

query why A and B are similar by the simple answer that they are similar, since the answer is tautologous. We hold that there is no justification for holding similarity to be an ultimate concept either as a category or as a relation and this is shown by the fact that the questioner is not silenced until a common characteristic is pointed out.

But the later Jaina philosophers have contended that the relation between universal and particular does not involve or presuppose identity of being. The element of identity in the *identity-in-difference* as the presupposition of relation is to be understood negatively as the absence of separate locus and positively as the necessity of coincidence. We have shown that this is the character of inherence as set forth by the Vaiśeṣika. If relation between universal and particular were one of mere necessary coincidence, the elaborate refutation of inherence and the positing of identity-in-difference as the ground of relation would be so much waste of labour. Nay it would be an act of make-believe inasmuch as it makes a show of difference when it is in entire agreement with the conception of inherence as propounded by the Vaiśeṣika. Not only this, the dismissal of identity as a case of invariable coincidence would make the whole philosophy of non-absolutism a hollow pretence. The relation of modes to the substance in which they occur is asserted to be identity in difference and the contradiction involved in it is solved by positing a separate category (*jātyantara*), which is not explicable in terms of identity or of difference, being an embodiment of both the elements in its being. But the assumption of such a separate category would be absolutely uncalled for if the theory of necessary coincidence could meet the situation. Furthermore, the postulation of *avaktavya* (inexpressible) as a separate category, which we have discussed in Chapter V, would have no *raison d'etre*, if the element of identity involved in the relation only meant necessary coincidence and nothing more. It is the concept of *avaktavya*, however, which gives the Jaina philosophy its distinctive character and individuality. But the later Jaina philosophers, who were rather frightened out of their wits by the flourish of Dharmakīrti's criticism, have given a wide berth to the Jaina conception of *avaktavya* by unconsciously reinstating the conception of inherence as the solvent of the logical difficulty involved which has led the Vedāntist and the Śūnyavādin to declare the phenomenal world to be an illogical and irrational appearance. We are deliberately of the opinion that the later Jainas have unwittingly played false to their ancient philosophy and we are positive that the older account of universals as given by us is not only in harmony with the philosophy of non-absolutism, but is the only possible account that can be accepted as the correct position. It is fortunate that we have Vimaladāsa on our side and it is desirable that students of Jaina philosophy should devote greater attention to him.

INDEX

absolute 154
absolutism 23, 75, 154
absolutist 53, 82
ādhārādheyabhāva 119
ādhārādheyabhūta 199
adhyavasāya 85, 87, 88, 242
agnosticism 3
ahiṁsā 272
Akalaṅka Bhaṭṭa 79, 266, 272, 273
ākārasārūpya 250
alika 213
analogy 206, 231
anekānta 27, 174
anekāntavāda 23, 62, 66, 86, 149, 173, 174, 175, 176
anubhava 4
anyāpoha 213, 257
apārokṣya 247
apoha 217
Āptamīmāṁsā 266
arthakriyā 238
ātman 22n. 207
atyantābhāva 29
avacchedaka 127
avācya 83
avaktavya 131, 133, 285
avayavāvayavin 199
avyāpyavṛtti 157
ayutasiddha 199
ayutasiddhi 207

Bhagīratha Ṭhakkura 218
bhaṅga 118
Bhartṛhari 31n., 101, 102
Bhattacharya, K. C. 133
bhāva 119
Bhoja of Dhārā 272
Bradley 178, 186
Brahman 31
Buddhist 3, 14, 18, 26, 27, 32, 34, 40, 50, 50n, 51, 69, 70, 74, 83, 85, 87, 88, 89, 90, 92, 93-97, 101-104, 113, 115, 127-128, 158, 175, 179, 181, 185, 190-192, 194, 196, 214-227, 229-243, 245-259, 262-267, 269, 272, 273, 274
Buddhist fluxist 5, 12, 24, 26, 46, 83, 113, 152, 212, 272, 277
Buddhistic 266
Buddhist idealist 27, 50, 51
Buddhist nihilist 153, 173

Candrakīrti 71, 75
Cārvāka 43, 44
Cārvāka materialist 38, 175
Causality 184, 195, 197
Causation 194
..., law of 71
Categories 29, 270, 271
Chala 159
Cognition, non-perceptual 235, 247, 248
Concepts, emergence of 2
Concomitance, the law of 268
Conjunction 206, 210
... Universal 204

determination, specific 161
dharma 167
Dharmakīrti 1, 173, 180, 181, 189, 242, 258, 262, 273, 274
Dharmottara 219, 225, 249
dhūmatva 249
Dignāga 1, 173, 175
dravya 119, 142, 143, 271, 301
dravyārthikanaya 271
dravyakṣetrakālabhāvātman 79
doubt 160

ekārthasamavāya 201
empiricism 5
epistemology 54, 86
Euclid 188
expressibility 126
extramental reality 2

flux, philosophy of 25
fluxism, Scylla of 65
fluxist 12, 29, 64, 69, 70, 73, 74, 141, 178, 197

gotva 6
guṇa-dravya 199

Hegel 101, 272
Hegelians 2
hetu 162

idealist 8, 14, 15, 16, 19, 23, 65, 164, 165, 172, 195
idealist, Buddhist 32
ihedampratyayahetu 199
illusionism, charybdis of 65
inexpressibility 125, 128, 150
inference 202, 225
inherence 201, 202, 204, 206, 208, 210, 259, 276
intuition, Pure 17

Intuition, Transcendental 17
itaretarābhāva 29, 44

Jagannātha 28n.
Jaina grammarians 200
Jainism 272
James 164
Jāti 213
Jāti-jātimat 200
jātyantara 187
Jinabhadra 266, 272, 273
Jīva 146
Jñānaśrī 217, 219, 225, 228, 241, 244, 245, 246, 248, 249
Joint method 195, 239

Kāla 119, 142
Kant 3, 17, 19, 88, 94, 181, 196
Karma 182
Kramārpaṇa 133
Kṣetra 119, 142, 271

law of causation 25, 28, 193
law of contradiction 7, 9, 11, 12, 14, 15, 19, 139, 164, 169, 174
law of excluded middle 7, 14, 15, 19, 61
law of identity 7, 8, 9, 19, 21
law of opposition 15, 16
law of parsimony 262
laws of thought 3, 4, 7, 12, 14, 16, 18, 19, 20, 23, 71, 163, 198
law of uniformity of nature 183
logic 6, 63, 69, 70, 73, 77, 78, 86, 107, 111, 130, 158, 172, 173, 176, 181, 223, 240, 243
...absolutist 97, 174
...abstract 14, 76, 77, 131, 149, 186, 268
...*a priori* 65, 86, 173
...empirical 165
...formal 12, 105, 129
...formal pure 164
...Jaina 66, 174
...mīmāṁsist 175
...non-absolutist 175
...realistic 165
...pure 8, 54, 56, 70, 82, 88, 104, 128, 164, 165, 197, 225, 226
...idealistic 128, 172

Madhva 279
major premise 84
McTaggart 189
method of agreement 195
method of difference 195
method of elimination 202
Mill, J. S. 195
Mīmāṁsist 2, 6, 15, 30, 36, 37, 38, 42, 92, 97, 107, 108, 109, 168, 175, 262
mithyaikānta 155
monism, Scylla of 164
monists of Śaṅkara school 173
mutual non-existence 29

Nāgārjuna 61, 62, 71, 75, 79
Nairantarya 178
Naiyāyika 4, 6, 12, 13, 61, 93, 108, 138, 139, 140, 149, 157, 166, 167, 169, 201, 202, 212, 214, 215, 222, 224, 226-228, 229-231, 235-237, 241, 244, 247-251, 256-257, 259, 261, 264, 268, 274-275
naya 154
negation of the opposite 247, 249
negativism 75
...absolute 73, 75
negativist absolute 23
nihilism 150, 165
...Charybdis of 165
nihilist 12, 163, 165, 253
non-absolutism 23, 36, 153, 154, 155, 163, 175, 261
...Jaina 173
non-absolutist 82
...logic 82
non-discrimination, theory of 246
non-existence, absolute 30, 49
...of mutual identity 49
Nyāya 61, 65, 209, 212, 247
Nyāya Vaiśeṣika 61, 174

ontology 175
opposition, absolute 15
...destructive 15
...of noncongruence 15
...of obstruction 16
...types of 15

pakṣasattā 267
Pāṇini 110
pararūpa 142
pararūpasattā 164
particularism, absolute 73
paryāya 192
paryāyārthikanaya 271
Patañjali 109
perception 146
petitio principii 226, 258
post-non-existence 29, 38, 41, 46, 47
Prabhācandra 272
Prabhākara 170
...school 175, 279
pradhāna 82
pradhvaṁsābhāva 29
prāgabhāva 29
prakṛti 29, 151, 174
pramāṇa 155, 232
Prameyakamalamārtaṇḍa 272
pratibadhyapratibandhakabhāva 16

pre-non-existence 30, 35, 36
puruṣa 174
Radhakrishnan 272
Raghunātha Śiromaṇi 218
rajas 174
Rasagaṅgādhara 18n
rationalist 5
Ratnakīrti 219
realism 22, 253, 272
realist 8, 14, 16, 21, 164, 165, 166, 167, 172, 253, 254
...Buddhist 252
...Jaina 173
reasoning 5
reductio ad absurdum 23, 115, 252
regressus ad infinitum 145, 173, 203, 204
relation 137, 158, 177, 185, 186, 187, 188, 189, 191, 194, 196, 197, 198, 200-202, 204, 208, 210, 212, 227
...of similarity and dissimilarity 3
sahānavasthānalakṣaṇa 16
Sahārpaṇa 133
Sāmānādhikaraṇya 147
Samanantarapratyaya 85
Samantabhadra 112, 113, 177, 266, 278
Sāmānya 109, 213, 256
Samavāya 149, 158, 182, 198, 199
Samaya 232
Saṃvṛti 79
Samyagekānta 155
Saṁyoga 157, 199, 205
Śaṅkara 115, 163, 164
...ācārya 164
...Miśra 218
saṅketa 92, 245
Sāṅkhya 29, 30, 35, 36, 37, 38, 39, 49, 61, 64, 66, 69, 81, 82, 151, 152, 174, 193
...Yoga School 82
...philosophy 82
Sapakṣa 127
...*Sattva* 267
Saptabhaṅgīnaya 21, 117
Saptabhaṅgītaraṅgiṇī 111, 192
Sautrāntika 24, 64, 86, 175
...realist 28
Savikalpaka 87
Sceptic 24, 56, 59, 60, 76, 77, 102, 122, 186
Scepticism 56, 186, 225
Self-existent principles 5
Sevenfold dialectic 130, 132
...predication 117, 130, 154, 155, 159, 160, 161, 163, 173, 176
...Theory of 153
Sophistry 177, 243
Stcherbatsky 75
Substance 208
Śūnyavāda 149, 150, 164, 165
Śūnyavādin 23, 25, 53, 59, 67, 120, 145, 152, 153, 173
Svalakṣaṇa 83, 88
Svarūpa 104, 142, 146
...bheda 216
...sambandha 210
...Satta 164
Syāt 83, 99, 121, 122, 133, 135, 150
Syllogism 35
tādātmya 171
tamas 174
Udayana 218, 222, 223, 224, 242, 245, 248, 253
Uddyotakara 206n
Ūha 5
Universal 2, 3, 6, 18, 153, 174, 203, 204, 206, 212, 213, 214, 218, 219, 220, 221, 225, 226, 227, 228, 234, 240, 241, 242, 244, 249, 254, 256, 257, 258, 259, 260, 261, 262, 263, 264, 266, 268, 269, 270, 273, 274, 275
...Unitive 5
Upādhi 256
Upakārakopakāryabhāva 180
Vācyavācakabhāva 200
Vadhyaghātakabhāva 15
Vahnitva 232, 249
Vaiśadya 146
Vaiśeṣika 30, 33, 41, 43, 45, 64, 182, 198, 201, 202, 204, 205, 206, 207, 208, 210, 211, 273, 276
Vaiṣṇava 175
Vākyapadīya 101
Vartamānatva 230
Vāsanā 244
Vedānta 21, 64, 66, 67, 70, 148, 164, 165
Vedāntic 66, 67, 263
idealist 28
Vedantist 8, 9, 12, 23, 28, 30, 31, 33, 34, 35, 37, 49, 51, 53, 63, 65, 70, 71, 72, 75, 80, 81, 86, 101, 120, 132, 139, 141, 145, 148, 152, 153, 158, 165, 178, 254, 272
Vidyānandi 266, 272, 274
Vimaladāsa 111, 277-79, 284
Vipakṣavyāvṛttatva 267
Viṣaya-viṣayibhāvasambandha 248
Viśeṣāvaśyakabhāṣya 273
Voidist 75-81
Vyatikara 163
Yaśovijaya 266, 272, 276, 277
Yoga 34
Yogācāra 25, 28, 175
...Buddhist 101
Yogasūtra 109
Yogyānupalabdhi 74
Yutasiddhi 207